The Guide

One of the most visited and praised regions of the UK, the Lake District lies within the county of Cumbria in north-west England. The 885 square miles that constitute the National Park are crammed with some of the most dramatic scenery, beautiful views and picturesque villages England has to offer. And it's no surprise that its famed beauty attracts millions of visitors each year from high profile celebrities to serious outdoor pursuits enthusiasts, all of whom travel here to vouch for what all the fuss is about.

It's hard to imagine anywhere else in the country where you can find such an incredible diversity of magnificent scenery in such a contained space. Rugged mountains, glacial lakes, forests and untamed fells fill the Lake District, as well as pretty villages linked by country lanes, bridleways and ancient trails. And just beyond the south and west boundaries of the National Park lies the Cumbrian coast, home to old maritime communities, areas of outstanding natural beauty and numerous historical sites.

The Lake District's magnificent scenery has inspired writers and artists for generations and many of the former homes and attractions related to the likes of Wordsworth, Beatrix Potter and Ruskin are one of the region's biggest draws. However, the Lakes remain a honey-pot for creative types and the range of new work produced by the region's artists, crafts people and writers all validates the enduring capacity of the Lake District's landscape to inspire.

If you think all this sounds a bit dull for children, think again. Families have been holidaying here for generations and many return year upon year to enjoy the outdoors with their children. And there's a host of excellent indoor family attractions to keep young visitors occupied on a rainy day.

All ages travel to the Lakes to experience the wide variety of outdoor pursuits on offer and activities for visitors include walking, climbing, pony trekking and cycling – either on the road or via one of the many off-road trails that snake through the region's forests. And of course there are water sports galore to choose from, all of which can be enjoyed by the complete beginner upwards. Getting out onto one of the National Park's 14 main lakes is a must for all visitors and if canoeing or kayaking isn't your thing, you can choose to cruise on a range of different crafts from solar powered passenger ferries to romantic steam yacht gondolas.

The Lake District is also establishing a reputation as a cultural destination, beyond the many writers and artists the region is already famous for. Visitors are now discovering an increasing variety of new cultural festivals to enjoy year-round, which perfectly complement the age-old calendar of agricultural shows and sheep dog trails.

This combination of old and new is one of the Lake District's most appealing characteristics and one that can be increasingly applied to its visitors. For, in addition to those who have been travelling here for years, a new generation of tourists is developing – one which is becoming increasingly concerned about the detrimental environmental impact of flying, and turning instead to destinations on their doorstep for weekend breaks and annual holidays. Those who wish to reduce their carbon footprint further will find that the Lake District is easy to reach and explore by public transport, especially in summer.

Cumbria also boasts a supportive and growing infrastructure that promotes local produce, thus allowing visitors to enjoy good, often organic, food minus the air miles. Self-caterers can shop for supplies at a growing array of first-class farm shops and the number of fine restaurants, gastro pubs and country tea rooms using local produce is increasing all the time. In addition, the days of average accommodation are long gone in the Lake District and visitors today have an ever diversifying choice of places to stay, from luxury country house hotels to camping in a wigwam.

All of these changes make the Lake District an increasingly appealing place to visit. Paradoxically, however, it is the timeless nature of the landscape underpinned by layers of traditions, folk lore, superstitions and myths, and where no view ever looks the same twice, that is the real reason so many travel here. And no matter how many times you visit, in whatever season or weather, the Lake District always takes your breath away.

Unmissable highlights

01 Ullswater Steamer ride

Whatever the weather, the Ullswater Steamer ride from Glenridding to Pooley Bridge is the way to enjoy a beautiful lake and picture perfect Lake District scenery.
See p.30.

02 Hill Top

Hill Top, the former home of Beatrix Potter, provides a fascinating glimpse into the author's life and inspirations. Visit off season if you can.
See p.89.

03 Honister Slate Mine

Popular with all ages, the Honister Slate Mine is the place to gaze at magnificent underground views and learn how generations of slate miners have worked in its vast caverns.
See p.231.

04 Wast Water

Nothing prepares the first time visitor for the breathtaking sight of Wast Water – the National Park's most dramatic lake and officially Britain's favourite view. See p.210.

05
Hardknott Pass

The infamous Hardknott Pass might be steep, but it's also good fun in the right conidtions and home to the remote and atmospheric ruins of an ancient Roman fort.
See p.178.

06
St Herbert's Island

Messing about on the waters of the Lake District doesn't come better than hiring a canoe or kayak and paddling out to St Herbert's Island in Derwent Water. See p.232.

07 The grand ruins of Furness Abbey

The grand ruins of Furness Abbey near Barrow-in-Furness are often overlooked by many visitors and remain one of Cumbria's most peaceful, yet also most spectacular, attractions. See p.142.

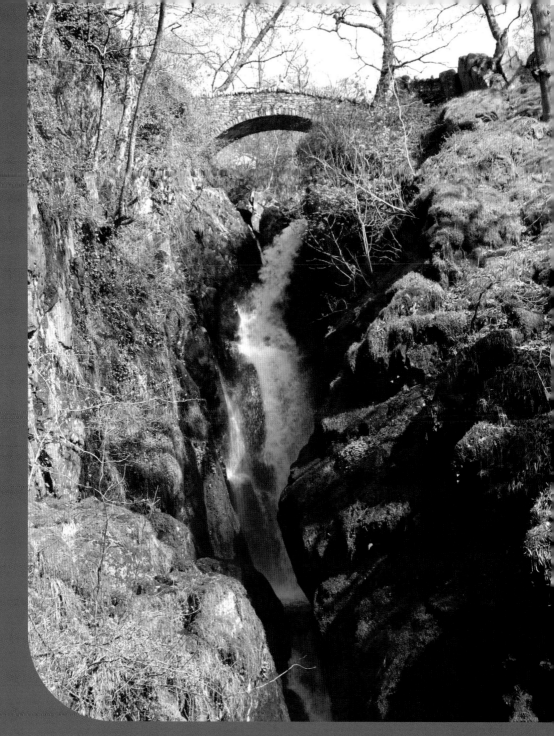

08 Aira Force

Aira Force, on the north side of Ullswater, is the most spectacular waterfall in the lakes. En route to its 21-metre dramatic decent visitors pass through a beautiful arboretum crammed with native and ornamental trees. See p.283.

09 The cross-sands walk

The cross-sands walk over Morecambe Bay with Cedric Robinson, Queen's Guide to the Sands, is a unique and unforgettable experience. You'll follow in the footsteps of centuries of travellers and watch the route disappear once the tide comes rolling in. See p.145.

10 Low Sizergh Barn

Low Sizergh Barn near Kendal is a treasure trove of delicious and often organic local foods and produce. You can also browse through regional crafts and watch cows being milked from the café. See p.114.

Secret
Lake District
Local Recommendations

01 The Capitola Wine Bar

The Capitola Wine Bar in Ulverston is a small and popular taste of Italy in the heart of the South Lakes.

See p.157.

02 Grizedale Forest

Walking in Grizedale Forest in the rain when the air is rich with the heady aroma of woodland fragrances.

See p.125.

03 Doi Inthanon Thai restaurant

Takeaways from Doi Inthanon Thai restaurant in Ambleside are every bit as delicious as eating in at this colourful eatery.

See p.100.

04 Gosforth Bakery

Locals travel for miles to feast on Gosforth Bakery's famously delicious and hearty pies.

See p.219.

05 Ulverston's International Music Festival

An unexpected feast of top quality classical music and jazz events in the South Lakes.

See p.150.

06 Bar 26

Bar 26 on Lake Road in Keswick is known for its great atmosphere, good selection of beers and wines and free peanuts. See p.237.

07 Greystones Coffee Shop

Standing at the foot of Helvellyn, Greystones Coffee Shop in Glenridding serves first class food and is also a fine contemporary art gallery. See p.289.

08 The Great Langdale Christmas Pudding 10km race

The Great Langdale Christmas Pudding 10km race is a weird and wonderful Lake District tradition – watch out for jogging santas. See p.77.

09 Silver How near Grasmere

Silver How near Grasmere is one of the finest places in the National Park to spread out a picnic. See p.175.

10 Majestic Skies

The lack of light pollution in most parts of the Lake District ensures majestic skies on a clear night.

Fact File

01 The Lake District National Park is England's largest national park.

02 It was established on 15 August 1951.

03 The National Park authorities only own approximately 3.9% of the land. Organisations such as the National Trust, United Utilities, Forest Enterprise and private landowners own the rest.

04 The Lake District is 33 miles across (east to west) and 40 miles long (north to south).

05 It contains England's highest mountain, Scafell Pike (3,210ft), deepest lake, Wast Water (243ft), steepest road, Harknott Pass (1 in 3 – 1 in 2.5) and largest stone circle, Long Meg and her Daughters.

06 Only one lake in the National Park is actually called 'lake' – Bassenthwaite Lake.

07 The Lake District contains 6,000 known archaeological sites, 1,740 listed buildings and 21 conservation areas.

08 Tourism is the National Park's biggest industry. It receives around 12 million visitors each year.

THE FACTS

WHEN TO GO

An increasing number of hotel managers throughout the Lake District claim that they never have any down time and that the Lakes are busy with visitors year round. That said, there are peaks in numbers throughout the year and certain months when one type of visitor is more prevalent than any other.

Easter to September is the Lake District's busiest time when hordes of visitors from Britain and across the globe descend on the most popular places such as Windermere and Grasmere. At this time, accommodation rates are at their highest, traffic is at its heaviest and finding car parking spaces or gaining entry into the more popular attractions is often very difficult – especially at weekends. You can also expect coach loads of foreign tourists to roll into certain attractions en masse and literally take them over.

During this time the Easter and summer school holidays see an increasing number of families visiting the Lakes (as do the two half-terms), and any attraction that appeals to children is bound to be busy at these times.

Following the end of the summer holidays, the number of retired people holidaying in the Lake District increases and September and October are busy months for older visitors. At this time the weather is often still good, the landscape is ablaze with autumn colours and the weekends remain popular with all ages.

Some attractions close or operate reduced hours between October and Easter and it's often, but not always, possible to find bargain breaks during this part of the year. The Lakes become quieter throughout November and December with early to mid-December often being the quietest time. For those who don't mind cooler temperatures this is a good time to make the most of low visitor numbers and get stuck into some Christmas shopping.

Numbers obviously peak again throughout Christmas and New Year and any festive break should be booked well in advance. Early spring, prior to the Easter rush is another relatively quiet period and one of the best times to visit. The countryside is awash with spring flowers, including the Lake District's famous daffodils, and new born lambs are bouncing all over the fells.

If you can only visit the Lakes during school holidays and are put off by high visitor numbers, stay in areas away from the main tourist drag such as the western lakes and Furness and Cartmel peninsulas. In these areas, and certain other less well-known pockets of Cumbria, it's possible to find solitude even at peak times.

GETTING THERE

Cumbria and the Lake District are easy to reach both by road and rail.

By road

The M6 motorway runs parallel to the eastern border of the National Park with junctions 36 to 41 providing access west into the Lakes.

The M6 is often very busy on Friday evenings when visitors are heading into the Lakes for the weekend, and equally chocked with traffic on Sundays in the late afternoons and evenings when many are heading home. If the motorway is slow moving or at a standstill, leave the M6 and travel along the A6 instead, which runs to the east and parallel with the motorway from Preston to Carlisle and provides equally easy access into the Lakes.

Approximate miles and driving time to Windermere are:

London	220 miles	5 hrs
Edinburgh	152 miles	3 hrs
Cardiff	265 miles	4 ½ hrs
Bristol	238 miles	4 hrs
Birmingham	157 miles	2 ¾ hrs
Manchester	82 miles	1 ½ hrs
Newcastle upon Tyne	100 miles	2 ¼ hrs
Aberdeen	290 miles	5 ½ hrs

The AA (www.theaa.co.uk) and RAC (www.rac.co.uk) feature route planners on their websites and for regular traffic updates tune into either a local radio station (see p.42) or Radio Five Live.

By coach

Inside the Lake District, National Express (08717 818181 www.nationalexpress.com) has stop off points for its services at Windermere railway station (whose forecourt is also the main bus stop in town), Ambleside, Grasmere and Keswick. Outside of the National Park, stop off points include Kendal, Penrith, Whitehaven, Cockermouth, Ulverston and Grange-over-Sands.

By rail

The West Coast Mainline, which runs between London and Glasgow and Edinburgh, also travels along the eastern edge of the Lake District. This service has stops in Lancaster, Oxenholme on the outskirts of Kendal, Penrith and Carlisle.

From Lancaster a fairly regular Transpennine (www.tpexpress.co.uk) branch line runs to Windermere with stops at Oxenholme, Kendal, Burneside, Staveley and Windermere. And another more frequent and exceptionally scenic branch line travels around the curve of Morecambe Bay to Barrow-in-Furness with stops including Grange-over-Sands, Cark and Cartmel and Ulverston. This service often originates at Manchester Airport and stops at up to four stations in and around Manchester including Piccadilly, Bolton, Chorley and Preston en route.

From Carlisle a further scenic branch line operated by Northern Rail (www.northenrail.org) runs via Wigton around the west Cumbrian coast to Barrow-in-Furness, with stops including Maryport, Whitehaven, St Bees and Ravenglass. Some of the smaller stations on this route are request stops only and these services sometimes continue straight on to Lancaster from Barrow-in-Furness.

Apart from a couple of short steam railways, these train services are the only ones in operation in Cumbria and the Lake District. For information on the scenic Carlisle to Settle Railway see p.300.

For further information on rail travel contact National Rail Enquires (08457 48 49 50 www.nationalrail.co.uk) and for up-to-the minute information on train times each day contact Train Tracker (0871 200 4950).

Stop-offs en route

On the M6 north of Kendal, Tebay services, located just north of junction 38, is the only motorway service station in England that was built by, and is now run by, local people. There are 24-hour filling stations on both sides of the motorway and each includes a farm shop (open 7am–11pm) that sells local produce and regional specialities.

Located close to the Carnforth junction (no. 35) of the M6 is Carnforth railway station (www.carnforth-station.co.uk). The station was the setting for David Lean's 1945 British film classic *Brief Encounter* and has recently undergone extensive renovation that has included the re-instalment of the famous clock from the film. The new Heritage Centre includes a recreation of the station tea rooms in *Brief Encounter* and displays detailing the rich history of the station (open 10am–4pm Tues–Sun; free).

A good stop for families en route into the Lakes is Rheged (see p.287) as its large child friendly restaurant is better than many motorway service station cafés and includes Fairtrade drinks, children's favourites and Cumbrian dishes on its menu.

GREAT STOP OFF – THE MIDLAND HOTEL

Stop offs en route to the Lake District don't come better than the magnificent art deco Midland Hotel. The hotel is accessible from either junction 35 or 34 of the M6 and stands on a prime spot on Morecambe's wide promenade overlooking Morecambe Bay and the low foothills of the south lakes.

The Midland, which featured in an episode of *Coast*, was originally built in 1930 and in its heyday the hotel's guests including Coco Chanel, Wallace Simpson and Lawrence Olivier. As the popularity of the British seaside waned with the rise of inexpensive package tours abroad, the Midland Hotel went into decline and finally closed in 1998 in an almost ruinous state.

However, the fortunes of this Grade II listed masterpiece are now on the rise again as the award winning property developers Urban Splash have completely restored the Midland to its former glory. The refurbishment has included the restoration of many of the original art deco features including several works of art by the British designer and sculpture Eric Gill. The iconic seahorses on the front of the hotel and the large relief in the lobby featuring Odysseus and Nausicaa were both sculpted by Gill.

Those stopping en route for lunch can enjoy a range of dishes dedicated to the British seaside in the stylish sea-facing restaurant and sun terrace. While those who are tempted to stay the night can choose between eight different types of rooms including six fabulous roof top suites that come with their own private terraces, hot tubs and uninterrupted, panoramic views over Morecambe Bay.

The Midland Hotel is due to open in June 2008. For further information or to make a reservation contact: 01524 424000 www.midlandhotelmorecambe.co.uk

10... places to avoid in the Lake District

1 Bowness-on-Windermere on weekends in the summer when it's swarming with tourists and the roads are clogged with cars.

2 Cat Bells. It's one of the most popular walks in the Lake District, horribly busy at the top and not the easy stroll visitors think it is. Also, because so many people have scrambled up the same rock before you, it's become very polished and slippery.

3 Barrow-in-Furness' bar district around the Abbey Road area on Friday and Saturday nights. It's one of the roughest places in Cumbria at this time.

4 Some of the small towns and villages that line the A5086 just beyond the western edge of the National Park such as Cleator, Cleator Moor and Frizington. They aren't the prettiest places in Cumbria.

5 Driving over Hardknott Pass in winter conditions when even the best of cars and drivers don't make it up the steep and often icy slopes.

6 Swimming in the lakes before July, it's simply too cold. Also, be warned that the water is much colder after a rain shower and make sure you follow the safety advice issued by the National Park authorities (see p.38).

7 Walking out onto the sands of Morecambe Bay without a locally trained guide. There can be patches of treacherous quicksand even close to the shore and the tide comes in very fast so it's easy to get cut off from land.

8 Cartmel village on race day – unless you are planning a day at the races.

9 Trying to find a car parking spot in Grasmere on weekends in the summer. This tiny village is inundated with cars at this time and has limited parking spaces, so catch the bus instead.

10 Wearing designer outdoor gear anywhere in the Lakes, but not actually doing any serious walking or climbing – the locals will laugh at you.

GETTING AROUND

The mountainous terrain of the Lake District severely restricts the number of main A roads that serve this region. Most of these roads skirt around the edges of the National Park and include the A66 in the north, which travels from Penrith to Workington, the A590 in the south, which leads from junction 36 of the M6 to Barrow-in-Furness, while the A595 traverses the west Cumbrian coast.

The only major road to cut through the Lake District is the A591, which links Kendal with Keswick travelling through Windermere, Ambleside and Grasmere on the way. Needless to say the A591 is exceptionally busy at peak times when you can expect to sit nose to bumper on the parts of this road that are single lane only.

A limited number of smaller A roads, smaller still B roads and very narrow lanes snake through the less mountainous parts of the Lake District, but huge swathes of the National Park are only accessible on foot.

The park authorities are doing as much as possible to reduce the amount of traffic in the Lakes and the environmental damage the ever increasing amount of emissions causes. Most places in the Lake District are reachable by bus and the number and frequency of services are higher in the summer.

There are practical as well as environmental advantages to using public transport. When the roads are busy it's much less stressful to let someone else do the driving: you can enjoy the amazing views, and not have to worry about finding a parking spot, which in many places in summer is nearly impossible. And once you take into consideration the price of petrol and often high car parking fees, public transport is not as expensive as you might at first think.

By bus

The major bus operator in the area is Stagecoach and you can call their Travel line on 0871 200 22 33 between 8am and 8pm daily, or find details of their services online at www.stagecoachbus.com/northwest. Stagecoach also produces a large free booklet called *The Cumbria and Lakes Rider* which can be picked up at Tourist Information Centres and contains full details on all the bus services in Cumbria. **Explorer Tickets**, which allow unlimited on travel on all Stagecoach bus services, can be bought for a day (£8.50), four days (£19) or a week (£26.50).

One of the main bus routes through the Lake District is the 555/6, which links Lancaster with Keswick and has stops at Kendal, Windermere, Brockhole Visitor Centre, Rydal and Grasmere along the way. This service meets trains that arrive in Windermere station and combination tickets that include train and bus travel plus a cruise with Windermere Lake Cruises (see p.71) called **Lakes Ranger Tickets** can be bought for £15 adult, £7.50 child, £29 families.

Another similar service is the **Cross Lakes Experience**, which links Windermere, with Coniston and includes stops at Hawkshead and Grizedale Forest. This seasonal service incorporates both bus and boat travel and will also transport bicycles. Timetables can be picked up at Tourist Information Centres or requested by calling 015394 45161.

For full information on public transport in Cumbria and the Lake District contact Traveline: 0870 608 2608 www.traveline-cumbria.co.uk.

By organised tour

There are a number of companies who offer organised tours around the Lake District. These companies include:

Mountain Goat, 015394 45161, www.mountain-goat.com
Lake District Tours, 017687 80732, www.laketours.co.uk
North West Tours, 01539 724026, www.nwtours.co.uk
Lakes Supertours, 015394 42751, www.lakes-supertours.com
Touchstone Tours, 017687 79599, www.touchstonetours.co.uk

ACCOMMODATION

There's a mind-blowing amount and variety of accommodation in and around the Lake District, and we've selected some of the most interesting and unique places to stay in The Guide. Most places get fully booked at peak times, so always book as far in advance as possible. Prices tend to be higher around the better known tourist destinations such as Windermere and Grasmere; and those on a budget, or who don't like crowds, are advised to consider areas around the edge or just outside of the National Park boundaries. During peak periods expect to have to book a minimum stay of two to three nights at weekends in most accommodation options.

Cumbria Tourism (www.golakes.co.uk) features a large amount of approved accommodation and details of late availability on its website and you can order a brochure or making a booking on 0845 450 1199. A £3 service fee applies to bookings.

Finding a self-catering cottage

An ever increasing number of self-catering accommodation is available in the Lake District. Some is privately owned and managed however but the vast majority is rented through agencies. Most properties have to be booked for a minimum of a week, especially during peak periods, but some can be rented for long weekends, midweek breaks or occasionally just one night.

Property Agencies in the Lake District/ Cumbria include:

Coniston Country Cottages, 015394 41114, www.conistoncottages.co.uk
Copper Mines and Lakes Cottages, 015394 41765, www.coppermines.co.uk
Cumbrian Cottages, 01228 599960, www.cumbrian-cottages.co.uk
Goosemire Cottages, 01539 731801, www.goosemirecottages.co.uk

Heart of the Lakes Cottages, 015394 32321, www.heartofthelakes.co.uk
Holidays in Lakeland, 0870 078 0162, www.holidays-in-lakeland.co.uk
Keswick Cottages, 017687 78555, www.kewickcottages.co.uk
The Lakeland Cottage Company, 015395 38180, www.lakeland-cottage-company.co.uk
Lakeland Cottages, 017687 76065, www.lakelandcottages.co.uk
Lakeland Hideaways, 015394 42435, www.lakeland-hideaways.co.uk
Lake Lovers, 015394 88855, www.lakelovers.co.uk
Wheelwrights, 015394 37635, www.wheelwrights.com
Windermere Lake Holidays, 015394, www.lakewindermere.net

National Holiday letting companies with properties in the Lake District/Cumbria include:

www.holiday-rentals.co.uk who have around 50 properties in the Lake District, most of which are within the boundaries of the National Park.
www.holidaylettings.co.uk who have over 50 self-catering properties available for short-term letting in the Lake District.
The National Trust (0870 458 4422 www.nationaltrustcottages.co.uk) also rents a number of unusual properties in the Lakes.
The Landmark Trust (01628 825925 www.landmarktrust.org.uk) is a building preservation charity that rescues and restores historic buildings and gives them a new future as holiday lets. The charity prefers people to buy a copy of their handbook which details 184 of their historic buildings, the cost of which (£11.50) is refunded on booking. There is only one Landmark Trust property in the Lake District which is Howthwaite near Grasmere, see p.172.

10... special places to stay

1 Moss Grove, an organic, environmentally conscious hotel in the centre of Grasmere, p.171.

2 New Dungeon Ghyll Hotel, in Great Langdale, steeped in history and surrounded by some of the best scenery in the Lakes, p.180.

3 Holbeck Ghyll Hotel, near Ambleside, laid-back luxury and amazing views, p.97.

4 Camping pods, cosy wooden shelters at the Eskdale Camping and Caravan Club site, p.217.

5 Yew Tree Farm near Coniston, B&B accommodation in a 17th-century farmhouse once owned by Beatrix Potter and film location for *Miss Potter*, p.133.

6 Brooklands, an immaculate luxury guesthouse in Penrith, p.274.

7 The Cottage in the Woods, a tranquil hotel in the heart of Whinlatter Forest, p.254.

8 The Lazy Fish, a luxury self-catering barn conversion near Cockermouth, p.204.

9 Sharrow Bay, a quintessential English country house hotel on the banks of Ullswater, p.291.

10 Wasdale Head Inn, a remote, historic inn at the head of Wast Water, p.217.

Farm stays

An ever increasing number of farms in the Lake District are throwing open their doors for B&B. This type of accommodation is often in a rural location and provides an insight into the working life of many Cumbrian farmers. Breakfast usually includes produce straight from the farm. The Lake District contains of number of National Trust owned farms, many of which offer B&B. Check the bed and breakfast section of their website for full details (www.nationaltrust. org.uk). Luxury farm stays in Cumbria are listed on www.luxuryinafarm.co.uk and further farm stays can be found via Farm Stay UK (www.farmstay.co.uk).

Camping

Camping is very popular in the Lake District, even with Cumbrians. There are a large number of sites to choose from, some owned and managed by the National Trust. All sites are listed in the *Caravan and Camping Guide* created produced annually by Cumbria Tourism – contact them via the accommodation booking line on p. 2 for a copy. This booklet can also be picked up at Tourist Information Centres around the region.

The Lake District also contains a number of camping barns, which offer basic indoor accommodation and cooking facilities. Leaflets detailing all of the barns can be obtained through Tourist Information Centres or see www.lakelandcampingbarns.co.uk. Another useful website for campers is www.find-a-campsite.co.uk/cumbria.html. And for a more unusual night under canvas in the Lake District try a night in a tipi (www.4windslakelandtipis.co.uk). All you need to bring is your own sleeping bag.

Hostels

Youth hostels are one of the cheapest forms of accommodation in the Lake District. There are YHAs in all the main communities and numerous others in more remote locations. You no longer have to be a member of the Youth Hostel Association to stay in one of its hostels, but rates are slightly cheaper if you are. Many contain individual rooms for couples and families as well as larger bunk rooms. Most include cooking and laundry facilities and many also have on-site restaurants and bike hire. The larger hostels remain open throughout the year, but some of the smaller and more remote ones close during the winter. A shuttle bus operated by the YHA runs between them all. Full information and booking can be made on the YHA website (www.yha.org.uk) and if you are booking less than seven days in advance you can use the Lake District Reservations Service to check availability and make a booking. This service operates daily between Easter and October (01539 431117).

The best... places to buy fresh local produce

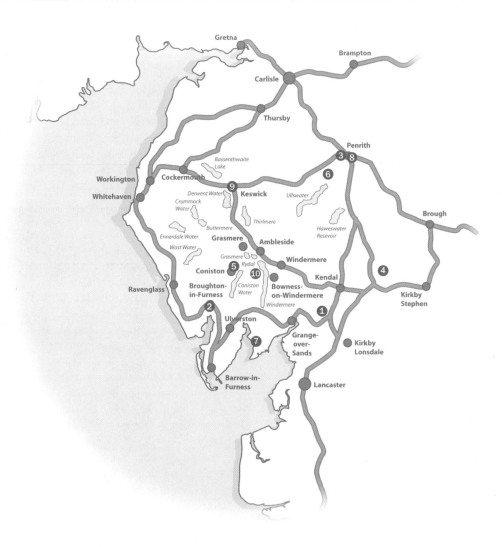

1. Low Sizergh Barn. See p.114.
2. Melville Tyson, Broughton-in-Furness. See p.135.
3. Cranstons, Penrith. See p.276.
4. Orton Farmers' Market. See p.277.
5. Yew Tree Farm, near Coniston. See p.135.
6. Greystone House Farm Shop, Stainton. See p.294.
7. Holker Food Hall. See p.154.
8. Brunswick Deli, Penrith. See p.276.
9. Fond Ewe Cheese Shop, Keswick. See p.244.
10. Hawkshead Relish Company. See p.99.

FOOD AND DRINK

Cumbria and the Lake District have a growing reputation for excellence in food and drink and the region is home to many first class regional producers and outstanding farm shops.

The obvious regional specialities are such as Herdwick lamb and mutton and Belted Galloway beef all reared on the Lake District's mountain slopes. Cumbria is also one of the largest 'milk fields' in the country and the region's delicatessens and farm shops are stocked with many varieties of cheese made from cow's, ewe's and goat's milk. You can expect first-class fish from the Lakes themselves including trout from Esthwaite Water, Windermere char and fresh seafood from Morecambe Bay's fishing communities. And many walkers and climbers still never leave home without a packet of Kendal Mint Cake tucked into their rucksacks – a high energy boost that both Shackleton and Sir Edmund Hillary swore by.

The drink that everyone associates with Cumbria is real ale and there is an ever increasing number of excellent micro breweries, producing a growing range of ales, bitters and stouts, springing up all over the Lakes.

Not so obvious regional specialities include damsons, which grow in abundance around the Lyth Valley and are used in products such as damson gin and beer and local jams. Homemade local condiments including Cumberland mustard and a wide variety of relishes, chutneys, preserves, and honeys are for sale in many regional stores. Fruit and vegetables from local farms, some organic, can be purchased from farm shops and at the region's markets. And the Lake District's bakeries are bursting with unusual breads, melt in the mouth cakes and, of course, pies galore.

Local restaurants, hotels and cafés are big supporters of Cumbria's regional producers and you can expect to see an abundance of regional specialities on menus around the Lake District. But as fantastic as many places to eat out in the Lake District are, on a fine day nothing beats tucking into a picnic on the fells or the edge of a lake. You can have a basket of fine local picnic foods delivered to your door from 1 May to 30 September from Lakeland Picnics (01539 568410 www.lakelandpicnic.co.uk).

Cumbria Tourist Board has produced an excellent booklet *The Taste District* (£2), which tells food and drink lovers everything they need to know about the gastronomic delights of Cumbria, from the best local retailers to the region's famed pubs. And their website also includes detailed information on where shop for local food and the region's many places to eat and drink (www.golakes.co.uk/do/food and drink).

Full details on the Lake District's farmers' markets, regional shows and recipes using local specialities can be found on the Made in Cumbria website (www.madeincumbria.co.uk). While Artisan Food is also a goldmine of information on Cumbrian food (www.artisan-food.com). And more information on the region's best real ale pubs can be found on the website of the Westmorland branch of the Campaign for Real Ale (www.camrawestmorland.org), who also produce a regular free newsletter that can be picked up in many pubs.

And if you want to spend a day discovering all there is know about regional food and drink, head to the annual North West Fine Foods Festival at the Westmorland County Show Ground at Crooklands on the outskirts of Kendal. Dates and full details can be found on the North West Fine Food website (www.nwfinefood.co.uk).

The best... Lake District real ale pubs

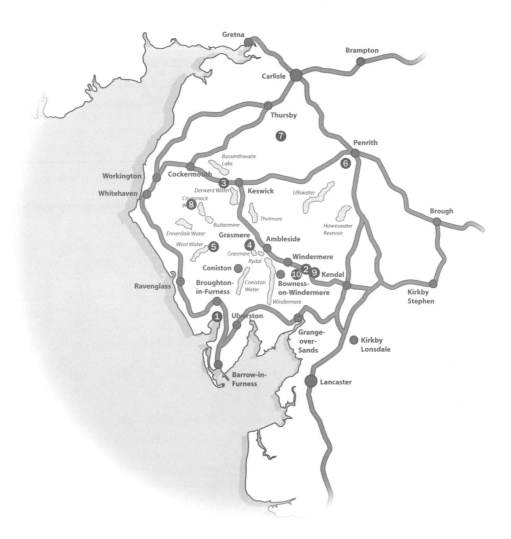

1 The Prince of Wales at Foxfield. See p.138.
2 The Eagle and Child at Staveley. See p.133.
3 Middle Ruddings in Braithwaite. See p.247.
4 Tweedies Bar at the Dale Lodge Hotel in Grasmere. See p.173.
5 Ritson's Bar at the Wasdale Head Inn, Wasdale Head. See p.219.
6 The Queen's Head at Tirril. See p.278.
7 The Old Crown at Hesket Newmarket. See p.258.
8 The Kirkstile Inn at Loweswater. See p.206.
9 Hawkshead Brewery Beer Hall, Mill Yard, Staveley. See p.116.
10 The Watermill at Ings. See p.116.

10... special places to eat

1 **The Jumble Room** in Grasmere is fun, friendly and serves fabulous food in eccentric surroundings, p.174.

2 Vegetarian restaurants don't come better than the gourmet **Quince & Medlar** in Cockermouth. It's even a big hit with meat eaters, p.206.

3 **The Pheasant Inn** at Bassenthwaite Lake is an award winning inn with a daily changing menu of far better than average pub food, p.256.

4 Locals travel for miles to enjoy top notch pub food at **The Blacksmith Arms** in Broughton Mills, near Broughton-in-Furness, p.136.

5 Relatively new in town, **Unique Fine Dining** in Keswick serves good food at reasonable prices, p.246.

6 **Fellbites Café** at Glenridding is a delightful café by day and a relaxed restaurant serving value for money unusual meals at night, p.295.

7 Michelin starred food is complimented by priceless views of lake Windermere at **Holbeck Ghyll**, a country house hotel near Ambleside, p.100.

8 **The Drunken Duck**, near Hawkshead is one of the Lake District's finest gastro pubs – reservations essential, p.100.

9 **Sharrow Bay** country house hotel boasts a Michelin starred gem of a restaurant on the banks of Ullswater – perfect for afternoon tea or a special night out, p.295.

10 **Wilf's Café** in Mill Yard, Staveley is a local institution and rightly famous for its reasonably priced hearty meals, Fairtrade coffee and superb cakes, p.116.

10... Lake District regional specialities

1 Cartmel Sticky Toffee Pudding, p.153.

2 Damson Gin from Strawberry Bank Liquors, p.114.

3 Real ale from one of Cumbria's many excellent micro breweries.

4 Traditional Cumberland Sausage, a distinctive fat coil of sausage made with coarsely chopped pork, black pepper, herbs and spices.

5 Sarah Nelson's Grasmere Gingerbread, p.173.

6 Herdwick mutton and lamb, Cumbria's very own sheep, bred on the fells and available at butchers and restaurants throughout the county.

7 Windermere char, a member of the salmon family found in deep lakes, most commonly Windermere, and available in many of the region's restaurants.

8 Quiggin's Kendal Mint Cake, the original producer of this minty flavoured slab of sugar, that's enduringly popular with walkers and climbers and for sale throughout the Lakes.

9 Morecambe Bay shrimps, farmed from the sands of Morecambe Bay. Sold in delicatessens and found on menus in Cumbria and beyond, p.154.

10 Farm-made ice cream, an increasing number of dairy farms in Cumbria are making ice cream with creamy milk from their own herds and selling it in tea shops.

LOCAL FESTIVALS

There are hundreds of events and festivals held in the Lake District every year. Many, such as the local agricultural shows and sheep dog trials have been running for centuries and are superb ways for visitors to find out more about the working life and traditions of the region. New festivals spring up all the time, especially those celebrating cultural life from within and outside the region, and some such as Keswick's *Words by the Water* literature festival have established a national reputation.

Many of the area's festivals and events are listed in each chapter throughout the guide, and for more detailed information see the 'What's On' section of the Cumbria Tourist Board's website (www.golakes.co.uk/do/whats-on) and the 'Events' section of the Lake District's National Park's website (www.lake-district.gov.uk/index/enjoying/ events).

The Lake District National Park also produces an extensive annual booklet detailing literally hundreds of events and activities taking place inside the National Park each year, called called *Out and About*. Cumbria Tourism produce a smaller *Events Guide booklet*. Both can be picked up from regional Tourist Information Centres.

10... Lake District local festivals

1 Windermere on Water, an annual three-day festival of events at venues around the lake, p.78.

2 Words by the Water, literature festival at Theatre by the Lake in Keswick, p.238.

3 The Kendal Mountain Film Festival at The Brewery Arts Centre in Kendal, p.112.

4 Potfest, the UK's oldest potters' market in Penrith and **Potfest in the Park** and at Hutton-in-the-Forest, p.272.

5 The World Gurning Championships in Egremont, p.216.

6 The Lake District Sheepdog Trials at Ings, p.112.

7 Printfest, an exhibition of work at Ulverston's Coronation Hall by the UK's leading printmakers, p.150.

8 The Keswick Jazz Festival, first-class jazz at various venues around the town, p.238.

9 The Hawkshead Agricultural Show, a showcase of local livestock and produce.

10 Ulverston's weekend-long Dickensian Christmas Festival, p.150.

Calendar of Events

March
Words by the Water is a high-profile literature festival hosted by Keswick's Theatre by the Lake and attracts top name authors and poets. See p.78.

April
Damson Day at Low Farm in the Lyth Valley celebrates the annual display of damson blossoms and includes craft demonstrations, children's activities and plenty of local produce made from this endangered fruit. See p.111.

Keswick's popular Film Festival features and eclectic mix of mainstream and specialist cinema. See p.238.

May
The **International Music Festival** held in Ulverston's Coronation Hall boasts an impressive array of top classical music events. See p.150.

Also hosted by Ulverston's Coronation Hall, **Printfest** is a large exhibition of work by the UK's leading printmakers. See p.150.

On spring bank holiday weekend, **Cartmel Races** take place at the villages' small racetrack – expect a fun family friendly day out and the opportunity to have a small flutter. See p.150.

Keswick's colourful **Jazz festival** livens up the town throughout the month. See p.238.

June
Windermere on Water, also known as WOW, is an annual festival of events at venues around the lake. See p.78.

Cockermouth's Summer Festival runs over June and July and includes a street entertainment and children's events. See p.201.

July
Ambleside Sports is a day of traditional Lakeland sports held on the last Thursday of the month in the town's Rydal Park. See p.96.

Coniston's week long **Water Festival** is a mix of sporting events, local traditions and arts and crafts. See p.132.

The **Langdale Gala** on the first Sunday in July is a day of local sports and traditional events. See p.179.

August
Potfest, the UK's oldest potters' market takes place in Penrith, while Potfest in the Park, an exhibition of selected potters' work is held in the grounds of Hutton-in-the-Forest. See p.272.

Held on the first Thursday of the month at Hill Farm in Ings, the **Lake District Sheepdog Trials** provide a unique insight into the working life of the fells. See p.112.

Grasmere's ancient rush bearing ceremony takes place on the nearest Saturday to St Oswald's Day (August 5th). See p.169.

Cartmel Races (see above) also take place over August Bank Holiday weekend.

September
Coniston's Walking Festival, held late in the month, is a mix of organised walks, events and family activities, all celebrating the surrounding landscape.

The **World Gurning Championships**, held on the third Saturday of the month in Egremont, sees the crowning of the world's ugliest man and woman. See p.216.

November
The **Kendal Mountain Film Festival** and associated Mountain Book Festival hosted by the town's Brewery Arts Centre is popular with climbers, film buffs and visitors wanting to find out more about those who pits their wits against the world's most challenging peaks. See p.112.

Ulverston's **Dickensian Christmas Festival** runs over the last weekend of the month and is a celebration of local arts, crafts, foods and history. See p.150.

December
Keswick's traditional **Christmas Fayre** takes place on the second Sunday in December and features craft stalls and local entertainment. See p238.

TRAVELLING WITH CHILDREN

The Lake District is an excellent destination for family holidays and many bring their children to this region year upon year. Families who want to spend time together enjoying the outdoors will be hard pushed to choose between the Lakes themselves, the inland fells and the seaside, all of which are brilliant places to while away fair weather days. But you don't have to rely on sunshine to have a good time with children as the Lakes and surrounding regions are home to many entertaining, educational and downright fun attractions for all age groups.

Families travelling to the region by train can save a fortune with a Family Rail Card (www.family-railcard.co.uk) and Virgin Trains hand out free activity packs to children travelling during the school holidays.

Whether you are driving with children or using public transport it's a good idea to have travel sickness tablets handy as the narrow windy lanes can upset even the hardiest of tummies. And for more information about travelling with children and useful products check www.travellingwithchildren.co.uk.

10... activities for children

1 An underground tour of **Honistor Slate Mine**, p.231.

2 Discovering the weird and wonderful animals at **Eden Ostrich World** at Langwathby, p.271.

3 Taking a trip on the **Ravenglass to Eskdale narrow gauge steam railway**, p.212.

4 Learning all about Whitehaven's maritime history at **The Rum Story**, p.200.

5 Enjoying a family day out at **Muncaster Castle**, p.214.

6 Finding out about the wildlife in and around the region's lakes at the **Lakes Aquarium**, p.94.

7 Horse trekking through the local countryside with the **Rookin House Farm Equestrian and Activity Centre**, p.287.

8 Getting to know animals from around the world at the **South Lakes Wild Animal Park**, p.148.

9 Standing in Peter Rabbit's vegetable patch at the **World of Beatrix Potter Attraction**, p.76.

10 Swinging through the trees at **Go Ape** in Grizedale Forest, p.132.

The best... things to do with children when it rains

1. Lakeland Climbing Centre, Kendal. See p.110.
2. The Beacon, Whitehaven. See p.198.
3. The Cars of the Stars Motor Museum, Keswick. See p.233.
4. The subtropical swimming paradise at Centre Parcs, Whinfell Forest. See p.270.
5. The Sellafield Visitor's Centre. See p.216.
6. RAF Millom Aviation and Military Museum. See p.139.
7. The Museum of Lakeland Life, Kendal. See p.109.
8. The Pencil Museum in Keswick. See p.234.
9. Honister Slate Mine. See p.231.
10. The Rum Story, Whitehaven. See p.200.

SPORTS AND OUTDOOR ACTIVITIES

Walking

There are all kinds of walks to suite all abilities in the Lake District. Many travel to the region to get stuck into some serious fell walking in all weathers, while others prefer to stroll around a small lake or tarn and enjoy the views without ever breaking into a sweat.

Some walks are detailed in this guide, and there are countless walking guides and leaflets available in the Lakes which start at 60p for a large laminated postcard detailing a single route, to well over £10 for more specialist guides. For a comprehensive list of walks online visit www.lakedistrictwalks.com. A useful website for information on walking in the Lake District is www.lakeswalks. co.uk and for inspiration to don your boots and get into the fells see www.stridingedge. net a photo diary of Lake District fell walks.

Families with buggies, wheelchair users and those who find walking a challenge should visit with the 'Miles Without Stiles' section of the Lake District National Park's website which lists 21 different manageable routes (www.lakedistrict.gov.uk /miles_ without_stiles) — all 'road tested' by local residents in wheelchairs.

One of the most sociable ways to get to grips with walking in the Lake District for new comers, or those who don't like to walk alone, is to hook into one of the region's Walking Festivals. Coniston, Ullswater and Ulverston all organise such festivals and you can pick up information on local history and geology along the way. Contact the relevant Tourist Information Centres for more information and dates.

There are also an increasing number of companies who lead organised walks in the Lake District and surrounding area. Just like Walking Festivals these are sociable and often informative events, and you can leave the map-reading to somebody else.

TOP TIPS FOR SAFE WALKING IN THE LAKE DISTRICT

- Choose a route that suites your level of fitness and ability. If it starts to get too difficult for you – turn back.

- The weather turns quickly in the Lakes, even in summer, so check the forecast before you leave with Weatherline (0870 055 0575 www.lakedistrict. gov.uk/weatherline) and plan a route that suites the conditions.

- Always wear appropriate sturdy shoes or walking boots.

- Take a waterproof and warm fleece or jumper, and enough food and drink to last the walk, plus a bit more just in case.

- Carry a map and compass if you are heading into the fells

- Let a third party know where you are going.

- Never rely on your mobile phone or GPS system.

Specialist walking tour operators

Fell Treks Guided Walks, 01946 810062, www.felltrek.co.uk

Guided walks lead by Susan Noake, a qualified mountain leader and member of the Wasdale Mountain Rescue Team, are tailored to suit each individual's or group's wishes and ability.

John Nash Guided Mountain Walks, 01539 725921, www.jwnash.co.uk

Qualified mountain leader John Nash worked for the Lake District National Park for 30 years and tailors his walks to suit all abilities. He also teaches navigational skills.

The best... Lake District walks

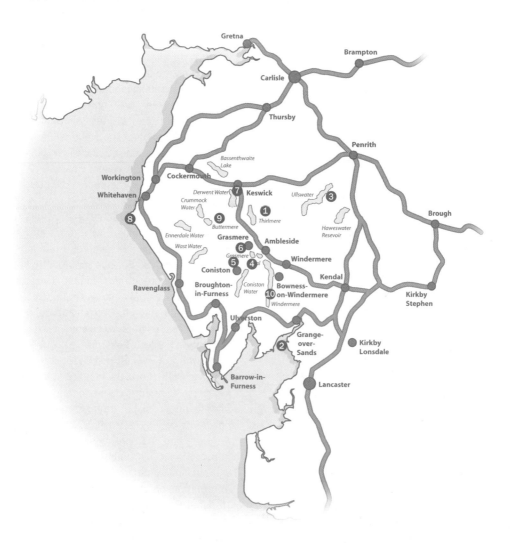

1. Helvellyn via Striding Edge and Swirral Edge. See p.283.
2. The cross-sands walk over Morecambe Bay. See p.145.
3. Pooley Bridge to Howtown and back via the Ullswater Steamer. See p.285.
4. The circular walk around Tarn Hows. See p.127.
5. Walking up The Old Man of Coniston from Coniston village. See p.127.
6. Easdale Tarn from Grasmere. See p.164.
7. Walla Crag from Keswick or Ashness Bridge. See p.229.
8. The coastal path along St Bees Head. See p.195.
9. The circular walk around Lake Buttermere. See p.193.
10. Gummer's How, a popular family walk. See p.74.

Striding Ahead Walking Adventures, 0845 638 1886, www.stridingahead.co.uk

A Kendal based company who offer starter to challenger trails for groups of up to eight.

Walks For Softies, 019467 25413, www.walks forsofties.co.uk

For full and half day guided walks around the western Lake District lead by experienced local guides.

For information on walking holidays see the Organised holidays section on p.41.

THE COUNTRYSIDE CODE

- Be safe – plan ahead and follow the signs.
- Leave gates and property as you find them.
- Protect plants and animals, and take your litter home.
- Keep dogs under close control.
- Consider other people.

Cycling

An ever increasing number of visitors are getting on their bikes in the Lake District and either bringing their own wheels or using one of the growing number of cycle hire companies around the region.

There is little in the way of cycle lanes on roads inside the National Park and some of the major routes can make for pretty stressful cycling in peak season. If you are a road cyclist head for the pockets of quieter lanes where you can usually find peace even in the height of summer. If you are a serious road cyclist you can test your fitness to the limit on the annual Fred Whitton Challenge that takes place in May. This gruelling 112-mile ride for charity starts and ends in Coniston and leads riders through all the Lake District's most glorious but most brutal scenery. Check www.fredwhittonchallenge.org.uk for details and to book a place, but get your entry form in early, as this event is incredibly popular and places are limited.

Off-road cyclists should be aware that mountain bikes are not permitted on footpaths but are allowed on bridleways. These snake all over the National Park and provide visitors with an appealing combination of good routes and excellent views.

However, some of the best cycling terrain, especially for families, can be found in the region's forests. Grizedale and Whinlatter forest are both laced with trails for all abilities from beginners' routes to seriously challenging rides. Serious mountain bikers can join September's annual Grizedale Mountain Bike Challenge (www.gmbc.co.uk) a 30-mile adrenalin fuelled whizz around the forest as fast or as slow as you like.

Cumbria Bike Fest is a week-long celebration of cycling across Cumbria and the Lake District and takes place in May. The festival includes organised rides for all ages and abilities, skills training, demos and children's cycling instruction. Details of the festival and comprehensive information about cycling in Cumbria can be found at www.cyclingcumbria.co.uk. And for more information on cycling in the Lake District National Park, ideas for routes, maps and details of cycle hire companies check out the cycling section on the park's website: www.lake-district.gov.uk/index/enjoying/outdoors/cycling. The park authorities also produce a cycling map (£2), which can be picked up at Tourist Information Centres.

The best... Lake District cycle rides

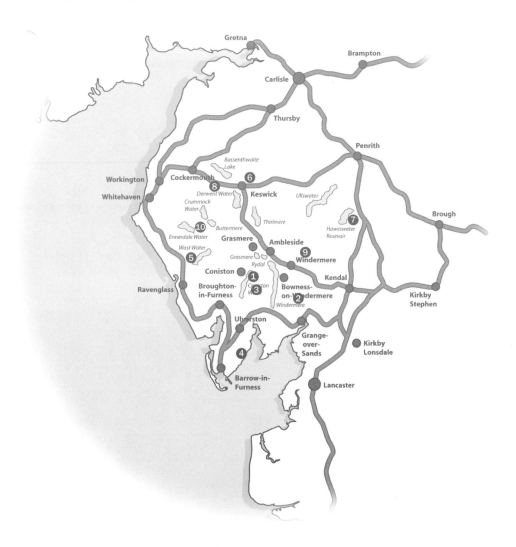

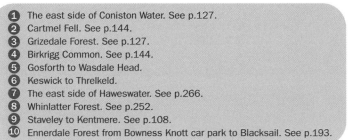

1. The east side of Coniston Water. See p.127.
2. Cartmel Fell. See p.144.
3. Grizedale Forest. See p.127.
4. Birkrigg Common. See p.144.
5. Gosforth to Wasdale Head.
6. Keswick to Threlkeld.
7. The east side of Haweswater. See p.266.
8. Whinlatter Forest. See p.252.
9. Staveley to Kentmere. See p.108.
10. Ennerdale Forest from Bowness Knott car park to Blacksail. See p.193.

Water sports and swimming

The region's many lakes provide visitors with ample opportunities to enjoy a large variety of water sports. Companies offering boat hire and organised water sport sessions are listed in each chapter of the guide. If you do hire a boat make sure that it is from a reputable company, has sufficient buoyancy, and that you never overload it. While on the water keep an eye open for boat wash and, as with walking, check the weather and head back to shore if conditions start to get too rough for you to handle.

On hot summer days the lakes and tarns are tempting places to swim. However, in some lakes such as Loweswater swimming is banned altogether and the National Park advises all would-be swimmers never to jump straight into the water. Even on a very hot day temperatures just below the surface are extremely cold and jumping in can cause your body to momentarily close down, which means you can't move your muscles or breath properly. Jumping off boats and bridges can be particularly dangerous.

Any would-be swimmer is advised to enter the water gradually and never venture out of their depth – remember that some lakes have steeply shelving sides. Always head along the shoreline rather than out into the lake and be aware that even if a lake is calm one minute, the wake from a passing boat can make conditions choppy.

Climbing

The Lake District was the birthplace of rock climbing and is home to many of England's top climbers. Needless to say climbing is an extremely popular pastime in this region and climbers can pick up climbing guides and gear in just about every town in the National Park. The numerous companies offering tuition and instruction for complete beginners include:

Above The Line, 019467 26229, www.wasdale.com
Based at the Wasdale Head Inn, Above the Line organises guided ascents for all abilities and runs courses just for women with female instructors.

Carol Climb Outdoor Adventures, 01946 862342, www.carolclimb.co.uk
For half and full day ascents plus evening climbs. This company also teaches scrambling and other outdoor pursuits.

Joint Adventures, 015394 41526, www.jointadventures.co.uk
A family-based company organises climbing and abseiling courses plus gorge walking.

Indoor climbing walls are great places to learn basic skills and can be found in Kendal (see p.110) and Keswick (see p.235).

THE LAKE DISTRICT NATIONAL PARK'S SAFETY TIPS FOR PADDLERS AND SWIMMERS

- Beware of windchill – the combined effect of wind speed and air temperature.
- Waves, natural wash and wash from boats can arrive without warning.
- Keep watch – be your own lifeguard! Few inland waters are patrolled.
- Supervise children closely at all times.
- Do not swim alone.
- Swim parallel to the shore, not out of sight or to the far distance.
- Inflatables should be securely tethered and used only in shallow water as they can quickly capsize, deflate or be blown into deep water.

Fell running

Fell running takes place throughout the year in the Lake District and is a popular pastime with many of the region's super fit. The sport essentially involves running up and down some of the Lake District's steepest scenery and is only undertaken by the hardiest of runners. Many of the Lake District's shows include a spot of fell running and to find out more about runs in the region check the websites of the Cumberland Fell Runners Association www.cfra.co.uk and the Borrowdale Fell Running Club www.borrowdale fellrunners.co.uk. The Eden Runners www.eden runners.co.uk also organise fell running events and the Hawkshead Half Marathon, which takes place in March. May's infamous Windermere Marathon is sponsored by the Brathay Hall Trust: details can be found on the organisation's website www.brathay. org.uk.

Traditional sports

The Lake District's annual shows such as Ambleside Sports (see p.96), Grasmere Sports and Show (see p.169) and the Langdale Gala (see p.179) are excellent places to witness local traditional sports such as fell running and Cumberland and Westmorland Wrestling.

Further information

For further information on outdoor pursuits in the Lake District see www.lakedistrict outdoors.co.uk and to get all fired up about outdoor activities visit the Keswick Mountain Festival in May (see p.238) and the Kendal Mountain Film Festival in November (see p.112).

REAL MEN WEAR THEIR UNDERPANTS ON THE OUTSIDE

It is thought that the Vikings brought Cumberland and Westmorland wrestling to England, although it may have developed out of a longer-standing Celtic tradition.

Wrestlers stand chest to chest, grasping each other around the body with their chins on their opponent's right shoulder. Once the wrestlers 'tekk hod', they attempt to unbalance each other, or make their opponent lose their hold, using any method other than kicking. If any part of a wrestler's body touches the ground aside from his feet then he loses. Matches are decided by the best of three falls.

The traditional costume of a Cumberland and Westmorland wrestler can make these usually very strong men look anything but butch – vests, white long johns, socks and embroidered felt 'underpants' worn on the outside. But if spectators go along expecting the preening and prancing associated with American wrestling, they'll be disappointed — competitors need power and skill, and they take their sport, and its traditions, very seriously.

The best... unusual attractions and activities

1 Hot air balloon ride with High Adventure. See p.74.
2 A beach horse ride with Murthwaite Green Trekking Centre. See p.139.
3 The Quaker Tapestry, Kendal. See p.110.
4 Homes of Football, Ambleside. See p.93.
5 Ghost spotting at the Kirkstone Pass Inn. See p.297.
6 Cartmel Races. See p.150.
7 Sea boat tour with Whitehaven Marine Adventures. See p.197.
8 Operating a JCB at Rookin House Farm. See p.287.
9 A tandem paraglide with Air Ventures Paragliding school. See p.250.
10 The Story Teller's Garden, Grasmere. See p.168.

ORGANISED HOLIDAYS AND COURSES

Walking and cycling holidays

Contour Walking Holidays
017684 80451; www.contours.co.uk
Contour Walking Holidays organises self-guided walking tours which include accommodation, luggage transport and a tour pack containing maps and a guidebook.

Discovery Travel
01904 766564; www.discoverytravel.co.uk
Discovery Travel organises a range of self-guided walking and cycling trips in the Lake District. Accommodation, luggage, transport and maps are all provided.

Free Range Walking Holidays
015396 20134; www.shacklabank.co.uk
Based outside of the National Park at Shacklabank Farm near Sedbergh, Alison O'Neil, otherwise known as the Lake District Shepherdess, runs walking holidays combined with a taste of life on the farm.

Holiday Lakeland Cycling Tours
016973 71871; www.holiday-lakeland.co.uk
Holiday Lakeland organises an annually changing programme of cycling holidays in and around the Lake District.

Knobbly Stick
01539 737576; www.knobblystick.com
Knobbly Stick runs five different walking holidays in the Lake District, or if you want to go it alone will provide details of routes, book accommodation and arrange baggage transport.

Outdoor pursuits holidays

Country Adventures
01254 690691; www.country-adventures.co.uk
Country Adventures offers a range of walking, multi-activity and scrambling holidays in the Lake District.

River Deep Mountain High 015395 31116;
www.riverdeepmountainhigh.co.uk
River Deep Mountain High organises a range of multi-activity holidays from weekend to week-long packages.

Cooking holidays and courses

Lucy Cooks Cookery School
015394 32288; www.lucycooks.co.uk
A top notch cookery school based in Staveley's Mill Yard near Kendal which offers a vast array of day long cookery courses.

Miller Howe
015394 42536; www.millerhowe.com/special
Miller Howe is a country house hotel on the edge of lake Windermere which has been running a four-night residential cookery course in November for around 30 years. The course includes a wine tasting session on the final evening.

Staff of Life Bakery
01539 738606; www.artisanbreadmakers.co.uk
Day-long bread making courses, usually on a Sunday, run by the fabulous Staff of Life bakery in Kendal.

Painting/photography holidays and courses

Bill Birkett Photography Courses
015394 37420; www.billbirkett.co.uk
Renowned landscape photographer Bill Birkett runs day-long photography courses for groups of up to three and longer residential courses, details of which can be found on his website.

Lakeland Art Courses
017687 72417;
http://web.ukonline.co.uk/janeward
Painting holidays in Grasmere and Keswick lead by professional landscape artist Jane Ward. Courses are aimed at all levels from beginners upwards and use a range of mediums.

Rothay Manor Hotel
015394 33605; www.rothaymanor.co.uk
Located on the outskirts of Ambleside, Rothay Manor Hotel runs a number of special interest holidays including various painting holidays for all levels and work with oil, acrylic and water-colours.

Residential colleges

Higham Hall
017687 76276; www.highamhall.com
Higham Hall is a residential college for adult education located at Bassenthwaite Lake. The college run an amazing array of year-round courses incorporating subjects such as art, history, literature and languages.

FURTHER INFORMATION

Local media

Radio
BBC Radio Cumbria 95.6, 96.1 or 104.1 FM, www.bbc.co.uk/cumbria/local_radio
The Bay 96.9, 102.3, 103.2 FM, www.thebay.co.uk
Lakeland Radio 100.1, 100.8 FM, www.lakelandradio.co.uk

Weekly newspapers
Westmorland Gazette
www.thisisthelakedistrict.co.uk
Cumberland and Westmorland Herald
www.cwherald.com
Cumberland News
www.cumberland-news.co.uk

Daily evening papers
North West Evening Mail
www.nwemail.co.uk
Evening News and Star
www.newsandstar.co.uk

Monthly magazine
Cumbria www.dalesman.co.uk

Bimonthly magazine
Cumbria Life www.cumbrialife.co.uk

Other useful webites

www.fld.org.uk
Friends of the Lake District.
www.madeincumbria.co.uk
A website dedicated to the foods and crafts produced in Cumbria.

www.gonmad.co.uk/cumbria
The place to learn Cumbrian slang before you arrive.
www.lakelandcam.co.uk
A website recording various daily images of the Lakes and surrounding areas.

Sustainable tourism

www.ourstolookafter.co.uk
The website of the Tourism and Conservation Partnership.
www.wildlifetrust.org.uk
The Cumbria Wildlife Trust
www.floraofthefells.com
Flora of the Fells is a project that celebrates and protects the Cumbrian landscape. This organisation also programmes a series of Cumbria Farm Days, which are excellent for visitors, especially families, to find out all about life on a farm in the Lake District. Details can be found on the website or look out for the Cumbria Farm Days leaflet.
www.thetravelfoundation.org
The Travel Foundation helps visitors care for the places they visit.
www.saveoursquirrels.org.uk
Website dedicated to saving red squirrels which can still be found in Cumbria.
www.naturalengland.org.uk
Natural England works to conserve and enhance the natural landscape.
www.fixthefells.co.uk
An online donation site that enables vital repairs to be made to the footpaths in the Lake District.

The Tourism and Conservation Partnership and Friends of the Lake District have produced a free *ABC Green Guide to Cumbria and the Lake District*, which can be picked up in Tourist Information Centres. And the free *Cumbria's Green Handbook* (www.greenhandbook.co.uk) is produced four times a year and can be picked up in local book and health food shops.

THE BACKGROUND

HISTORY

Pre-Roman

It is believed that the human settlement of the area of Britain now called the Lake District began around 5,000 years ago. However, history has left us little with which to flesh out the bare bones of dates and carbon remains to create an image of life for those who lived in the region at this time. Evidence of Cumbria's earliest settlers exists in the form of a so-called Stone Age axe factory in the Langdale Pikes, which was a major source of stone axes during Neolithic times.

However, the greatest legacy left behind from this era is the region's stone circles, which include some of the earliest in Britain. The purpose of these magnificent circles can only be speculated upon and the most spectacular ones to visit include **Castlerigg Stone Circle** (see p.226) near Keswick and **Long Meg and Her Daughters** (see p.262) at Little Salkeld.

Roman

The main Roman occupation of Britain began in AD43 under the command of Emperor Claudius. At the time of the invasion a large part of the north of England was governed by the Brigantes – a powerful matriarchal Celtic tribe ruled by Queen Cartimandua, the only woman other than Boudicca mentioned in ancient sources of British history. Roman historian Tacitus records that the impact of the invasion was not felt in Cumbria until AD77–84 when Agricola marched into what is now the Lake District with the 20th Roman Legion.

This view, and Tacitus's writings, have since been challenged. Roman coins unearthed in the Furness peninsula date back to the earliest days of their occupation and some local historians believe that the Romans were actually trading in the area and perhaps did not take it by force.

The biggest evidence of Roman occupation in the region is **Hadrian's Wall**. Completed in AD130, the wall travels from the Solway Firth in the north-west to the River Tyne in the north-east and once marked the far northern border of the Roman Empire.

However, little is known about the actual influence Romans had in the area and what life was like during their occupation for the average citizen. It is known that following the Roman occupation, the Brigantes rebelled several times from York and Carlisle, yet there is no way of knowing whether the inhabitants of the region were involved in any uprising against Rome or were content with life under its rule.

Other than the inevitable roads and hoards of coins, further evidence of Roman occupation in the region can be found in the form of ruined forts at Hardknott Pass (see p.178) and Waterhead near Ambleside (see p.87) and those wanting to find out more about the Romans in Cumbria should visit the **Senhouse Roman Museum** in Maryport (see p.199).

Post-Roman Saxons and Vikings

According to most historians, the Romans officially left Britain in AD409/410. Between 30 and 40 years after the Romans left, invading Saxons from north Holland arrived in southern and eastern Britain. However, the Saxon influence was not felt in Cumbria until the 7th century and the most enduring evidence of their occupation is on the region's place names. Any name ending in 'ton', 'mere' or 'ham' suggests a Saxon influence.

More evidence exists of Britain's next set of invaders – the Vikings – who arrived in Cumbria in the 9th and 10th centuries from Ireland and the Isle of Man. The Vikings who landed in this part of the country were from Norway (Norse) and less ferocious than their Danish counterparts (the Danes). Viking relics still *in situ* and accessible to visitors include the **Gosforth Cross** (see p.212) in the Western Lakes. However, like the Saxons, the most tangible legacy on the Vikings can be found in their influence of place names. Any name that incorporates 'kirk' (Norse for church), 'by' (Norse for farm or village) or 'thwaite (Norse for forest clearing or meadow) suggests Viking occupation or settlement. It is also suggested that even if places were named after the Vikings departed, their influence was so strong on the region that it lasted for hundreds of years after their initial arrival.

Domesday Book to Dissolution of the Monasteries

In contrast to the uncertainties that dominate the early Middle Ages, the period after the Norman Conquest of 1066 provides the first quantifiable evidence of the existence of settlements in Cumbria and their size. Written in Latin, the Domesday Book recorded the findings of the 1086 Domesday Survey and is the first official record of land ownership in Britain. Immediately following the Norman invasion, much of the north was laid to waste in a deliberate policy on the part of the Conqueror to make the unruly northern territories comply with Norman rule. Once they did, as with the rest of England, William assumed control over the framework of both secular and spiritual life through a system of manors and monasteries that worked together in support of each other.

Founded in 1127 the great Abbey of St Mary in Furness, otherwise known as **Furness Abbey** (see p.142), on the outskirts of Barrow-in-Furness, was once one of the most important religious centres in the country. As with many of Britain's great medieval abbeys, all that remains of what was once an epicentre of power and wealth in the region is a stone husk of ruined walls

that are owned by English Heritage and open to the public.

The monks of Furness Abbey smelted iron and it was the rich and plentiful supplies of high quality iron that attracted Robert the Bruce to the region in 1316 and provided him with a much needed boost to the Scottish economy. Not satisfied with their early plunder, the Scots returned again in their thousands in 1322 – the biggest Scottish raid in the north. This devastating raid laid waste to large areas and Robert the Bruce only agreed to spare Furness Abbey for a fee of £10,000 – an enormous amount of money at that time.

Many of the Cumbria's old houses such as **Levens Hall** (see p.106) and **Sizergh Castle** (see p.106) are built around old medieval pele towers, which are defensive structures with thick stone walls that could withstand short sieges and were built as protection from the invading Scots.

Dissolution of the monasteries in 1536 saw the rise of the 'statesman', or yeoman farmer, as land previously owned by the church was divided up. The most famous statesman house in Cumbria is **Townend** (see p.88) in Troutbeck, which dates back to the 17th century. In farms such as Townend, families would have carried on the domestic life of growing crops and farming sheep in ways that remained largely unchanged throughout this period.

Mining and quarrying in Cumbria also dates back to the beginning of this period, if not before, with graphite and slate being mined in Borrowdale and copper around Keswick and Coniston. Places to find out more about mining in Cumbria include the **Honister Slate Mine** (see p.231), the **Keswick Mining Museum** (see p.231), the **Threlkeld Quarry and Mining Museum** (see p.235) and the **Haig Colliery Mining Museum** (see p.191).

Industry and the Romantics

The Industrial Revolution, which began during the second half of the 18th century, was a period of transformation for the newly formed United Kingdom. Technological advances

The best... historic experiences

1 Castlerigg Stone Circle near Keswick. See p.226.
2 Furness Abbey on the outskirts of Barrow-in-Furness. See p.142.
3 Townend in Troutbeck near Ambleside. See p.88.
4 Honistor Slate Mine on Honister Pass. See p.231.
5 Hardknott Roman Fort on Harknott Pass. See p.178.
6 The Dock Museum in Barrow-in-Furness. See p.147.
7 Long Meg and her Daughters, stone circle at Little Salkeld. See p.262
8 The Senhouse Roman Museum in Maryport. See p.199.
9 Stott Bobbin Mill near Lakeside. See p.93.
10 Levens Hall near Kendal. See p.106.

such as the invention of the steam engine in 1774 by Boulton and Watt, initiated changes in manufacturing and transport, which in turn speeded up economic change.

Most of the changes brought about through these technological advancements affected areas in the outskirts of what is now the National Park. Carlisle developed a cotton manufacturing industry, Whitehaven prospered under the slave trade and Barrow-in-Furness, with its deep water port, grew in prominence as a ship building town. Attractions such as Whitehaven's **The Rum Story** (see p.200) and the **Dock Museum** (see p.147) in Barrow-in-Furness are places to find out more about this period of Cumbria's history. While within the boundaries of the National Park, **Stott Bobbin Mill** (see p.93) near Lakeside at the south end of lake Windermere is testimony to the once thriving wooden bobbin making industry that supported the north-west's many cotton mills.

The construction of passenger railways in the second half of the 19th century greatly aided the growth of tourism to the Lakes. And the work of poets such as Thomas Gray and painters including Turner and Constable, glorifying the region's natural beauty, helped to change the wider world's perception of the Lakes as dangerous border territory once terrorised by the Jacobite rebellions.

Early guidebooks such as the one produced by Thomas West in 1778 also promoted the virtues of the Lakes to the rest of the country and the formation of Wordsworth's circle of Romantics in the early 19th century further stimulated interest in the region. Wordsworth himself produced a guidebook to the Lakes that was first published in 1810.

For a taste of early railway travel in the Lakes take a trip on the **Ravenglass and Eskdale Railway** (see p.212) in the western Lakes or the **Lakeside and Haverthwaite Railway** (see p.131) in the south Lakes. While **Dove Cottage** (see p.166) and **Rydal Mount** (see p.167), both near Grasmere, are essential stops for anyone wanting to discover more about the Romantics in the region.

Establishment of the Lake District National Park

The Lake District National Park was created in 1951 as a means of conserving and enhancing the region's natural beauty, wildlife and cultural heritage, all under threat with the increasing amount of visitors and effects of farming and industrialisation. The National Park authorities have control over the planning and building development of the Lake District and are also responsible for promoting the understanding and enjoyment of the area. For more information on the work of the Lake District National Park, drop into their **Visitor Centre at Brockhole** (see p.76) on the north-east banks of Lake Windermere.

During the county boundary changes of 1974, 23 years after the formation of the Lake District National Park, Cumbria was formed from the older counties of Westmorland and Cumberland and sections of North Lancashire and North Yorkshire. At the top of Wrynose Pass the old **Three Shires Stone** (see p.177) once marked the meeting place of Westmorland, Cumberland and Lancashire; and many older residents of south Cumbria still defiantly consider themselves residents of Lancashire not Cumbria.

Recent history

In 2001 Cumbria was hit hard by the outbreak of foot-and-mouth disease. Many farmers lost all of their animals and related income, while local businesses suffered with the corresponding 'closing of the countryside' and decline in tourism.

Today around 12 million visitors descend upon the Lake District National Park each year, all of which presents the park authorities with the difficult balancing act of preserving and protecting the beauty of the region for future generations, while allowing the current one to enjoy all that it has to offer.

GEOGRAPHY AND GEOLOGY

The Lake District is England's only mountainous region and contains all of its land over 3,000ft above sea level including Scafell Pike (3,162ft), England's highest peak. The region's geology has taken 500 million years to develop from the surface of a great ocean far south of the equator, to the majestic scenery we see today.

The section of the earth's crust that now contains the Lake District crossed the equator 350 million years ago, stopping at the same latitude as the present-day Sahara Desert about 250 million years ago. And its slow movement to its current location explains some of the region's geological features such as its high peaks and the sandstone on its boundaries.

Bedrock

The Lake District's bedrock is predominately made up of three different bands of rock that run in a general south-west to north-east direction.

The most northerly and oldest band (about 500 million years) is the Skiddaw group, which runs from south of Whitehaven on the west coast and includes Keswick, Derwent Water and Skiddaw (3,054ft) – the highest peak in this geological area. These rocks were first laid down as sediment in the Lapetus Sea, which was a 2,500-mile wide southern ocean that once separated the North American and European continental plates before it formed a heavily compressed, folded grey rock as the plates converged.

The landscapes found in this area are characterised by either rounded hills, which have formed where the bedrock has been affected by volcanic activity, or much more rugged areas which have not been subjected to the heat generated from this activity, such as the dramatic south face of Blencathra.

To the south of the Skiddaw Group is the second band of bedrock – the Borrowdale Volcanic Group. This rock is the product of a period of volcanic activity some 450 million years ago and it makes up the rugged terrain much loved by walkers and climbers around Haweswater, Ullswater and Rydal Water, as well as some of the Lake District's highest peaks, Scafell (3,162ft), Scafell Pike (3,210ft), Helvellyn (3,116ft), the Old Man of Coniston (2,635ft) and the Langdale Pikes.

Further south again, and including the areas around Coniston Water, Windermere, the Duddon Estuary and Kendal, is the Windermere Group of bedrock which makes up a band of low hills made up of slate, siltstones and sandstones formed by sea deposits 420 million years ago.

Limestone exposed by later glaciation (see below) into a smooth pavement has since been eroded further by rainwater which has created a complex pattern of solid blocks called *clints* and fissures called *grikes*, as well as extensive cave systems and underground streams which are created as water percolates through the limestone pavement.

The Lake District contains 36% of the limestone pavement in Britain including areas around the Eden Valley, Whitbarrow to the south-west of Kendal and the spectacular sloping pavement in Farleton Fell. Great effort is being put into preserving these pavements and it's ironic that one of the best ways today to see and understand their extent is to visit an old limestone quarry, such as the one at Raisbeck to the north-east of Kendal.

The same period of uplift that produced limestone also compressed the remnants of the swampy forests that had replaced the receding tropical seas. This process created the region's coal deposits on the west coast that were heavily mined from the 12th century onwards.

Areas of sandstone

The areas skirting the National Park include significant areas of sandstone, which formed from deposits left while the 'Lake District' resided near the equator. Erosions by heat, wind and water resulted in sand dunes and salt lakes, and heavy downpours washed debris from the uplands to the lowlands. The famous red sandstone of St Bees, for example, believed to be the result of flash floods leaving thick deposits, while the sandstone found in the Eden Valley, Penrith sandstone and Lazonby sandstone, are the result of settling sand dunes.

Glaciation

The Lake District landscape we see today is most significantly, and most recently, shaped by glaciation. Starting around two million years ago, Britain experienced a series of cold glacial periods followed by warmer interglacial periods which saw ice sheets spread south and then recede north, gouging and grinding down the landscape. Melt water and the collapsing of slopes also had a significant effect on the landscape at this time and anyone studying glacial landforms can find text book examples throughout the region.

Even today the weather continues to change the shape of the Lake District. Limestone landscapes develop with each rainfall, and every winter, water in cracks in the rocks, especially the heavily fractured Skiddaw group, freezes, expands and tears rocks off the side of hills into fragment (scree) that builds up to form very steep scree slopes.

SOME LOWLAND FEATURES

U-shaped valley: These distinctive, wide valleys, literally U-shaped, gouged out by glaciers define the Lake District every bit as much as the peaks and lakes. Great examples of U-shaped valleys are Honister and Langdale.

Hanging valley: A glacial valley which has been cut off by a larger, deeper glacial valley which seems to hang half way up the larger valley's wall, often creating dramatic waterfalls. Little Langdale is an excellent example, as is Sourmilk Gill, a waterfall in Buttermere Valley.

Ribbon lakes: These long lakes, formed by glaciers carrying sharp-edged boulders while travelling over softer rock, are distinctive features of the Lake District. Windermere, Wast Water, Ullswater and Haweswater are all ribbon lakes.

Drumlins: Small, smooth, tear-shaped hummocks formed by passing glaciers of compressed clay and stone. Examples can be found in the Eden Valley and around the Langdales, while Keswick was built in an expanse of drumlins.

Erratics: Large boulders dragged for huge distances and left behind by glaciers. These oddities are often found in the middle of fields in the Lake District; look out for them around Ennerdale and Kentmere.

Terminal moraine: Moraines are piles of rubble left behind by receding glaciers, and terminal moraine is left by the glacier's leading edge or snub. Examples of terminal moraine can be found in Eskdale or Borrowdale south of Rosthwaite.

SOME UPLAND FEATURES

Cirque or Corrie: An 'armchair'-shaped hollow on the side of a mountain dug out by glaciation. Excellent examples can be found at Helvellyn, complete with tarn (see below) and Black Combe near Coniston.

Tarn: A glacial lake at the bottom of a cirque or corrie. Don't be fooled by the names, though, as in Cumbria the word 'tarn' (from the Norse word Tjern) is used to describe any small lake. For example Tarn Hows is not technically a tarn as it's man-made. However, there are many glacial tarns throughout the uplands of the Lake District – Langdale is littered with them – including Red Tarn on the east side of Helvellyn, and Little Langdale Tarn at the foot of Wrynose Pass.

Arête: A narrow, knife-like ridge between two corries. Helvellyn has two classic examples of arêtes, Striding Edge and Swirral Edge, and other examples include Steeple which connects Scoat Fell and Steeple Fell between Wasdale and Ennerdale.

A hill is never simply a hill. Most of us measure the height of a peak in relation to sea level. However, in Britain a system has also been created that classifies the relative height of hills, or the height of a peak from the lowest contour line fully encircling it – thus classifying a peak in relation to the land surrounding it, not sea level, and recognising a hill on top of a hill.

Nuttalls: Hills with a relative height of 15–29 metres. They take their name from John and Anne Nuttall who in their *The Mountains of England and Wales* (1990) listed all the of hills in England and Wales over 610 metres above sea level, that also have a relative height of at least 15 metres. These often quite insignificant peaks include Honister Crag and Striding Edge, and the only one requiring rock climbing to conquer it, is Pillar Rock, an outcrop on Pillar between Wasdale and Ennerdale.

Hewitts: Hills with a relative height of between 30 and 149 metres. These were initially called 'sweats' by Alan Dawson in his *The Relative Hills of Britain* (1992) – presumably because you'll break into a sweat climbing them. Dawson's classification, now more genteelly named Hewitts, eliminate the smallest of hills from the Nuttalls' list, offering walkers more significant peaks to challenge them. Hewitts do throw up slight anomalies, such as Scafell, which stands 133 metres above its parent hill, Scafell Pike. However, its absolute height (964 metres above sea level) is lower than Scafell Pike's highest peak (978 metres above sea level). Other significant Hewitts include Kentmere Pike and Skiddaw Little Man.

Marilyns: Hills greater than 150 metres above sea level and below 600 metres above sea level, regardless of its their surrounding land. Significant Marilyns include Blencathra, Grassmoor, Grizedale Pike, Pillar and the Old Man of Coniston. Amusingly, Marilyns are named in response to the Scottish Monros (mountains over 3,000ft or 914.4 metres above sea level named after Sir Hugh Munro, and early cataloguer of hills in the 19th century), as in Marilyn Monroe.

P600: Hills or prominences over 600 metres above the surrounding terrain. The only peaks considered in this category in the Lake District are Skiddaw in the northern Fells, Scafell Pike in the southern Fells (its parent is actually Snowdon) and Helvellyn in the eastern Fells.

Wainwrights: Less a classification than a list, Wainwrights include all the hills or fells included by Alfred Wainwright in his seven-volume walking guide classics *Pictorial Guide to the Lakeland Fells* and the supplementary *The Outlying Fells of Lakeland*. There are 214 Wainwrights.

WILDLIFE AND HABITATS

With a vast geographical range, from coastal beaches and cliffs to the highest peak in England, the Lake District includes a huge variety of habitats supporting distinct and often endangered flora and fauna. However, human activity has altered all of these habitats and little of the Lake District can truly be called 'natural' any more.

Much of the region was once covered with forest, most of which was cleared even before the Romans marched into the region, and agriculture and mining have also had a huge effect on the landscape, scarring hillsides with quarries and girding the slopes and valleys with stone walls. Ironically these activities have formed a new system of habitats, now heavily protected, especially within the National Park itself.

There are 30 Natural Reserves in Cumbria, eight of which lie within the National Park. Details of some these are listed below and all can be found at www.cumbriawildlifetrust.org.uk

Woodlands and forest

Pockets of **native woodlands** are scattered throughout the Lake District. These are predominantly made up of sessile oak, which thrives on the region's acid rocks, and ash in limestone areas; however, birch, hazel, and holly trees are also common. These woodlands are a vital habitat for the region's wildlife, providing breeding sites and hunting grounds for buzzards, warblers, tawny owls and pied flycatchers, while deer, fox, bats, weasels, stoats and more other animals use the woodlands for food and shelter.

Smaller life forms such as lichens, fungi and insects also thrive in the woodlands. Borrowdale's woodlands are particularly important with large colonies of lichens, mosses and liverwort, which require both high humidity and rainfall to thrive. In addition, woodlands provide habitat for plants common to limestone, like bluebell, primrose and the wild daffodils so loved by Wordsworth, as well as spindle, crab apple, alder buckthorn and the small shrub mezeron, which produces sweet smelling pink flowers in early spring.

However, much of the woodland we see today consists of plantations of fast growing, non native trees, like pine and spruce, grown for commercial purposes. While this woodland offers few benefits to local wildlife, native red squirrels are found here and several birds of prey, including the sparrowhawk, merlin and goshawk, use them as hunting grounds.

Recently plantation techniques have improved to benefit wildlife. For example, a patchwork system of harvesting and replanting in Grizedale Forest, creates a range of aged trees and varied habitats for small animals like voles, who in turn are prey for larger birds. Ospreys have recently returned to Dodd Wood near to the Forestry Commission's **Whinlatter Forest Park**, a managed forest near Keswick.

In between these two types of woodland there is what's known as ancient semi-natural woodland which has been continually harvested for hundreds of years and has a flora and fauna all of its own. For example, on the southern edge of the park, near Haverthwaite, is **Roudsea Woods** and **Mosses National Nature Reserve** which has been carefully harvested for centuries. Its unique combination of habitats, sitting on both limestone pavement and slate and merging with the Roudsea Mosses to the east, has meant that its special flora and fauna includes over 50 species of breeding birds such as the greater spotted woodpecker and reed bunting.

Dorothy Farrer's Spring Wood near Staveley, is another small area of this semi-natural woodland which has been coppiced (harvesting by carefully cutting back trees to a stump) for bobbins, charcoal and baskets for centuries. As a result, more light reaches the woodland floor providing conditions for early purple orchids, dog's mercury, primrose and bluebells in the spring, and fungi in the autumn. It also attracts birds including great spotted woodpecker, treecreeper, and pied and spotted flycatchers. Coppicing is also important for providing habitats for violets and the high brown fritillary butterflies that feed off them.

The Newlands Valley in Derwent Fells near Keswick provides a home for some of the highest woodland in Britain, including Keskdale and Birkrigg woods in Borrowdale, both of which may be original woods and have been managed over the years.

Grasslands

After centuries of deforestation for pasture, drainage and management (including seeding exotic grass species), grassland is now a significant feature of the region, supporting plant and animal life in both heavily used and less used areas.

The acid grasslands of upland areas, principally used as sheep pasture, are subject to high rainfall and grazing, which has resulted in habitat that supports few species, but the invertebrates common in these areas provide food for skylarks and meadow pipits amongst other birds, and small mammals such as voles and mice also thrive in these conditions. Where these acid grasslands meet springs and mires, they provide excellent habitats for a greater variety of plants, like sundew and butterwort.

In areas of limestone, calcareous grasslands are common, such as at **Whitbarrow National Nature Reserve**, where you'll find blue moor grass as well as rare plants like orchids and crested hair-grass. These grasslands provide breeding and feeding territory for a variety of butterflies.

Haymeadows, which prosper on neutral grasslands, support a large variety of life, from wild flowers to sward grasses, which in turn provide food for insects and other invertebrates. The smallest National Nature Reserve in England, at about three-quarters of an acre, **Sandybeck Meadow** in Lorton Vale in the north-west of the National Park is an excellent example of a haymeadow. Here

you can see a variety of grasses and flowers including, in June, greater butterfly ortchin and common bistort. Orange tip butterflies are common, while the river and woodland along it make excellent habitats for otters.

Upland heath

In the Lakes, heathlands, or open areas dominated by woody shrubs, would have been originally cleared for agriculture. However, as the acidic soil isn't very suitable for arable farming, they have been used as pasture and become a habitat for heather and other dwarf shrubs. Over 170 species of butterflies can be found in the important heathland of **Rusland Moss National Nature Reserve**, between Coniston Water and Windermere north of Haverthwaite, along with spiders, moths and beetles, and a variety of birds and reptiles.

Heathland is not natural and needs to be carefully maintained to keep it from returning to woodland. Traditionally this has largely been done on shooting estates by burning strips of heather to promote the germination of seeds and encourage the growth of new shoots, which in turn provide food for red grouse. Careful grazing can also retain heathland, but grazing sheep are indiscriminate eaters and kill the plants if left to their own devices. The merlin, Britain's smallest bird of prey, breeds in heathlands.

Upland lakes and tarns

Lakes and tarns, gouged out by glaciers and filled by melt and rainwater, vary greatly in size and depth and their contribution to the flora and fauna of the region are both important and varied. While we think of the lakes for their recreational uses, many have been left virtually undisturbed.

The deep, cold lakes, including Buttermere, Ennerdale and Wast Water, support a relatively small variety of plants and animals, but these include rare crustaceans, which have evolved to take advantage of nutrient poor environments.

A more diverse range of life can be found in lakes like Windermere and Bassenthwaite, whose wooded shorelines, and shallow bays and reed beds provide nesting places for swans, grebes and a variety of other birds. Windermere in particular is a nationally important site for wintering fowl and Bassenthwaite is home to Britain's rarest fish, the declining vendace, which are known only to live here and in Derwent Water. The rare floating water plantain is also found at Bassenthwaite.

The features of these lakes which make them so important are at risk from human use, as trampling feet and the wake from boats slowly wash away soil and organic material, and the reed protected shores decline into something akin to pebble beaches, taking with it the invertebrates and plant life which provide food and the reeds that provide shelter.

Mires

The Lake District is extremely important for peat bogs, or mires. Peat is nutrient poor and any vegetation relies on nutrients found in rainwater and settling dust, yet these mires support mosses, liverworts, lichens and dwarf heathers and sedges.

There are two types of mire found in the Lakes, both internationally scarce environments. Blanket mires, which are important to the breeding of moorland birds like the red grouse, golden plover and merlins, are endangered by burning, grazing and drainage, but still survive on flat fell tops.

Raised mires, flat, boggy areas of deep peat, can also be found in the area, including an excellent example near **Witherslack** at Meathop Moss, one of the first nature reserves in the country, which provides habitat for a wide range of plants and over 200 species of butterfly and moth, as well as dragonfly and damselfly. South of Bowness, you can visit the **South Solway Mosses National Reserve**, which is comprised of three peatlands, including

Glasson Moss, one of the best examples of raised mire. Along with red grouse, curlew and meadow pipit in the open areas, you'll find sparrowhawk, redpoll, reed bunting and willow tit in the woodlands and meadows around the moss. A variety of mosses can be seen, along with bog asphodel, bog rosemary, cranberry and three species of sundew.

Rivers

Rivers add another variant to the habitats of the Lake District, with its relatively pure waters supporting fish, native crayfish, freshwater pearl mussel and the otters that prey on them. Upland, the fast water provides good conditions for clippers and grey tails, along with other bird species.

Rock and scree

Despite appearances, the rocks and scree slopes affected by glaciation and frost-heave support a lot of life. Steep gills cut into fellsides provide shelter, inaccessible to animals, for unusual plant life, while crags, or steep rocky cliffs, support a mix of arctic-alpine flora and lowland plants and sheltered ledges are home to herbs and ferns. Rocks and scree are also home to birdlife, including stonechat and wheatear, and nesting sites for raven, peregrine falcon and the rare golden eagle.

Coast

The dunes, salt marshes and banks of tidal rivers that make up the region's coastal habitats include five internationally significant conservation sites. **Drigg Local Nature Reserve** south of Silcroft is an area of dunes that was formed when shingle brought to the coast by glaciation was eroded by wave action into ridges of rounded stones. These ridges then forced the River Esk to divert and in doing so deposit shell sand. This area has been farmed and used to collect fish for thousands of years, and today it provides habitats for wading birds such as curlew, oystercatcher and heron. The fine sediment deposited inland enables glasswort, sea lavender and other plants to thrive, and marram grass binds the dunes together. Insects, including butterflies, thrive here along with their predators such as the green tiger beetle and the rare natterjack toad which spawns in freshwater pools.

The edges of Morecambe Bay and the Duddon Estuary are also important and provide breeding and wintering grounds for birds. These areas have both received protection under the European RAMSAR programme to protect wetlands.

The cliffs of St Bees offer an impressive counterpoint to other coastal features, with its myriad of ledges in the sheer sandstone hosting the largest sea bird colony on the west coast of England. This is the only place in the country where black guillemot breed, while razor-bill, kittiwake, fulmar and herring-gull all turn up in large numbers during the summer, as do puffins in smaller numbers. While out to sea, gannets are common and occasionally eider duck and shearwaters can be seen.

Flora of note

Sessile oak: These large deciduous trees were once the dominant tree on the Lakes' upland acidic soil, recognisable by their distinctive leaves with rounded lobes. The remaining stands of sessile oak are important for native lichens, fungi, insects and other micro-organisms.

Ash: Common on calcareous soils, like limestone pavements, ash are distinguished by their feather-like leaves. They also produce a distinctive black bud in around April.

Yew: Ancient groves of these medium-size evergreen trees sporting red berries in the autumn are common on the limestone around Morecombe Bay and the Borrowdale yews found at Seathwaite may be over 2,000 years old. The leaves and seeds of Yew tree are poisonous so you are most likely to find the oldest of this species in churchyards and other places where cattle can't get to them.

Alpine catchfly: These tiny, pink and rare alpine flowers can be found in one small colony above Whinlatter Pass.

Grass of Parnassus: Also known as bog-stars, this white flower with greenish veins was the county flower of old Westmorland.

Alpine gentia: Amongst the rarest of British flowers, alpine gentian is found in only two areas in Britain: Cumbria, and Perth and Kinross. Its petals are bright blue and pointed.

Wild daffodil: Thanks to Wordsworth, the wild daffodil is the most famous flower in the Lake District. But they are much rarer today than they were when the Romantic poet stumbled across them, as intensive agriculture and the clearing of woodland have had a strong effect, as has digging up bulbs to plant in gardens. They are found in woodlands.

Touch-me-not-balsam: The exclusive food of the netted carpet moth, this plant (with small yellow flowers and, later, pods which explode when ripe, spreading its seeds widely, and almost transparent stalks) shrink away when touched, hence the name. Found in wet woods and on limestone pavements.

Juniper: Found on the high fells and on limestone, this is an evergreen shrub with small blue berries.

Eelgrass: Related to sea grass and also known as zostera, eelgrass can be found on the mudflats and shallows around Morecambe Bay.

Quillwort: Common along the shores of the lakes and tarns in the region, but rare in the rest of England, quillwort looks like a small tuft of spiny grass in clear water.

Fauna of note

Artic charr: These slender fish, with a small adipose fin found between the dorsal and tail fin, rarely grow larger than 30cm and have been present in the region's alpine lakes since the Ice Age. The lakes are about the most southerly habitat to support them and, sadly, climate change will adversely affect them.

Vendace: One of only three freshwater white fish native to Britain, vendace are amongst the most rare of British fish, found in Bassenthwaite Lake and Derwent Water.

Schelly: Another rare fish found in the lakes, the schelly can be found in Brothers Water, Haweswater, Red Tarn and Ullswater.

White clawed crayfis: Britain's only native crayfish is found in the Eden and Kent rivers (the latter thought to have the highest density in England), but is at risk due to the introduction of the larger and more aggressive exotic crayfish.

Freshwater pearl mussel: These rare bivalves, with heavy, yellow-brown shells (brown when mature) can live to be 100 years old and can number into the thousands in each colony, but known British colonies, found only in Cumbria and Northumberland, rarely develop to more than 30.

Black grouse: Only the male of this rare species of gamebird is actually black – apart from a red eyebrow-like wattle and white bars on the wings – while the female is greyish brown (hence their folk names blackcock and greyhen). Virtually wiped out by fox predation and reduction of habitats, they have been recently reintroduced to the Upper Derwent Valley and the Peak District.

Common raven: The largest of the crow family, these large black birds with a prominent forehead are common in the Lakes and are thought to be the smartest of birds with intelligence on a par with wolves.

Golden eagle: These huge birds of prey with broad fingerlike wings and a long tail are now virtually extinct (only 442 breeding pairs in the UK, according to the RSPB) but can be seen year-round, looping above you as they surf the wind currents looking for prey. There is a watchpoint at the RSPB's Haweswater reserve.

Osprey: These beautiful fish-eating birds of prey, white and mottled black, with black tipped wings, have recently been reintroduced to breed in Bassenthwaite, where you can see them from a viewpoint in Whinlatter Forestry Park near Keswick.

Kingfisher: Common on the Eden, Lune and Derwent rivers, kingfishers are unmistakable with their bright blue and orange plumage.

Knot: This grey and white little wading bird is commonly seen in autumn and winter around Morecambe Bay and the Solway Firth.

Dotterel: A rare, medium sized wader in the plover family, the dotterel is an unusual bird as the female has brighter plumage, grey and orange to the male's grey brown. It can be found either on the shores or in breeding grounds on hilltops.

Nuthatch: This plump, blue-grey and orange bird with a long, sharp black bill, resembles a small woodpecker and rarely ventures far from woodlands. A success in Cumbria, their numbers have expanded greatly since the 1980s.

Peregrine falcon: These large, blue-grey birds of prey were in decline until the 1960s, but there are more than 100 nesting pairs in and around the Lake District today, mostly in the upland fells.

Hen harrier: One of the most persecuted of the UK's birds of prey for their habit of taking free-range fowl – grouse in particular – these elegant birds (males are light grey, with black wing tips and white rump, while females are brown, with a white rump and striped tale) breed in the heather of upland moorland, but winter in more lowland areas and coastal marshlands.

Red squirrel: Cumbria is one of the last refuges of Britain's favourite little rodent.

Otter: Otters are returning to the streams and rivers of the Lake District.

Water vole: One of Britain's most endangered native animals and the creature that gave us Ratty in *The Wind in the Willows*, water voles have declined in the past 50 years to near extinction. Efforts to bolster the populations in Cumbria have centred around the Eden River.

Natterjack toad: The rarest of Britain's native amphibians, the natterjack breed in shallow pools and have developed short limbs to help with digging burrows to protect them from changes in temperature and moisture, and from predators. They are distinguished by a black stripe down their backs and can be found in the sandy dunes and lowland heaths, especially around the mouth of the Esk River.

Fells ponies: Fells ponies have been bred in the Lakes for thousands of years. If you are around Shap and the Howgills, keep your eyes open for these distinctive horses, today normally black or dark brown and with plenty of fine hair at their heels and long mane and tail.

Herdwick sheep: Found mostly in the central to western dales, the Herdwick (or Herdy) is a particularly hardy sheep that can deal with the terrain and survive with little vegetation, making them perfect for Cumbria's fells – indeed over 90% of Herdwicks live in the Lake District. They have white faces and dense, grey fleece, and their lambs are generally black. They have been farmed here since the 9th century and the name most likely comes from the Norse *herd-vick* or sheep farm. Beatrix Potter, a master breeder of Herdwicks, suggests the breed can survive for six weeks in the snow from the oil in their fleece alone. So important are the Herdwick that it has become a local celebrity and is now the face of the Lake District. See www.herdy.co.uk for more information.

Rough fell sheep: Common in the east of the region, especially around the Howgill and Orton fells where the ground is drier, these large sheep, with patchy black faces and long white fleece are valued for their long wool fibres and high meat yield.

Swaledale sheep: Distinguished by their black faces with white noses and curled horns, these hardy sheep number over 2.5 million in the country, about a third of which are in Cumbria. They are found on the high northern and eastern fells.

Border collies: Initially bred in the border regions of England and Scotland, these black and white sheep dogs are common in the Lakes. But be warned, these are mostly working dogs, not family pets and should be treated as such.

Belted Galloway: At first glance, these could be designer cattle, either black, red or dun with a distinctive white band around their middle. Originally bred in Scotland, 'belties' are very hardy, with a double layer of hair, a coarse outer layer to protect from rain and a downy under layer for warmth. They survive well on poor land and are sensitive eaters, avoiding rare heathers. They also produce a rich flavoured meat with omega-3 fat.

Deer: Thousands of deer can be found in the Lakes, including Britain's only pure-bred population of its largest native land mammal, the red deer, which thrives on the heather around Thirlmere, Haweswater and Shap Fells. Keep an eye out from April to November when they descend from the high fells to graze and mate, including their dramatic antler-locking battles for supremacy. Deer parks around Grange-over-Sands are also good places to spy these shy animals, including the lovely, dusty coloured fallow deer.

Butterflies

High brown fritillary: This rare, large (wingspan of 60mm) brown butterfly, distinct for its silver dots and a row of orange spots on the underwing, is found around Morecambe Bay and depends on abundant violets which grow around the around limestone outcrops.

Mountain ringlet butterfly: Scarce in the UK, this small brown butterfly with rows of orange-ringed dark brown spots can be found in the high fells of the central Lakes.

Man-made features
Stone walls

Stone walls are a constant in the Lake District. Traditionally built without cement or mortar, the skill is to build the wall so that its weight is transferred downward to the large footing stones that hold the wall together.

Dry stone walls support a variety of wildlife including lichens and other small plants, invertebrates and small mammals, such as voles, mice and hedgehogs, while birds like wrens, robins and small owls use the crevices for food and nesting places.

To find out more about any aspect of Cumbria's Wildlife visit **The Cumbria Wildlife Trust** (01539 816300, www.cumbria wildlifetrust.org.uk), Plumgarths, Crook Road, Kendal, LA8 8LX. Open 9am – 5pm Mon – Fri.

CULTURE

The Lake District is synonymous with the Romanic Poets and although echoes of their famous works and wanderings permeate much of the region, don't expect to find Cumbria's cultural life nostalgically stuck in the past. Contemporary new authors such as Sarah Hall are equally inspired by the landscape and its history and the region's literary scene reflects an appealing combination of respect for past masters and support for new voices.

Likewise views of Cumbria's dramatic scenery have been captured and interpreted by successive generations of artists and many of the region's fine galleries are places to view or buy an impressive range of work in a plethora of mediums, from impressionist paintings to landscape photography. Attractions such as Grizedale Forest's sculpture trail are showcases for large scale art, inspired by, and embedded into, the landscape.

Crafts in the Lake District are also thriving. Expect to find a range of outlets in most towns and villages and numerous stalls at local fairs and festivals where you can pick up a growing array of creative textiles, contemporary and traditional pottery and local woodcrafts – most conforming to a consistently high standard.

Those seeking a culturally orientated nightlife should head to the region's larger towns such as Keswick and Kendal. Here Cumbria's theatres and arts centres programme a varied selection of regionally produced theatre, touring shows, dance, music and both mainstream and specialist films.

Writers

Melvyn Bragg (1939–). Perhaps best known as the genial, intellectual host of BBC television's *The South Bank Show* and Radio 4's *In Our Time*, Melvyn Bragg (now Lord Bragg of Wigton) was born and brought up in Wigton, where he went to school before reading Modern History at Oxford in the late 1950s. He began his broadcasting career as a producer with the BBC, and since 1967 he has been a successful writer and broadcaster.

In both fact and fiction, Bragg has championed the stories and poetry of the Lakes and Cumbria. His non-fiction books have included *Cumbria in Verse* (editor 1984) and *Land of Lakes* (1983), while his fiction writing includes *The Maid of Buttermere* (1987) – based on the life of Mary Robinson, a shepherdess whose 1802 marriage to a fake aristocrat ended with his hanging for being an imposter, bigamist and forger. He also edited the children's compendium, *My Favourite Stories of Lakeland* (1981).

WG Collingwood (1854–1932). Author and artist William Gershom Collingwood was first introduced to the Lakes as he travelled with his artist father on sketching trips. In 1873 he visited John Ruskin at Brantwood and later worked there before studying art. While in the Lakes he became interested in Norse and Anglican archaeology, in particular Northumbrian crosses. His artistic skill and knowledge of these crosses led to post-First World War memorial commissions, including those still found in Grasmere, Ulverston, Otley and Coniston, while the Hawkshead cross was sculpted by his daughter Barbara to his design. Collingwood also set up an exhibition dedicated to Ruskin at the back of the Mechanics Institute in Coniston which later became the Ruskin Museum.

Hunter Davies and **Margaret Forster.** Brought up in Carlisle, husband and wife writers Hunter Davies and Margaret Forster split their year between London and Loweswater.

Author, journalist and broadcaster **Hunter Davies** (1936–) is best known as a long-time columnist for *Punch* and writer of books on the Beatles, but amongst his 30 plus books are biographies of Lakeland notables including Wordsworth, Beatrix Potter and Wainwright as well as *The Good Guide to the Lakes*. He also wrote *From London to Loweswater*, the story of his year-long journey between the two localities, following in JB Priestley's footsteps, and he is a collector of Beatrix Potter artefacts, from letters about Herdwick sheep to an early copy of *Ginger and Pickles*.

Author **Margaret Forster** (1938–) married Davies the day after her final exam for her honours degree at Oxford. Forster is famous for her novel *Georgy Girl*, made into a film staring Lynn Redgrave, and she is an award winning biographer whose subjects have included Daphne Du Maurier, and her own grandmother in *Hidden Lives*, and the Carr family of biscuit fame.

Their daughter Caitlin is also a noted novelist and campaigner against domestic violence.

Sarah Hall (1974–). Considered to be one of the best young writers in Britain, Cumbrian born novelist Sarah Hall's fiction is heavily influenced by the landscapes of the Lake District. The Commonwealth Writers Prize winning *Haweswater* (2002), her first novel, is a tragic tale of a Cumbrian hill farming community threatened by the building of a reservoir, while her most recent, *The Carhullan Army* (2007), winner of the John Llewellyn Rhys prize, is a distopian tale set in the Cumbrian fells. In between she wrote the Man Booker nominated *The Electric Michelangelo*, set in both Morecambe and Coney Island.

Norman Nicholson (1914–1987). Born in Millom on Cumbria's south coast, where he lived for most of his life, writer Norman Nicholson published numerous collections of verse, four verse plays, two novels and, in 1975, *Wednesday Early Closing*, his autobiography. His poetry is direct, often using the local vernacular and focuses on the work of the region, mining, quarrying and ironwork, as well as religion and faith. Nicholson was awarded the Queen's Gold Medal for Poetry in 1977 and the Order of the British Empire in 1981. Local writer Nell Curry edited a collection of his poems published in 1994.

Beatrix Potter (1866–1943). Best known as the author of the *Peter Rabbit* stories, Beatrix Potter (subject of the 2006 film *Miss Potter* starring Reneé Zellweger) has much more than children's stories in her arsenal. She was also a noted illustrator, botanist, conservationist and breeder of Herdwick sheep.

Potter was born in London, but visited the Lakes while quite young. She studied botany in private as her family discouraged her intellectual development, and was one of the first to suggest that lichens were a symbiotic relationship between fungi and algae. This and other observations led to her being a well-respected mycologist, while her need to illustrate her work brought her to notice as a botanical painter. In 1897, she had a paper on spore germination read at the Linnaean Society by her uncle (women were not allowed to attend society meetings), but her botanical work was never published.

She published her first story, *The Tale of Peter Rabbit*, in 1902 when she was 36 and soon after – following the death of her fiancé – she moved to Hill Top farm near Hawkshead in the Lake District (see p.89). Over the course of her life, Beatrix Potter published 23 books, became a respected breeder and farmer of Herdwick sheep and President of the Herdwick Sheep Breeders' Association.

Arthur Ransome (1884–1967). British author and journalist Arthur Ransome was born in Leeds in 1884 and received part of his formal education in Windermere. On moving to the Lake District, Ransome moved away from journalism and turned his attention to children's books; and he penned the novel he is most famous for *Swallows and Amazons* (1930), which recounts school holiday adventures, and is one of the best-

The best... cultural sites

① Blackwell, an Arts and Crafts gem near Windermere. See p.75.
② Abbot Hall art gallery in Kendal. See p.105.
③ Ruskin's former home Brantwood on the north-east shores of Coniston Water. See p.131.
④ Dove Cottage, one-time home of the Wordsworths and de Quincey near Grasmere. See p.166.
⑤ Hill Top, Beatrix Potter's former home near Hawkshead. See p.89.
⑥ Wordsworth House, birthplace of William and Dorothy in Cockermouth. See p.189.
⑦ The Beatrix Potter Gallery in Hawkshead. See p.92.
⑧ The Heaton Cooper Studio in Grasmere. See p.169.
⑨ Rydal Mount, the long-time home of William Wordsworth and family near Grasmere. See p.167.
⑩ Castlegate House Gallery in Cockermouth for a taste of the work produced by present day artists from the region. See p.189.

known children's books of all time. Although all of the places in the book are imaginary, many are inspired by locations around Windermere and Coniston. A number of other books in the *Swallows and Amazons* series followed, some inspired by Ransome's later travels as a foreign correspondent. Arthur Ransome died in 1967 and is buried at Rushland near Grizedale Forest.

Sir Hugh Walpole (1884–1941). Born in New Zealand, novelist Hugh Walpole moved to Catbells in the Lake District in 1924 where he lived until he died in a house built from local slate and containing around 30,000 books. The best known works Walpole wrote in the Lakes include a Cumberland family saga, *The Herries Chronicle*, and although his former home is not open to the public numerous volumes of his diary can be viewed in the Keswick Museum and Art Gallery (see p.233).

The Romantics

William Wordsworth (1770–1850). Born in Cockermouth and educated at Hawkshead Grammar School, before attending Cambridge, one-time Poet Laureate William Wordsworth helped found the Romantic Movement in English Literature.

Both William and his sister, Dorothy, left the Lakes for their education and to travel. They moved to Dorset in 1795 where they met Samuel Taylor Coleridge and the trio travelled to Germany together in 1798. The same year Wordsworth and Coleridge published their *Lyrical Ballads*, which included Wordsworth's 'Tintern Abbey' and Coleridge's famous 'The Rime of the Ancient Mariner' and is considered the launching of the Romantic Age of English Literature.

The Wordsworths returned to the Lakes to live in Dove Cottage, Grasmere in 1799 and were followed by Coleridge and his friend Robert Southey (who preceded Wordsworth as Poet Laureate). The three writers became known as **the Lake Poets** during the years they all lived and worked in the region. After marrying his childhood friend Mary Hutchinson, Wordsworth moved, along with Dorothy, to nearby Rydal Mount, where he lived out his life and became Poet Laureate in 1843.

Amongst Wordsworth's most famous poetry are remembrances of his Lake District childhood and observations after his return to the region, making him not just a poet from the Lakes, but of the Lakes. The famous, 'The Daffodils' (or 'I Wandered Lonely as a Cloud'), for example, was written as a remembrance of daffodils seen while out walking with his sister, probably around Ullswater.

The posthumously published *The Prelude*, written throughout his poetry career, includes the depiction of several journeys, which are used as metaphors for spiritual challenges, such as the 'Vale of Grasmere'. Travelling around the Lakes you are never far from Wordsworth landmarks, be it the family home in Cockermouth (see p.189), or Dove Cottage (see p.166) and Rydal Mount (see p.167) near Grasmere, or the views and nature that inspired him.

Samuel Taylor Coleridge (1772–1834). Born in Devon, the poet and philosopher Samuel Taylor Coleridge would help found the Romantic Movement in English literature with the publishing of *Lyrical Ballads* in 1798.

Coleridge followed the Wordsworths to the Lake District in 1800, eventually settling his family at Keswick. Coleridge left the Lakes in 1804 hoping the warming climes of Malta would cure his illnesses and reduce his opium use. In the years that followed, his opium addiction would cost him his marriage, his friendship with the Wordsworths and, ultimately, his life as he died of a lung disorder probably related to smoking the drug. The great passion of his life, which tormented his poetry, was Sara Hutchinson, Wordsworth's sister-in-law.

Best known for 'The Rime of the Ancient Mariner' and the shorter 'Kubla Khan', Coleridge is credited with introducing Wordsworth to meditative conversation poems, which the latter would use successfully, and his lectures in Bristol between 1810 and 1820 are credited with renewing literary interest in Shakespeare.

Thomas de Quincey (1785–1859). Author and intellectual Thomas de Quincey is most linked to the Lake District through his relationship with the Lake Poets. Born in Manchester and educated at Oxford, de Quincey became interested in Wordsworth after reading the *Lyrical Ballads*, which he felt consoled him during fits of depression. He met Coleridge and Wordsworth in 1807 and moved to the Lake District for ten years, living in Dove Cottage after the Wordsworths vacated. De Quincey is most famous for his *Confessions of an English Opium-Eater*, an account of his long-term opium addiction serialised in *London Magazine*.

Robert Southey (1774–1843). Romantic poet and biographer Robert Southey became Poet Laureate in 1813 (after Sir Walter Scott refused the post) and is considered one of the Lake Poets, having lived in Keswick, at Greta Hall with his wife Edith Fricker, sister of Coleridge's wife, Sara Fricker. Southey's poetry was often historical, having written epic poems on Joan of Arc, Wat Tyler and Robespierrre. Like his Romantic poet friends, he was an early radical supporter of the French Revolution, but, disillusioned by the aftermath of the Revolution, and he tended to conservatism later in life – much to the disgust of Lord Byron. Following Edith's death, Southey married the poet Caroline Anne Bowles in 1838, but his health deteriorated after a stroke and he died in Keswick in 1943 of 'softening of the brain'.

Artists

The Heaton Coopers. Grasmere is home to the studio of the Heaton Cooper family, whose artistic dynasty has, for the past four generations, produced outstanding work inspired by the Lake District landscape.

Alfred Heaton Cooper (1863–1929) was born into a Lancashire family of mill workers and after gaining an art scholarship moved to London to study. Alfred become fascinated by the Norwegian fjords and settled in Norway, marrying a local girl. Unable to support his wife away from home, Alfred returned to the Lakes and caused a sensation by bringing his Norwegian log house with him. He converted the house into a studio and divided his time between painting the Lakes and illustrating Edwardian guidebooks. Alfred's distinctive log house still stands in Ambleside – just south of the town centre off the A591 – and is currently a restaurant (www.loghouse.co.uk).

Alfred's third child, **William Heaton Cooper** (1903–1995), followed in his father's artistic footsteps and studied at the Royal Academy in London, before spending time living in an experimental commune in southern England. William moved back to the Lakes and in 1937 built a studio in Grasmere, which is still thriving today.

William's work, influenced by his expert knowledge of the Lakes' geology and deep spiritual beliefs, is more impressionistic than his father's and some of the most instantly recognisable ever produced on this region. William married the sculptor **Ophelia Gordon Bell** (1915–1975), who, amongst other work, produced sculptures of farmers, climbers, sheep and even William and Dorothy Wordsworth – you can view a plaster cast of her portrait of Sir Edmund Hillary in the Grasmere studio and her sculpture of St Bede in St Oswald's Church.

William and Ophelia's third child, **Julian Heaton Cooper** (1947–), continued to feed the family's landscape-inspired artistic output. Mountains form the focus of this third generation of Heaton Cooper work and Julian's interpretations of ranges including the Andes and Himalayas have earned him an international reputation.

Alfred's great-granddaughter, **Rebecca Heaton Cooper** (1970–) (see Local Knowledge p.175), has taken her artistic inheritance in a new direction. Although still deeply inspired by the Lake District landscape, Rebecca's work draws on her fashion and textiles degree and her intricate mixed media collages reflect the continually changing moods of the Lake District, intertwined with strands of her own family history.

The Heaton Cooper Studio (015394 35280 www.heatoncooper.co.uk) is located opposite Grasmere's village green. Open Mon–Sat 9am–5.30pm, Sun noon–5.30pm, closing 5pm in winter.

Andy Goldsworthy (1956–). Artist, sculptor and photographer Andy Goldsworthy is famous for site-specific pieces that use natural, found objects. As well as incorporating his work into natural settings, Goldsworthy often places pieces in urban settings and photographs them as they decay, or in the case of huge giant snowballs left in London, melt.

Goldsworthy studied at Bradford College of Art and Preston Polytechnic (now the University of Central Lancashire) and received an OBE in 2000. From 1996 to 2003 Goldsworthy produced the Sheepfolds Project in which he repaired, rebuilt and added symbolic elements to 48 derelict dry stone wall enclosures around Cumbria, originally built as places where sheep could shelter from the elements. In 2001 a documentary film called Rivers and Tides was made about Andy Goldsworthy's work and you can view one of his works on the Sculpture Trail at Grizedale Forest (see p.125).

LS Lowry (1887–1976). Most famous for his paintings of working class Salford, the artist Lowry travelled widely in the north and produced his distinctive urban landscapes with tiny matchstick-like human figures along the way. From the late 1940s, Lowry visited friends in Cleator Moor and produced several paintings of the area including the impromptu *Cowles Fish and Chip Shop, Cleator Moor* in 1948.

George Romney (1734–1802). Born at Beckside near Dalton-in-Furness, George Romney trained in Kendal and is one of England's best known portrait painters. Romney refined his training in Rome and Parma and did most of his work in London before returning to Kendal in 1799. His famous paintings, such as *The Death of General Wolfe*, his portraits of fellow painters and his self-portraits, are held in major collections around the world including the National Portrait Gallery and the Musée du Louvre. His work can also be seen at Abbot Hall in Kendal (see p.105) and Sizergh Castle (see p.106).

Arts and crafts

John Ruskin (1819–1900). Author, poet, artist and critic Ruskin was born in London and educated both in London and Oxford. Ruskin moved to Brantwood (see p.131) on the banks of Coniston Water in 1871, buying it from the engraver, poet and social reformer William James Linton, and used the house as a centre for his teaching in art, literature and sociology. He is perhaps most famous for his scathing criticism of the paintings of James Whistler, which he believed were the epitome of reductive mechanisation, and as a champion of decorative and 'craft' art in the face of the Industrial Revolution, which inspired the Arts and Crafts movement. As a social critic, Ruskin was influenced by Christian Socialism, but while mainstream socialism tended to favour strong leadership, Ruskin promoted the concept of community and social economy, or networks of co-operative organisations and charities, as a leadership model. He also opposed the division of labour which he felt turned workers into tools of production, be that capitalist or socialist in nature. His ideas influenced the development of Britain's Labour party, and, more widely, inspired the creation of Ruskin communities in the USA and Canada, while his ideas influenced Leo Tolstoy, Marcel Proust, Mahatma Gandhi and Oscar Wilde.

ARTS AND CRAFTS IN THE LAKE DISTRICT

Arts and Crafts was inspired by the writings and romantic idealisation of the craftsman John Ruskin. As such this 19th-century aesthetic movement found a spiritual home in the Lake District. Arts and Crafts was a reaction to the standardisation and reduction of objects to their utility – a result of the Industrial Revolution – and looked back to the time of hand-worked pieces of art and function (be it lace or a building) believing that these objects should be imbued with morality and humanity. While its most famous exponents, from William Morris to Charles Rennie Mackintosh, spanned Britain and the globe, significant elements were made and are preserved in the Lakes. Most obvious are the houses built in Arts and Crafts style, which include Ruskin's former home Brantwood (see p.131) and Blackwell to the south of Windermere (see p.75). However, other examples of Arts and Crafts work once produced in the Lakes include metal work from the Keswick School of Industrial Art, which was the longest running Arts and Crafts group, furniture made by Arthur Simpson, a Quaker and craftsman who lived in Kendal, and Langdale linen. Examples of Arts and Crafts work can be found at Brantwood, and Blackwell, and the Abbot Hall and the Museum of Lakeland Life in Kendal (see p.109).

Kurt Schwitters (1887–1948). Born in Hanover, Germany, Modernist artist Kurt Schwitters settled in Kendal after fleeing Nazism in both Germany and Norway and spending time interned in Douglas Camp, Isle of Man. In the Modernist way, Schwitters experimented with collage, sculpture, graphic design, sound art, poetry, painting and typography, but is most famous for what is now called installation art. His Merzbau were structures made of found objects, which could range from small to room-size, and moved two-dimensional collage to three-dimensional installations. His final installation was Merzbarn, built in a farm building at Cylinders Farm, Elterwater, near Ambleside. After his death, in obscurity and poverty, Merzbarn was moved to the Hatton Gallery at the University of Newcastle. Examples of his work can be seen at the Armitt Gallery in Ambleside and Kendal's Abbot Hall and the barn itself still stands at Elterwater.

Keith Tyson (1969–). Born in Ulverston and having briefly worked at the Barrow shipyards, the artist Tyson's 'scientific' art focusses on physics, philosophy, probability and computers, won him the 2002 Turner Prize. He is most famous for his piece *The Thinker (After Rodin)*, a huge, black hexagon containing rows of computers and producing a constant low hum. It was exhibited at the 2001 Venice Biennale.

LOCAL HEROES

Sir John Barrow

Sir John Barrow was born in a small cottage in Dragley Beck near Ulverston on 19 June 1764. From these relatively humble beginnings he went on to become Secretary of the Admiralty, a position he held for 40 years. He was also a traveller and explorer and helped establish the Royal Geographical Society in 1830, becoming one of its Fellows. Barrow was also a prolific writer and is perhaps most famous for being the original author of *The Mutiny on the Bounty* – the story of the navel mutiny in the Pacific in 1789 against Captain William Bligh, led by Fletcher Christian, who Barrow knew personally.

A lasting testimony to his life of exploration are the trips to the Arctic that he helped organise – trips which resulted in various places in the Northwest Passage to the Pacific Ocean being named after him, such as Barrow Point in Alaska and the Barrow Straits of northern Canada. He also assisted in the planning of Sir John Franklin's ill-fated expedition to find the Northwest Passage.

It's also believed that while Barrow was Secretary of the Admiralty he suggested that Napoleon be exiled to St Helena, following the emperor's defeat at the Battle of Waterloo on 18 June 1815. Barrow received a knighthood from William IV in 1835 and died in London on 23 November 1848.

The **Sir John Barrow Monument** (see p.114) stands on top of Hoad Hill in Ulverston and the Fergus Fleming book *Barrow's Boys* (Granta Books 2001) recounts the history of Sir John Barrow's many expeditions.

Donald Campbell CBE

British car and motorboat racer Donald Campbell was born in Horley in Surrey on 23 March 1921 to Dorothy and Sir Malcolm Campbell, holder of 13 world speed records in the early 20th century. Following his father's death, Donald bought Malcolm's old *Bluebird* K4 speed boat and 1935 *Bluebird* car and began racing himself. And Between 1956 and 1959 he raised the world water speed record four times on Coniston Water.

In July 1964 Campbell set a new land speed record of 403.10mph in Lake Ayre in Australia in terrible conditions – it is said that had conditions been better he could have achieved 450mph. On New Year's Eve of the same year he set a new water speed record of 276.33mph on Lake Dumbleyung in Western Australia. He remains the only person ever to have set both the land and water speed records in the same year.

Campbell returned to Coniston in 1966 with a new boat, *Bluebird K7*, and the intention of breaking the 300mph record on water, and in perfect conditions on 4 January 1967 Campbell made his record-breaking attempt. His first run clocked 297.60mph, but Campbell then made the fatal mistake of not stopping to refuel or let the wash from his first attempt subside and turned straight round to try again. At a reported speed of 328mph *Bluebird K7*'s stability began to break down in the rough water; its bow rose from the surface before the boat somersaulted backwards and smashed back into the lake at a 45° angle. *Bluebird K7* disintegrated and Campbell was killed instantly. Even though Royal Navy divers made an extensive search at the time, Campbell's body was not recovered from the lake until May 2001.

Campbell was a superstitious man and the night before he was killed he drew an unlucky hand in a card game – the ace and queen of spades. He knew that Mary Queen of Scots had drawn the same hand the night before she was beheaded and took this to be a bad omen for the following day. Some believe this is why he turned around so quickly: he knew his attempt was doomed and decided there was nothing he could do about it.

To find out more about Donald Campbell and to see the actual tailfin of *Bluebird K7*, visit the **Ruskin Museum** in Coniston (see p.131).

George Fox

George Fox, founder of the Religious Society of Friends (or Quakers), was born in 1624 in Drayton, Leicestershire. The son of a weaver, his father was an exceptionally religious man who belonged to the Church of England, which George also joined. In 1643 George Fox became a religious itinerant and, in 1647, he began his public ministry during which he openly attacked the Church and preached against what he perceived to be the lewd behaviour of the age.

The most controversial feature of the religion he advocated was its inwardness and belief in the light within each person that allowed everyone direct communication with God. As such George Fox would not address any person by a title, instead calling everyone by their first names or 'thou' instead of 'you'.

The name 'Quaker' was first given to George Fox and his followers in reference to their 'quaking' during Meetings for Worship, when believers are moved to speak by the Holy Spirit. During the reign of the Catholic James II (1685–1688) the Quakers suffered greatly from the religious intolerance of the Clarden Code of Laws, which advocated their persecution. It was not until 1688 during the reign of the Protestant William and Mary that the Quaker religion was finally officially tolerated in Britain.

George Fox's ministry took him to Ireland, Scotland and America, as well as all parts of England and he was frequently persecuted. In 1652 he arrived at Swarthmoor Hall near Ulverston and recorded in his journals that the town's inhabitants 'are liars, drunkards, whoremongers and thieves and follow filthy pleasures'. However, eleven years later, Fox married Margaret Fell, the owner of Swarthmoor Hall, and the pair travelled extensively and were imprisoned many times for their beliefs. Fox died on 13 November 1690 in White Hart Court, London and is buried in the Quaker Cemetery near Bunhill-Fields. Although he spent relatively little time at Swarthmoor Hall it became the central base behind the Quaker movement. Swarthmoor Hall (see p.143) is open for visitors. To find out more about the Quaker's visit the Quaker Tapestry in Kendal (see p.110).

Stan Laurel (Arthur Stanley Jefferson)

Arthur Stanley Jefferson, the famous comedian known to the world as Stan Laurel, was born on 16 June 1890 in Ulverston. He was the second of five children born to the theatre owner Arthur Jefferson and his actress wife, Margaret. Stan was 16 when he made his stage debut with an act called *Stan Jefferson – He of the Funny Ways*. Although Stan remembered the act to be terrible, it was good enough for him to be employed by Fred Karno who owned 'Fred Karno's Army', one of the most famous music-hall companies of all time. Many comedians of the silent era came from 'Karno's Army', including Charlie Chaplin who Stan understudied.

In 1910 'Karno's Army' moved to America and in 1917 Stan was spotted by Carl Laemmle, the head of Universal Studios, and he made a series of short, relatively unsuccessful films for Universal. It was during this time Stan met the actress Mae Charlotte Dahlberg, who, thinking that Stan Jefferson was an unlucky name because it contained 13 characters, persuaded him to change to Laurel. The vaudeville act Stan and Mae created together was spotted by Gilbert Anderson, who formed the Essanay Film Company, and it was here that Mr Laurel met Mr Hardy and one of the most famous comedy duos in film history was formed.

Laurel and Hardy went on to appear in a total of 106 films together, including both shorts and feature films, silents and talkies, as well as performing their stage show throughout America and Europe. Their most popular films include *Sons of the Desert*, *Way Out West* and *Block-Heads*. After making their last film *Atoll K* in 1951, the pair retired from the screen. Oliver Hardy died of a massive stroke in 1957, after which Stan stopped performing and he himself died of a heart attack on 23 February 1965.

Visit the **Laurel and Hardy Museum** in Ulverston (see p.147) to find out more about this comedy duo and to watch a clip from their films.

Harriet Martineau

English writer, philosopher and feminist Harriet Martineau lived in Ambleside from 1845 until her death in 1876. Although her name is unknown to many today, she was in her time a famous and controversial figure who gained prominence among English intellectuals.

Born in Norwich in 1802 and left penniless following her father's death in 1826, Harriet began to write for a living. She wrote religious books before turning to economics and politics. Novels and children's stories followed and after moving to Ambleside in 1845, Harriet's house The Knoll received many literary guests including Charlotte Bronte, Matthew Arnold and Mrs Gaskell, although she was famously at constant odds with the Wordsworths.

Harriet Martineau was far from an ordinary woman for her time: she never married, travelled extensively and was known for bathing in Windermere at night and smoking a pipe. She was also an ardent champion of women's rights and wrote on the employment of women and, state education for girls, and argued for the admittance of women into the medical profession. In 1850 she wrote a *Guide to Windermere* and five years later published the *Complete Guide to the English Lakes*.

Although her former Ambleside home The Knoll is not open to the public, the town's **Armitt Library and Museum** (see p.92) contains many of her books and personal belongings, plus Harriet's death mask and a cast of her right hand.

Alfred Wainwright MBE

Alfred Wainwright is famous for his handwritten, illustrated walking guides, which include the seven-volume standard reference books of the Lake District the *Pictorial Guide to the Lakeland Fells*.

Alfred was born in 1907 in Blackburn, Lancashire to a relatively poor family. He left school at 13 to work at Blackburn's Borough Engineers Department, but loved walking even at an early age. Wainwright first visited and fell in love with the Lake District aged 23, and in 1941 was finally able to move to Kendal where he lived and worked for the rest of his life.

Wainwright started to plan and create his *Pictorial Guide to the Lakeland Fells* in 1952 and working at the rate of a page a day he finally finished the enormous task of detailing 214 lakeland fells 13 years later. The fells he detailed in this series are now known collectively as the Wainwrights and it' is a popular sport among Lake District walkers to 'bag' them all. Other walking guides followed the *Pictorial Guides* including the *Pennine Way Companion* (1968). In 1972 he devised the *Coast to Coast* walk from St Bees to Robin Hood's Bay.

Wainwright died in 1991 and although he refused to allow any revision to his guidebooks during his lifetime, so many paths and walls had altered since he first wrote his books that updating became essential after his death. The onerous task of revising Wainwright's work has fallen to the cartographer Chris Jesty who is imitating Wainwright's handwriting in an attempt to make his alterations blend into the original work.

For more information on Wainwright visit the website of the Wainwright Society www.wainwright.org.uk and the **Kendal Museum** (see p.109).

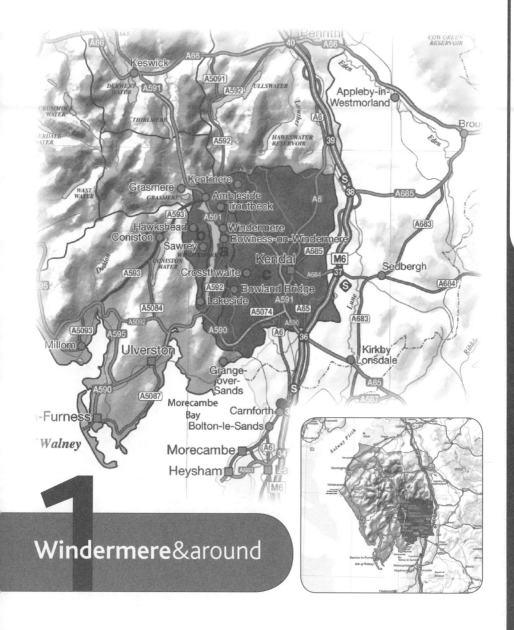

1

Windermere&around

a. Windermere and Bowness-on-Windermere

b. Ambleside and west of Lake Windermere

c. Kendal and around

Unmissable highlights

WINDERMERE
AND AROUND

Windermere stretches a picturesque 10.5 miles from Ambleside in the north to Newbury Bridge in the south and is England's longest and best known lake. Wordsworth, in his 1835 Guide to the Lake District, claimed that Windermere 'ought to be seen from both its shores and from its surface' and his advice rings true today.

The two sides of Windermere are completely different in scenery and personality, offering visitors two very different experiences of the same lake. But getting out onto the water itself is the only real way to appreciate the whole of Windermere's magnificence.

The east side of Windermere is the region's most visited area. Its proximity to the M6 ensures that millions arrive by road every year, so getting anywhere fast on major routes in high season is impossible. It's hardly surprising then that this side of the lake has more of a tourist focus and is largely set up to meet the needs of visitors.

However, this is the best side for those wanting to take to the water as the majority of cruises, boat hire companies and outdoor pursuits operators are found along the eastern shoreline. And those preferring dry land don't have to stray far from the tourist orientated Bowness and Ambleside to reach the attractive market town of Kendal, with its good shopping and numerous attractions, and the tranquil fells that lie between it and the shores of Windermere.

Hawkshead is the largest community on the west side of Windermere and this region has a much wilder feel to its fells. This is Beatrix Potter country and her former home Hill Top, just south of Hawkshead, receives thousands of tourists through its tiny doors each year. Further south, Lakeside, along with the Lake District Visitor Centre at Brockhole located north of Bowness, are magnets for visiting families.

A frequent and inexpensive car ferry crosses the waters at Windermere's narrow mid-point, making travel between the two sides easy. Both sides offer endless walking trails for all abilities plus a fine collection of real ale pubs all served by top quality micro breweries. Good food lovers will find some excellent local producers here, many of which supply the areas' restaurants and cafes. Of the mind-blowing array of accommodation to choose from, some of the best places to stay are tucked away in small communities such as Troutbeck and Staveley.

In high season this famous lake is best experienced early in the morning before day trippers arrive, when a low mist often clings to its serene waters and the low foothills of the southern fells that rise from them. Even in the middle of a tourist-soaked summer's day, Windermere remains one of Britain's most wistfully beautiful sights.

WINDERMERE AND BOWNESS-ON-WINDERMERE

The dark slate town of Windermere doesn't actually touch the shores of the lake that shares its name, but stands a mile inland and elevated above its waters. The railway first came to town in 1847, before which this Lakeland community was known as Birthwaite, and the station on its eastern outskirts still transports reams of tourists into the area. Attractive as Windermere is, unless you have accommodation here there's little reason to linger on its busy streets as there are no tourist attractions in town, only a selection of local shops clustered around its small one-way system.

Seamlessly linked to Windermere via Lake Road, a B&B lined main drag, Bowness-on-Windermere (always shortened to Bowness) is the region's main tourist hot spot and biggest community on the banks of the lake. Most visitors make a beeline for Bowness piers where you can catch a cruise aboard one of the frequent steamers and launches that ply the lake's waters. In high season this area is a milieu of tourists from around the globe and no place for those who've travelled here to get away from it all.

The other main draws to Bowness are the ever popular World of Beatrix Potter Attraction and fascinating Steamboat Museum. However, if you've time, wander

St Martin's church, Bowness-on-Windermere

away from the busy main streets and potter around the tiny lanes behind St Martin's Church. There's been a church on this spot from at least 1203 and, small though it is, this old area of town embodies a sense of a history that Bowness's main tourist areas lack.

Set back from the shores of Windermere and a mile and a half south of Bowness, is Blackwell, an Arts and Crafts house, restored by the Lakeland Arts Trust and one of Cumbria's finest cultural attractions. A stroll around this elegant mansion and its ever growing art collection is well worth travelling to this region for alone.

For many the main draw to the Windermere/Bowness area is the views of the lake itself. One of the best places to feast on them is from Fell Foot Park – a chilled out National Trust gardens at the far south-eastern tip of the lake. This tranquil spot is also close to Gummer's How, one of the area's most popular walks.

WHAT TO SEE AND DO

 ## Fair weather

Getting out onto the waters of Windermere is one of the best ways to make the most of good weather in this region. There's a range of opportunities to suit all ages and abilities, with the cruise ships having undercover areas if the weather turns. All of the below are located at, or close to, Bowness piers to the south of the main town centre off the A592.

On the water
Bowness piers are the central hub for **Windermere Lake Cruises**, the main cruise operator on Windermere. This company runs regular sailings on steamers and launches throughout the summer (April to October) and less frequent departures during the winter (November to March), making stops at Lakeside in the south, Waterhead near Ambleside and the Lake District Visitor Centre at Brockhole. There are various cruise options to choose from including sightseeing tours and a 24-hour ticket allowing holders to hop on and off boats all day. Combination tickets can also be bought for entry to the Lakes Aquarium and the Lakeside and Haverthwaite Railway. Additional Santa Specials and Christmas Cruises are laid on in December.

WINDERMERE LAKE CRUISES, Bowness piers off the A592, Bowness-on-Windermere; 015394 43360; www.windermere-lakecruises.co.uk; from £5.25 adult and £3.15 child from Bowness to Ambleside, £14 adult, £7 child for a Freedom of the Lake 24-hour ticket; family tickets available; first cruises depart 9.30–10.30am in summer and 10–10.30am in winter; last cruises depart 5.35–6.10pm in summer, 3.45pm in winter; every day except Christmas Day.

BOAT HIRE, 015394 40347; rowing boats £5 per adult, £2.50 per child over 5, per hour; open motor boats £15 per hour for two adults, cabin boats £18 per hour for two adults; children under 16 free; hire cabin opens daily at 9am Apr–Oct.

Windermere lake cruises

If you fancy plying the waters of Windermere under your own steam, wooden rowing boats and small motor boats can be hired from the Bowness pier area. Two types of motor boats are on offer: open traditional models with a steering tiller and cabin models with sliding cabin roofs and steering wheels.

WINDERMERE CANOE KAYAK, off the A592 south of Bowness on Ferry Nab Road, near the car ferry terminal, LA23 3JH; 015394 44451; www.windermerecanoe kayak.com; canoe/kayak hire £20–£35 half day, £30–£45 full day; tuition from £13–£35 per hour.

Get right up close to the lake and its wildlife by hiring a canoe or kayak from **Windermere Canoe Kayak**. Half and full day hires are available and you're provided with a map detailing where you can kayak and recommended routes, along with information on rules concerning the lake's islands and wildlife. Tuition is also available.

Lakes Leisure is the place to head if you want to have a go at kayaking, canoeing, windsurfing or sailing. Introductory taster sessions with qualified instructors are available for all of these water based activities and full equipment is provided. Longer courses are also on offer, along with a range of land-based outdoor pursuits such as climbing, orientation and Nordic walking.

Rowing boats, Windermere

LAKES LEISURE, located north of Bowness on Rayrigg Road (A591), LA23 1BP; 015394 47183; www.lakesleisure.org.uk; introductory sessions £24 adults, £19 children.

The Visitors' Book

A family adventure in Windermere

'Cumbria may be famous for its vast fells and lakes but it is possible to enjoy some gentle family biking here, and still have the energy for a spot of boating and afternoon tea. Our active day out began with breakfast in Bowness, followed by a bike ride to Hawkshead, with the older children pedalling and the youngest relaxing in her trailer.

'A highlight of the day for the children was the old-fashioned ferry ride across Windermere, which took us away from the main road and on to quiet lanes and forested mountain bike track, following the spectacularly moody lake Windermere.

'After lunch in one of Hawkshead's very 'English' cafés, we made our way by bike back up the road to Far Sawrey.

'A return trip on the ferry took us to Bowness, then a short drive around the lake to the south shores of Windermere brought us out at Fell Foot Park, a National Trust-owned Victorian country park with views of the fells. At the tea shop we hired two rowing boats and crossed the lake (a relaxed ten minute paddle, not an Olympic endurance test).

'We recharged our batteries with a silver service afternoon tea at the Lakeside Hotel; the tiny sandwiches, cakes and coffee in the sunlit conservatory fuelling us up for a race back across the Lake.

'On the short stroll back to the car at Fell Foot we stumbled upon the children's playground and a quick zip wire challenge with the sun going down over the lake brought an atmospheric end to our family adventure in the central Lakes.'

Kirstie Pelling, Burton-in-Kendal, Lancashire

Hot air balloon rides

Gently drift high above the spectacular scenery surrounding Lake Windermere with a **High Adventure** hot air balloon ride. All sights of interest are pointed out along the way as the lakes and their surrounding fells roll out beneath your feet. A glass of champagne awaits you on landing.

Parks and gardens

A former Victorian country park, **Fell Foot Park** rambles along the north-east shores of Windermere. These beautiful, free gardens have been lovingly restored by the National Trust and are a fabulous place to mess about on a sunny day. Picnic tables and benches command prime views over the waters and fells beyond and countless swans, ducks and other birdlife flock around the park's shores. Rowing boats can be hired in the summer and anyone visiting in the spring will be treated to spectacular displays of rhododendrons and daffodils.

Walking

Orrest Head is a rocky hill that stands 784ft above sea level to the north of Windermere town. The easy walk to its summit starts to the right of the Windermere Hotel which is across the road from the railway station and is paved as far as Steve Hick's blacksmith's studio (015394 42619), where you can stop for a tea and to look at his work. The path then winds through scenic woodland – spot the rabbits and squirrels – and wooden benches look

Popular route: Gummer's How

out over numerous viewpoints. If it's not too windy the summit is a great picnic spot and provides undisturbed views of Windermere and the surrounding hills.

At the southern end of Windermere **Gummer's How** provides equally impressive views of the lake and the Coniston fells. This easy walk is popular with families and to reach the footpath that leads to the summit take the very steep minor road that turns off the A592 near Fell Foot Park. About a mile along you'll come to a small car park from where the footpath to Gummer's How is marked.

CELEBRITY CONNECTIONS

Hollywood star **Renée Zellweger** fell in love with both the role of Beatrix Potter and the Lakes when she came to Windermere and the surrounding area to film *Miss Potter*. She is recorded as saying that she was 'completely stunned by the beauty of the landscape and the tranquillity of the scene'. Rumours abound that Renée adores the region so much she's looking to buy property in the area and is known to have made return visits to enjoy the views minus the pressures of a busy filming schedule. Renée celebrated a birthday while she was filming in the Lakes and Beaulea's Cake Studio (015394 48204 www.beauleascakestudio.com) on Lake Road in Bowness made her birthday cake.

 ## Wet weather

One of the most impressive attractions in the area and a 'must see' for Arts and Crafts enthusiasts, **Blackwell** is a turn of the 20th-century architectural delight that marries an outgoing Victorian style with incoming modern design. The house was originally a holiday home for wealthy Manchester brewer Sir Edward Holt and its intricate beauty, characterised by detailed stained glass, tiled fireplaces, period furniture and exquisite wall coverings, has survived remarkably well – with the help of restoration. Blackwell has none of the roped off areas of many historic homes and visitors are free to roam and linger throughout the property and its

collection of work by Arts and Crafts artists, including Ruskin pottery and carvings by Eric Gill. Blackwell's elevated location above Windermere commands stunning views over the lake and fells beyond, making the outdoor terrace of its café one of the best places in the Lakes to enjoy afternoon tea.

BLACKWELL, Lyth Valley Road, 1.5 miles south of Bowness on the B5360, off the A5074, LA23 3JT; 015394 46139; www.blackwell.org.uk; £5.45 adults, £3 children, £15 family; open daily 10.30am–5pm, closing 4pm Feb, Mar, Nov, Dec; café open from 10am.

 ## What to do with children

The **World of Beatrix Potter Attraction** is the closest to Disney that the Lake District gets and kids love it. Scenes from Potter's tales have been carefully recreated in 3D, allowing the young, and young at heart, to stand in Peter Rabbit's vegetable patch or take virtual tours to the author's favourite Lakes locations.

THE WORLD OF BEATRIX POTTER ATTRACTION, Old Laundry, Cragg Brow, Bowness, LA23 3BX; 015394 88444; www.hop-skip-jump.com; £6 adults, £3 children; open daily at 10am, closing 5.30pm/4.30pm summer/winter.

QUAYSIDE KIDS, The Quays, Glebe Road, Bowness, LA23 3HE; 015394 45354; www.quaysidekids.co.uk; £4.50 per child for up to two hours play; open 9am–6pm Mon–Fri, 9.30am–6pm Sat and Sun with extended hours during school holidays.

A visit starts with a short film about Beatrix's life and ends with a visit to the Tailor of Gloucester's Tea Room and there are plenty of activities and interactive attractions to keep little ones entertained along the way.

Quayside Kids is an indoor play centre and brilliant place for young children to let off steam and have fun in an area that has more to keep adults occupied than youngsters, especially on rainy days. Two colourful play areas aimed at toddlers and juniors are crammed with the likes of spiral slides, tunnels and air balls, and while kids wear themselves out, adults can chill in a lakeside lounge area and enjoy coffee, cakes and great views.

The house and grounds of Brockhole on the northwest edge of lake Windermere make up the main **Lake District Visitor Centre** and is a popular spot for both local and visiting families. This is an ideal place for children to learn about the geology and wildlife of the Lake, through hands-on exhibits (check out the magic carpet ride over the Lakes!), changing displays and a short slide show at the Information Centre. Outside a fab adventure play area, complete with wooden fort and rope walks, will keep youngsters occupied for hours. Adults seeking a peaceful, and often fragrant, retreat should head for Brockhole's impressive landscaped gardens, all maintained using environmentally friendly methods and rich with birds and wildlife including deer, badgers and foxes. All ages enjoy exploring the acres of rambling woodland and meadows that make up the grounds of Brockhole where visitors can seek out various pieces of public art. The numerous benches nestled along the waterfront offer stunning views of the Langdale Pikes on the opposite shore and make for one of the best picnic spots for families in the region (children's picnics are available in the café). Windermere Lake Cruises stop at Brockhole, which, with its plentiful parking, is often a better place to hop aboard a launch than the more crowded Bowness.

THE LAKE DISTRICT VISITOR CENTRE, Brockhole, 2 miles north of Windermere, off the A591, LA23 1LJ; 015394 46601; www.lake-district.gov.uk; admission free; gardens and grounds open daily dawn to 6pm all year, house, café and shop open daily 10am–5pm Apr–Oct.

Local Knowledge

Nurse practitioner and partner of the Windermere Health Centre, **Dr Alison Crumbie** first came to the Lake District aged 17 to work for the Lakeside YMCA at the south end of Lake Windermere. Although spending bouts of time away, Ali has always considered the Lakes to be home. She now lives with her husband, Chris, in a 300-year-old, solar powered barn conversion on the outskirts of Windermere. Ali tends a large vegetable patch and keeps bees, producing buckets of veg and even her own honey each year.

Favourite takeaway: Many people don't know that Zeffirellis in Ambleside also do takeaway. So you can enjoy their great pizzas at home or in the park on a summer's evening.

Best kept secret: The east side of Coniston Water is a peaceful haven far removed the tourist crowds and a perfect picnic spot.

Annual event not to miss: The Great Langdale Christmas Pudding 10km race takes place the weekend before Christmas. The race starts at noon at the New Dungeon Ghyll Hotel and Sticklebarn Tavern on the B5343 near Ambleside, from where runners head out into the valley for 5km and back again. Some hardy souls dress up as Santa Claus or fairies and all who finish are presented with a Christmas pudding.

Favourite treat: Damson gin from the Crossthwaite Valley – a splash in a glass of champagne is especially good.

Best thing to do on a rainy day: Head to Grizedale Forest. Its treetop canopy protects you from the worst of any wet weather and the forest smells wonderful in the rain.

Favourite haunt: The Mill Yard in Staveley is a great local development. Wilf's is my favourite café in the area and the number of shops and arts and crafts outlets are growing all the time.

Best thing about living in the Lakes: The connection with the natural environment, its seasons, wildlife, weather and peace and quiet.

Entertainment

Theatre and cinema

The Old Laundry Theatre is a 260 seater, relatively new theatre in the heart of Bowness which hosts an annual autumn festival of touring theatre, music events and one person shows, all supported by big name stars including Victoria Wood and Alan Ayckbourn.

The Royalty is a charming old three-screen cinema which plays a mix of mainstream and non-commercial films – the intimate screen 3 even has a couple of 'double seats' for the romantic film buffs.

THE OLD LAUNDRY THEATRE, Crag Brow, Bowness, LA23 3DX, 01539 400 444; www.oldlaundrytheatre.co.uk; box office is located at entrance to World of Beatrix Potter Attraction; open 10am–5pm or noon–7.45pm on performance days.

THE ROYALTY CINEMA, Lake Road, Bowness, LA23 3BJ; 015394 43364; www.nm-cinemas.co.uk; tickets £4–£5 adults, £3–£4.50 children.

Special events

Windermere on Water (015397 26442 www.wow2008.co.uk) or WOW as it's known locally, is an annual three-day festival that takes place on and around the lake. Dates for 2008 are 6–8 June and, although at the time of writing details of the big name acts have yet to be released, you can expect an action packed programme of events such as street theatre, sailing regattas, treasure hunts and firework shows.

Every August this region hosts **Lake District Summer Music** (0845 644 2144 www.ldsm.org.uk) an internationally renowned classical music festival when top name artists from around the world perform at various venues including local parish churches. Check the website for details of exact dates.

Nightlife

During the summer **Windermere Lake Cruises** (015394 42600 www.windermere-lakecruises.co.uk) operates Summer Evening Cruises on the waters of Windermere. Cruises depart from Bowness Pier and you can choose between BBQ or buffet cruises, both of which include live entertainment. Advance booking recommended. Tickets £25 adults, £20 children.

The best... **PLACES TO STAY**

BOUTIQUE

Angel Inn

Helm Road, Bowness, LA23 3BU
015394 44080
www.the-angelinn.com

An informal stylish hotel in the heart of Bowness against the backdrop of lake Windermere. An outside terrace overlooks the town's busy streets and the lake beyond. The lively bar and restaurant serves dishes featuring local cheeses and meats plus numerous veggie options.

Price: B&B £65–£100 per room per night midweek, £90–£140 weekends. Special offers available.

HOTEL

Applegarth Hotel

College Road, Windermere, LA23 1BU
015394 43206
www.lakesapplegarth.co.uk

Time stands still in this elegant Victorian mansion in the heart of Windermere. The style and atmosphere is reminiscent of the 1920s and its individually designed rooms offer guests sedate luxury with all the mod cons. The ground floor consists of comfy lounge areas and a wood panelled bar and the evening menu is fine dining.

Price: B&B from £40 for single or twin pppn, from £35 for a double pppn. Two-night minimum stay at weekends.

FARMSTAY/ORGANIC

Bannerigg Farm

Kendal Road (A591), LA23 1JL (one mile south of Windermere)
015394 43362
www.lakedistrictletsgo.co.uk/bannerigg.html

Bannerigg is a family-owned National Trust working farm on the outskirts of Windermere, surrounded by stunning scenery. Guest rooms in the farmhouse are all en-suite and come with TVs. Their hearty breakfasts include local bacon and sausages, and the option of trying the farm's duck eggs.

Price: B&B £27.50 pppn.

B & B

1 Park Road

1 Park Road, Windermere, LA23 2AW
015394 42107
www.1parkroad.com

Recent winner of Les Routiers Best B&B Award. Stylish, cosy rooms have an Art Nouveau influence and there's an abundance of 'special touches' such as tea and cakes on arrival and the daily paper. Breakfast includes fruit smoothies, locally smoked kippers and home-made marmalade and the dinner menu is superb.

Price: B&B £35–£40 pppn, special rates available for families and discounts for longer stays.

The best... PLACES TO STAY

UNUSUAL

Aphrodite's Lodge 🍴 🖼

Longtail Hill, Bowness, LA23 3JD
015394 45052
www.aphroditeslodge.co.uk

The large rooms and suites of this funky B&B each have their own wacky theme. Choices include the Flintstone suite, complete with reams of fake fur and cave like interior, or an Egyptian suite containing fake columns and a chariot chair. Breakfast is hosted in an elegant conservatory overlooking the heated outdoor pool.

Price: B&B £35–£55 pppn midweek, from £70 pppn weekends with a two-night minimum stay.

Holiday Houseboats 🚤 🏠

Mereside, Ferry Nab, Bowness, LA23 3JH
01539 443415
www.lakewindermere.net

Accommodation with lake views don't come better than these luxury houseboats, moored on private jetties close to Bowness. The boats contain separate sleeping cabins, showers, sundecks, a salon area with TV, video and CD player and a fully equipped kitchen. Boats are fully heated and can be rented year round.

Price: Three-night weekend or four-night midweek rent £300–£465, weekly rents £500–£820.

The best... FOOD AND DRINK

Away from the main tourist drag and more orientated towards local food shoppers than Bowness, Windermere is well set up for self-caterers seeking regional fare. Its status as a Fairtrade town ensures there are many of their products available alongside local produce. And shoppers are encouraged to invest in a hessian shopping bag to save plastic. Those wanting to eat out will find more choice in Bowness and many of the surrounding hotels offer fine dining to non-residents.

Staying in

Famous for good quality kitchenware, the enormous **Lakeland Plastics** store (015394 88100 www.lakeland.co.uk) adjacent to Windermere train station and where each checkout is named after a different lake, sells a varied selection of honeys, chutneys, preserves, herbs, pickles and snacks.

For local delis try **Ashworth's** on Main Road, Windermere (015394 45900 www.ashworthsofwindermere.co.uk) for a decent range of local meats, preserves, eggs and cheeses plus a pre-order picnic service from their sandwich bar; or **Butterworth's** (015394 43119) on Quarry Rigg, Bowness for an enormous range of sarnies, baguettes, home-made pies and pasties and veggie specials, plus a selection of jams, biscuits and teas.

Meat lovers will find two excellent butchers in Windermere; **Clayton's** (015394 43071) on Main Road, where meat travels 29 food miles and staff can name the local farms where produce has come from, or **Huddlestones** (015394 43080 www.cumberlandsauage.co.uk) on Crescent Road, famous for its traditional Cumberland sausage and award-wining pies. While the **Oak Street Bakery** (015394 48284) sells a range of freshly baked breads, takeaway sandwiches and Fairtrade coffee.

A good range of local ales, quality wines and malt whiskies can be found at the **Windermere Wine Store** (015394 46891) on Crescent Road.

Takeaways

The Little Chippy on Beech Street in Windermere (015394 44132 open Mon–Sat 11.30am–10pm, Sun noon–9pm) is an upmarket chip shop selling poached salmon and chips, haggis, a good vegetarian selection and milk shakes. For Indian takeaways head to the **Prince of India** (015394 45244 open daily 5pm–midnight) on Crescent Road in Windermere, or the **Emperor of India** (015394 43944 open daily noon–2.30pm and 5.30pm–1.30pm) on Cragg Brow in Bowness, both offer a good range of traditional and unusual dishes plus specialities.

EATING OUT

FINE DINING
Jerichos
Birch Street, Windermere, LA23 1EG
015394 42522
www.jerichos.co.uk

Tucked away on a side street, Jerichos is Windermere's finest restaurant. The menu features modern British cuisine and meals are prepared in an open kitchen using seasonal local ingredients with main courses averaging at £16. Open for dinner only. Closed Sundays and Mondays in winter. Reservations recommended.

RESTAURANT
Francine's Coffee House and Restaurant
Main Road, Windermere, LA23 1BL
015394 44088

A rustic restaurant characterised by hardwood floors and wooden furniture. Their long specials board includes many seafood and vegetarian dishes with lunch costing around £5 and dinner mains £15. Lakeland sticky toffee pudding is one of a number of tempting deserts. Open daily for lunch, Wed–Sun for dinner.

Nissi Restaurant
Lake Road, Bowness, LA23 3BJ
015294 45055

A colourful restaurant with bold red and blue décor and memorable mural of the Trojan War. The menu consists of Mediterranean dishes and wines and includes Cumbrian fell breed meat and fresh fish. Main courses cost £12–£15. Open Mon–Sat from 5.30pm.

The White House
Robinson Place, Lowside, Bowness, LA23 3DQ
015393 44803
www.whitehouse-lakedistrict.co.uk

A contemporary restaurant close to Bowness's St Martin's church. The menu features top notch pub grub including burgers from traditionally reared local beef (£7) and Cartmel Valley Oak smoked platter (£7.50). A pleasant outside terrace is perfect for fair weather dining.

Lucy4 at the Porthole
Ash Street, Bowness, LA23 3BE
015394 42793
www.lucy4attheporthole.co.uk

A funky wine bar-style restaurant with simple décor and a long wine list. The Mediterranean-style menu features tapas, platters and dips from £5–£10. Veggies are spoilt for choice and everything is best washed down with a glass or two of Lucy4's sangria. Open evenings only and from noon on Sundays.

EATING OUT

CAFÉ
The Purple Chilli

**4 Windermere Bank, Lake Road,
Bowness, LA23 2JJ
015394 45657**

Groovy Internet café with a young vibe and friendly feel. The menu is dotted with organic and Fairtrade options and includes salads, cheeses and pressed fruit juices. A bowl of home-made soup and 20 mins on the Internet is a steal at £3.50. No credit cards. Open daily 10.30am–6.30pm, closed on Sundays in the winter.

Colour Pots

**59 Quarry Rigg, Lake Road,
Bowness, LA23 3DU
015394 48877
www.colourpots.co.uk**

A good option for families with young children. Visitors get to decorate a piece of pottery over inexpensive coffee and home-made cakes. Your masterpiece is then fired for you to collect and keep. Children's drinks include Babycino, steamed milk sprinkled with chocolate, and a range of organic cold drinks.

Drinking

There's a limited range of pubs in Windermere and visitors are better off heading for Bowness for a friendly pint. Here a number of pubs cluster around the back of St Martin's church including the **Hole int' Wall**, the oldest tavern in town (and former drinking spot of Dickens) characterised by flagstone floors, very low ceilings and a range of real ales. **The Royal Oak** next door to the World of Beatrix Potter Attraction (see p.76) is a more modern option serving local cask ales and guest beers in stylish surroundings. And for somewhere more vibrant, the **Bodega Bar** on Ash Street specialises in beers from around the world and cocktails.

ⓘ Visitor Information

Tourist Information Office: Victoria Street, Windermere, 015394 46499, www.lakelandgateway.info, Mon–Sat 9.30am–5pm, Sun 10am–5pm.

Hospitals: Nearest hospital to Windermere with a minor injuries unit is Westmorland General Hospital, Burton Road, Kendal, LA9 7RG, 01539 732288; the Windermere Health Centre (see below) will also deal with minor injuries; for more serious problems Lancaster Royal Infirmary, Ashton Road, Lancaster, LA1 4RP, 01524 65944; or Furness General Hospital, Dalton Lane, Barrow-in-Furness, LA14 4LF, 01229 870870.

Doctors: Windermere Health Centre, Goodly Dale, Windermere, LA23 2EG, 015394 45159, www.windermerehealthcentre.co.uk, Mon–Fri 8.30am–6pm.

Pharmacies: Windermere Health Centre (see above) has its own pharmacy; Boots, Crescent Road, Windermere, 015394 43093; out of hours Asda Pharmacy, Burton Road, Kendal, LA9 7JA, 01539 731151, Mon–Sat 8am–9pm, Sun 10am–4pm.

Police: Lake Road, Windermere, 0845 330 0247.

Supermarkets: Boothes, next door to Windermere railway station; Tesco Express and Co-op in Bowness.

Parking: Very limited in Windermere. A small car park at Windermere railway station (£3.50 per day) or limited street parking; in Bowness, Rayrigg Road car park north of the town off the A592 has 200 spaces (£1.20 per hour), or turn onto The Glebe, the road next to Tourist Information at Bowness piers to reach a 600-space long-stay car park at Braithwaite Fold; seasonal park and rides are located further out of town.

Internet Access: Lakeland Plastics, next door to Windermere railway station, free Internet access at its first floor café; The Purple Chilli café; Windermere Public Library, Broad Street, 015394 62400.

Car Hire: Lakes Car Hire, New Road, Windermere, LA23 2LA, 015394 44488 www.lakeshire.co.uk.

Left Luggage: Darryl's Café, Church Street, Windermere, 8am–6pm, £1.50 per item.

Bike Rental: Country Lanes, next door to Windermere railway station, 015394 44544, www.countrylanes.co.uk, daily 9am–5pm (Easter–November and by arrangement Nov to Easter), bikes £15 a day; in Bowness, Windermere Canoe Kayak (see p.72) hire bikes, from £15 per half day, £22 full day.

Taxis: Abacus Taxi Service, 015394 88285, www.travelabacus.co.uk; Pegasus Taxis, 015394 48899.

AMBLESIDE AND WEST OF LAKE WINDERMERE

Standing firmly at the north end of Windermere is the thriving town of Ambleside, whose streets are the haunt of serious climbers and walkers attracted to the impressive fells that close in around the town. This is one of the best places in the region to get stuck into some good walking. To the east of Ambleside is the tiny, exceptionally pretty village of Troutbeck, whose big draw is the National Trust property Townend and the two nearby gardens of Holehird and Stagshaw.

Heading around the tip of the lake to Windermere's western shores you enter deep into the heart of Beatrix Potter country. Here the fells and tiny communities but up against the wilds of Grizedale Forest to the west and a strong sense of landscape and nature untamed prevails. Beatrix's ashes are scattered in this countryside in an area known as Claife Heights whose attractive trail-filled woodland are a pleasant spot for some easy walking.

Hawkshead is the main town on this side of the lake and its biggest draw is Hill Top, Beatrix Potter's one-time home. Hill Top is located one mile south of Hawkshead and is one of many of the farms and acres of land she purchased in this region. The town's other two attractions are its old Grammar School, once attended by Wordsworth, and the Beatrix Potter Gallery. The town is also home to the Hawkshead Relish Company and numerous micro breweries making it a serious destination for foodies and real ale aficionados.

Immediately south of Hawkshead is Esthwaite Water, a relatively small lake with a remote feel that's stuffed with top quality trout. Contact the Esthwaite Water Trout Fishery (015394 36541 www.hawksheadtrout.com) to have a bash at fishing these peaceful waters. The fishery provides free instruction to beginners and even if all you leave with are tales of the ones that got away, time spent sharing the lakeside with wildlife such as otters and kingfishers is well worth the cost of a permit fee.

No visit to this side of Windermere is complete without heading down to Lakeside at its extreme south-western tip. Here you'll find the lakes' swanky aquarium, a popular attraction for all ages, and the chance to catch a ride on the old Lakeside to Haverthwaite steam train. And maybe, if you watch the waters closely on a calm day, you might catch a glimpse of the mysterious giant eel-like creature that many swear to have sighted over the past half century.

To Grasmere
To Kirkstone Pass
To Kirkstone Pass

The Green
Smithy Brow
Kirkstone Road
Chapel Hill
Peggy Hill
Fair View Rd
The Falls
Rydal Road
Stockghyll Lane
Stock Ghyll
Stockghyll Lane
Cheapside
Market Pl
Compston Road
Vicarage Road
The Slack
St. Mary's Ln
Cheapside
High Gale
Gale How Park
Lower Gale
Compston St
Church St
King St
Lake Road
Kelsick Rd
Gale Rigg
Low Gale
Old Lake Road
Knott St
Rothay Road
Wansfell Road
Blue Hill Road
Loughrigg Avenue
A591
Fisher Beck Park
A593
Rothay Road
Borrans Road
River Rothay
Waterhead
To Galava Roman Fort
To Windermere
Lake Road
Skelghyll Lane
Old Lake Road

Ambleside

1. Bridge House
2. Rothay Park
3. The Armitt Library & Museum
4. Homes of Football
5. Zeffirellis
6. Artists' Courtyard
7. Lucy's
8. Organico
9. The Sweet Jar
10. Walnut Fish Bar
11. Tagore Tandoori
12. Bizzy Lizzy's
13. Lucy's On a Plate
14. Doi Intanon
15. The Golden Rule
16. Lucy's 4
17. Lake Road Wine Bar
18. Biketech
19. Ghyllside Cycles
20. Pippin's

WHAT TO SEE AND DO

 Fair weather

Ambleside is located five miles north of Windermere and is split into two distinct areas, the main town centre and Waterhead, a small harbour spilling over the northern end of the lake a mile to the south off the A591. Many visitors arrive on one of the frequent lake launches that dock at Waterhead and never venture further than its gift shops and cafes. In the town itself, narrow streets jumble around a small one-way system and a wide stream called Stock Ghyll passes through to the north over which stands the distinctive **Bridge House**. Built around 300 years ago this tiny property was constructed over water as a way of escaping land tax and is now owned by the National Trust operates an information centre and shop from its cramped ground floor. Shoppers will enjoy rummaging around the town's varied collection of stores and the many cafés and friendly pubs are good places to relax if the weather turns. Those seeking a decent walk from the town centre should head for Rothay Park to the west of St Mary's church. From here follow the signposts located at the humpbacked bridge that point the way to the hike up Loughrigg Fell.

Bridge House, Ambleside

Townend, a 17th century National Trust property

TOWNEND, 3 miles south east of
Ambleside at Troutbeck, LA23 1LB; 015394
32628; www.nationaltrust.org; adults
£3.80, children £1.90, family £9.50; open
Apr–Oct, Wed–Sun 1pm–4.30pm, may close
early if the light is poor.

Townend is a fascinating house built in the early 17th century as a home for a wealthy farmer, George Browne, located to the east of Ambleside in Troutbeck. The property remained in the possession of generations of the Browne family until 1943 when it passed into the hands of the National Trust which opened the doors to this typical Lake District style house and grounds to the public. Townend has survived remarkably well and today, with its ornate carvings, library, old-fashioned domestic appliances and homely feel, it opens a window through which visitors can catch a glimpse of how people in the Lakes used to live.

Travel five miles from Ambleside around the northern tip of Windermere, then head south down its western shore and you'll come to the ancient community of **Hawkshead**. Once owned by Furness Abbey (see p.142), under whose governance the town prospered as an important wool market, today much of Hawkshead stands on land belonging to the National Trust. Wool trading is the reason the town centre has two squares – one was used to sell sheep, the other fleeces. And one of the big attractions to this old Lakeland community is the muddle of narrow alleys and small streets leading off these two squares that are a pleasure to potter around. Cars are banned from the town centre (visitors park in a large car park on the outskirts of town just off the B5285), which makes discovering the collection of quaint shops, bargain outdoor stores, cosy cafés and friendly pubs that line these streets all the more enjoyable.

Hawkshead Post Office

Also take time to walk up to **St Michael and All Angels** parish church, which dates from 1500 and stands above the centre of Hawkshead. Here you can feast on memorable views over the town's whitewashed stone cottages and uneven slate roofs and onto the fine countryside beyond, still populated with traditional working farms.

The most popular historic property in this region is **Hill Top**, a small 17th-century Lakeland farmhouse which Beatrix Potter bought in 1905 with the royalties from her first books. She then moved out of her parents' London home to live and write some of her best-loved children's tales in the Lakes, inspired by the nature on her doorstep. Hill Top remains much the same as it was when Beatrix lived here, with many of her possessions, such as furniture and books, on view. A visit includes a wander around the rambling cottage garden filled with flowers, herbs and vegetables and the extraordinary amount of tourists attracted here each year guarantees that the limited quota of tickets often sells out early in high season.

HILL TOP, 2 miles south of Hawkshead at Near Sawrey, LA22 0LF; 015394 36269; www.nationaltrust.org.uk: adults £5.40, children £2.70, families £13.50; discounts for ticket holders to the Beatrix Potter Gallery (see below); house open daily Apr–Oct, 10.30am–4.30pm (but can be closed for cleaning on Fridays) and weekends in March; shop and garden open daily 10.30am–4pm closing at 5pm Mar–Oct.

HOLEHIRD GARDENS, a mile along the A592 off the junction with the A591 past St Anne's School, LA23 1NP; 015394 46008; ww.holehirdgardens.org.uk; admission/ parking free, donations welcome; open daily year-round; reception desk open and warden present Apr–Oct, 10am–5pm; guided walks Wed 11am in season.

Parks and gardens

Once voted by BBC gardeners to be one of the Nation's Favourite Gardens, **Holehird Gardens** consists of ten beautiful acres sitting high above Windermere and tended by volunteers from the Lakeland Horticultural Society. There are numerous different areas to explore including rock, heather and walled gardens and herbaceous borders, all bursting with colourful plants and enhanced by stunning views. Spring and autumn are the best times to visit, but you can expect to enjoy fine gardens whatever the time of year. The society holds regular free daytime lectures and hosts a large plant sale at a local school each May.

A couple of miles north of Holehird and on the outskirts of Windermere is **Stagshaw Gardens**, a delightful 8-acre rambling woodland garden known for its annual riotous displays of flowering shrubs such as rhododendrons, magnolias and azaleas. A large part of this garden clings onto steep hillside down which a woodland beck and its

STAGSHAW GARDENS, half a mile south of Ambleside off the A591, LA22 0HE; 015394 46027; www.nationaltrust.org.uk; admission £2, paid into an honesty box at the entrance; open daily Apr–June 10am–6.30pm.

small waterfalls stream. Magnificent views of Windermere can be seen through the trees and the gardens provide access to nearby fells for those who want to explore further.

Over on the western shores of Windermere, the handsome **Graythwaite Hall Gardens** surround the equally impressive Graythwaite Hall (not open to the public), home of the Sandys family – founders of Hawkshead Grammar School. Designed in the late 19th century, the gardens have formal and more rambling areas and include an Arts and Crafts style rose garden. Graythwaite's woodlands were a favourite haunt of Wordsworth and the setting for Beatrix Potter's *The Fairy Caravan*.

GRAYTHWAITE HALL GARDENS, 4 miles north of Newbury Bridge on the west side of Windermere past Lakeside, LA12 8BA; 015395 31333; www.graythwaitehall.co.uk; adults £3, children under 14 free; Apr–Aug 10am–6pm.

The Visitors' Book

Hill Top Farm

'If you're anywhere near Sawrey, it's worth battling the hordes of Japanese tourists and car parking queues to pay a visit to Beatrix Potter's house at Hill Top Farm. Apparently she wrote lots of her stories there and the cottage and gardens are very sweet — not sure if it's deliberate, but the garden outside the cottage is a pretty good likeness for Peter Rabbit's adventures...

'We had a lovely chilled-out day in the picturesque surroundings of Near Sawrey. It's very pretty, with farmland and rolling green hills, and if you fancy something in the lakes that doesn't involve walking it's a nice alternative — although perhaps more appealing to those who remember Jemima Puddleduck or appreciate chocolate-box cottages, than those who own their own walking boots!

'On busy days, you get given a timed ticket to the cottage when you pay, so you can go and amuse yourself while you wait. If you're not feeling particularly energetic you could do what we did and go to a nearby hotel (the Sawrey House Hotel I think) and have some tea and scones!

'We eventually went to Beatrix Potter's cottage; it is small, so you can see why they time entry. There is plenty to see though — the rooms and furniture in the cottage are replicated in the drawings of her characters dotted around, so you can see how much inspiration Beatrix Potter got from her surroundings, and the garden is great. It does get quite crowded, so you can almost trip over your fellow tourists while trying to walk around, but it's well worth a visit!'

Nicola Slavin and Mark Aplin, London

Wet weather

THE BEATRIX POTTER GALLERY, Main
Street, Hawkshead, LA22 0NS; 015394
36355; www.nationaltrust.org.uk; adults
£3.80, children £1.90, families £9.50;
discounts for ticket holders to Hill Top; open
Apr–Oct daily (except Fri) 10.30am–4.30pm
and weekends in March.

The other highlight on the Beatrix Potter tourist map on this side of Windermere is **The Beatrix Potter Gallery**, a charming art gallery housed in a 17th-century Lakeland town house in Hawkshead. The gallery is the former offices of Beatrix Potter's solicitor husband William Heelis, and during busy periods a timed ticket system is in operation to control the flow of visitors. For fans of Potter's work this is the place to get up close to many of her original illustrations, paintings, sketchbooks and letters. Those who enjoyed the recent film of her life can view displays dedicated to *Miss Potter*.

The other indoor attraction in Hawkshead is the Elizabethan **Hawkshead Grammar School**. Founded in 1585 by the former Archbishop of York and local lad Edwin Sandys, the school closed its doors to pupils in 1909. Fletcher Christian's brother Edward served a short stint as headmaster in 1781, but the most famous name attached to the school is

HAWKSHEAD GRAMMAR SCHOOL, off
Main Street near St Michael's Church,
Hawkshead, LA22 0NT; 015394 36735;
www.hawksheadgrammar.co.uk; admission
£2; open Apr–Sept Mon–Sat, 10am–1pm
and 2pm–5pm, Sun 1pm–5pm; 1–31
October Mon–Sat 10am–1pm and
2pm–3.30pm, Sun 1pm–3.30pm.

ex-pupil William Wordsworth who arrived in 1778 when it was one of the best grammar schools in the country. Today this simple, flagstoned building houses worn wooden school desks, some dating from the 16th century and all carved with the names of old pupils including young William himself. A visit includes a short talk on the school's history and a chance to explore the old classroom and headmaster's study. The school's foundation trust still provides educational grants to the young of Hawkshead and the governing body is still chaired by a member of the Sandys family.

THE ARMITT LIBRARY AND MUSEUM,
off Rydal Road (A591) adjacent to the
University of Cumbria campus, LA22 9BL;
015394 31212; www.armitt.com; adults
£2.50, children £1; open daily 10am–5pm,
library Tues/Fri 10am–4.30pm.

The Armitt Library and Museum is a treasure trove of local history, art and literature including Neolithic and Roman artefacts discovered around Ambleside, items relating to famous Lakes residents such as Dorothy Wordsworth's scarf, and Victorian photographs of Lakeland life. The upstairs library houses an impressive collection of Lake District titles from early guidebooks to works by Arthur Ransome and Beatrix Potter. The Armitt also holds a large collection of books and personal belongings of the writer, philosopher and feminist Harriet Martineau who lived in Ambleside from 1845 until her death in 1876. For more information on Harriet Martineau see p.65.

Don't be fooled into thinking **Homes of Football** is just for football fans. This fascinating collection of photography by Stuart Clarke documents his 3,500 visits to football grounds around the world. The images of fans, teams and grounds are outstanding and have an

> HOMES OF FOOTBALL, 100 Lake Road, Ambleside, LA22 0DB; 015394 3440; www.homesoffootball.co.uk; admission free; open Wed–Sun 10am–5pm.

appeal that reaches far beyond the game's loyal fan base. An unlikely attraction to find in the Lakes, but one not to be missed all the same.

Further afield wet weather attractions

The other historic property in this region is **Stott Park** a steam-powered Victorian bobbin mill – once one of 65 in the area – located at the far western tip of Windermere. Stott Park is one of the few places to explore the Lakes industrial heritage in this region. The abandoned mill was bought by English Heritage in the 80s and restored to working order and now allows visitors to see how this old technology works and the bobbin making process. The dark slate mill, instantly recognisable by its tall chimney, nestles low into a valley near the water's edge and wooden outdoor buildings house displays detailing the history of bobbin making. Picnic tables in the grounds make for a pleasant lunch spot on a sunny day.

> STOTT BOBBIN MILL, on south-western tip of Windermere, 2 miles north of Newbury Bridge; 0870 333 1181; www.english-heritage.org.uk; adults £4.20, children £2.10, family £10.50; guided tour only; open Apr–Oct Mon–Fri 10am–5pm.

 ## What to do with children...

Lakeside, at the extreme south-west tip of Windermere, is a great place to head with children of all ages, whatever the weather. Rambling woodland slopes down to the water and the whole area has a much calmer feel than the busy communities at the Lake's northern end. The Lakeside and Haverthwaite Railway (see p.131) steams into a tiny lakeside station, offloading passengers next door to the Lakes Aquarium and a pick-up point for Windermere Lake Cruises (see p.71). Too good to be true views of the length of Windermere stretch out before you and a jaunty café, with indoor and outdoor seating, makes the most of its scenic location. Bikes

LAKES AQUARIUM, Lakeside, a mile north of Newbury Bridge off the A590, LA12 8AS; 015395 30153; www.lakesaquarium.co.uk; adults £7.50, children £5, family from £22, combined tickets are available with Windermere Lake Cruises (see p.71); open daily 9am–6pm, closing at 5pm in winter.

can be hired at the station for those who want to explore the surrounding hills and woodland further.

At the **Lakes Aquarium** you can learn about the fish and wildlife to be found in the rivers, lakes and coast of Cumbria. At this entertaining and educational attraction visitors follow the journey of water as it falls onto the region's mountaintops and travels down to the sea, and also discover all the creatures who live in or around it at the various habitats along the way. A visit includes films, interactive displays and plenty of children's activities such as quizzes and daily talks. And although everyone loves the otters, the best bit is a walk through the tunnel aquarium where you're surrounded by a recreation of Windermere's lake bed.

Lakes Aquarium tunnel

On a dry day a good area to aim for with children is **Waterhead**, the harbour area to the south of Ambleside. Here you can pick up a bag of duck food from the Waterhead Coffee Shop and have fun feeding the countless birds that strut their feathered stuff around the water's edge. And to the west of this busy waterfront area, just a short distance along the A593, is Borran's Park a tranquil landscaped area, which, with its long lake views, is a perfect picnic spot and play area. The Romans named this area Galava and built a fort in a field adjacent to the park. Little remains of Fort Galava, but it's still an interesting and often peaceful place to explore, populated by local sheep and far fewer tourists than the town centre.

 ## ... and how to avoid children

The Lakeside Hotel at the far south-west of lake Windermere is the place to head for some serious pampering. The hotel organises **Luxury Day Passports** at their spa and pool, which allow the holder a full day to relax in the pool, Jacuzzi, sauna and steam room. The passport also includes a two-hour spa treatment of your choice and a three-course lunch in the hotel's conservatory which overlooks the lake.

LAKESIDE HOTEL, Lake Windermere, Newbury Bridge, LA12 8AT; 015395 30001; www.lakesidehotel.co.uk; £149 per person or £199 per person with customised beauty products; luxury day passport lasts from 7am–7.30pm.

 ## Entertainment

Named after the Italian cinema director Franco Zeffirelli, Zeffirellis is an independent four-screen cinema showing mainstream and specialist films on both traditional 35mm format and state of the art HD digital.

ZEFFIRELLIS, Compston Road, Ambleside, LA22 9AD; 015394 33845; www.zeffirellis.com; £5.80 after 6.45pm, before 6.45pm: £4.50 adults, £3.50 children; dinner and cinema deals available.

As well as being a cinema and restaurant, **Zeffirellis** hosts regular jazz events throughout the year – call or check the website for details. And every Friday night from February to October the **Outgate Inn** (015394 36413 www.outgateinn.co.uk) on the B5286 at Outgate just north of Hawkshead, hosts a popular live jazz night. The music kicks off at 8.30pm and if you also want to eat at the pub (upmarket pub fare from £11–£15), it's essential to book a table in advance. If you prefer classical music Yewfield Guesthouse (www.yewfield.co.uk) at Hawkshead Hill hosts free regular concerts that are open to all.

Special events

Well over two centuries old, **Ambleside Sports** is a whole day of traditional Lakeland sports held on the last Thursday of July at Rydal Park half a mile north of Ambleside off the A591. Catch a glimpse of Cumberland and Westmorland wrestling, believed to have been brought to the area by the Vikings, watch the super fit take part in the Rydal Round Fell Race and enjoy other events including hound trails and bike races. There are also craft stalls to browse through, children's activities and a beer tent that never runs dry. Admission costs £5 per adult, £10 per family. For more information on Ambleside Sports contact the town's Tourist Information Centre.

 # Shopping

Next door to Homes of Football at 101 Lakeside Road in Ambleside is the **Artists' Courtyard**. This quaint little yard, tucked away off the main road is home to the studio and shop of local potter Sue Bartholomew (www.suebartholomew.co.uk), Caribou Arts, a contemporary arts store whose wares include handmade books and cards, and Novel Café, a bookshop and cosy café. Also in Ambleside, **the Cook House Gallery** on Church Street (www.cookhousegallery.co.uk) sells a fine range of artists' work in different mediums all creatively expressing the way they see the Lake District. And in Hawkshead, **Poppi Red** on Main Street (www.poppi-red.co.uk) is an unusual gifts, clothes and furniture store as well as cute café.

The best... PLACES TO STAY

HOTEL

Holbeck Ghyll

**Holbeck Lane, Nr Ambleside,
LA23 1LU
015394 32375
www.holbeckghyll.com**

Multi-award winning luxury hotel that combines excellent service with the aura of an old country home. Its hillside location commands impressive views of Windermere and facilities include a pleasant spa, putting green and tennis courts. Sherry and relaxing music await in every room and celebrity guests include Renée Zellwegger and Joseph Fiennes.

Price: B&B £100–£225 pppn.

FARMSTAY/ORGANIC

Howe Farm

**Hawkshead, Nr Ambleside, LA22 0BB
(from Hawkshead follow the road
signposted to Newbury Bridge for
half a mile)
015394 36345
www.howefarm.co.uk**

A friendly working farm dating back to the late 17th century on the outskirts of Hawkshead. The farmhouse features oak panels and log fires and delicious breakfasts are cooked with home-grown and locally sourced produce.

Price: B&B £27.50 pppn.

INN

The Drunken Duck

**Barngates, Nr Ambleside, LA22 0NG
015394 36347
www.drunkenduckinn.co.uk**

A deservedly popular 400-year-old inn, whose contemporary makeover has destroyed none of its charm. Deep sofas, open fires and Kipper the cat await in the residents' lounge. Private gardens beside a small tarn are the perfect summer chill out spot. Book well in advance.

Price: B&B and afternoon tea £95–£225 per room per night.

The Queens Head

**Townhead, Troutbeck, Nr
Windermere, LA23 1PW
015394 32174
www.queensheadhotel.com**

An appealing mix of comfort and style set in a stunning location. Rooms are available in the old coaching inn itself or an adjacent barn conversion. The friendly pub is a local favourite and the on-site restaurant (see below) makes it worth the stay alone. Special offers can include a half day cookery course or a sailing trip.

Price: B&B £50–£68 pppn.

The best... PLACES TO STAY

B & B

Ivy House Hotel

Main Street, Hawkshead, LA22 0NS
015394 36204
www.ivyhousehotel.com

An attractive Georgian house in the centre of Hawkshead whose comfortable rooms (some four poster) are set in elegant surroundings. An on-site restaurant serves an excellent choice of à la carte evening meals, accompanied by a good wine list.

Price: B&B £40–£50 pppn, £5 extra for a four poster room.

SELF-CATERING

Ann Tyson's

Wordsworth Street, Hawkshead, LA22 0PA
015394 36405
www.anntysons.co.uk

This Grade II listed Lakeland cottage is linked to Ann Tyson's B&B in Hawkshead. The cottage was home to Wordsworth from 1779 to 1787 and has a central location in the village. It features two bedrooms, exposed beams and an open fire (coal provided).

Price: £280–£460 a week. Can be rented as a three-night minimum stay mid-Nov–Feb. Sleeps 4–5.

The best... FOOD AND DRINK

Staying in

The multi-award winning **Hawkshead Relish Company** (015394 36614 www.hawksheadrelish.com) has a small shop in the centre of Hawkshead that's crammed with a mind-blowing array of relishes and a selection of Hawkshead beers. Also in Hawkshead, **The Honeypot** (www.thehoneypotinhawkshead.co.uk) sells a range of specialist food such as home-baked filled rolls made to order, locally baked pies and local meats and cheeses.

In Ambleside, **Lucy's** (015394 32288 www.lucysofambleside.co.uk) on Compston Road is a specialist grocers and one of the most impressive delis in the Lakes. The shelves are stocked with an amazing array of produce from all over Cumbria and Lucy's will also deliver. The region's best wine shop, **Organico** (015394 31122, www.organi.co.uk) is located at Fisherbeck Mill at the back of the car park off the A591 on the southern outskirts of Ambleside. Organico is the world's first completely organic wine shop. You can browse around 200 organic wines purchased directly from vineyards around the world and buy by the bottle or sip a glass on the wooden terrace outside the shop.

And all those with fond memories of the old-fashioned sweets you used to spend your pocket money on should head for **The Sweet Jar** on Millans Park in Ambleside (www.thesweetjarambleside.co.uk) where you can relive your favourite childhood treats.

Takeaway

The Walnut Fish Bar (015394 33845) opposite Zeffirellis on Miliams Park serves gourmet fish and chips to eat in or takeaway (open Mon–Thurs 11.45am–9pm, Fri and Sat 11.45am–10pm and Sun 11.45am–8pm). **Tagore Tandoori Restaurant** (015394 34346) on Compston Road in Ambleside has a long take-away menu with a good choice for vegetarians (open daily noon–2.30pm, Sun–Thurs 5.30pm–11.30pm and Fri and Sat 5.30pm–midnight). For takeaway lunch try **Bizzy Lizzy's** in Ambleside on Lake Road which sells sandwiches, hot panini, hot baguettes and Fairtrade products.

EATING OUT

FINE DINING
Holbeck Ghyll
Holbeck Lane, Ambleside, LA23 1LU
015394 32375
www.holbeckghyll.com

Reservations are essential at this Michelin starred restaurant where the food is as fabulous as the lake views. The menu changes daily and features dishes made from locally sourced ingredients such as Herdwick lamb and Cumbrian venison. The wine list contains over 300 choices and for that special night, splash out on a gourmet menu of eight exquisite courses (£60).

RESTAURANT
Zeffirellis
Compston Road, Ambleside, LA22 9AD
015394 33845
www.zeffirellis.com

A mainly pizza (with wholemeal crusts) and pasta restaurant with a varied selection for vegetarians including butternut squash ravioli (£9.45). Booking is advisable most evenings especially for the two-course dinner with reserved cinema seats deal (£16.95). For details of the cinema see p.95.

Lucy's On A Plate
Church Street, Ambleside, LA22 0BU
015394 31191
www.lucysofambleside.co.uk

This chic restaurant is popular with locals and tourists alike. The imaginative menu is crammed with local meats and produce and you can feast on six glorious deserts on pudding night, held on the first Wednesday of the month (£25).

Doi Inthanon
Market Place, Ambleside, LA22 9BU
015394 32119

Housed in the old market building and decorated in striking orange and dark green, Doi Inthanon is a first rate Thai restaurant. The detailed menu features a good range of stir fries, curries and Thai salads all with varying degrees of spice and there's a whole page just for veggies. Open daily from 6pm, mains £8–£10.

GASTRO PUB
The Drunken Duck
Barngates, Ambleside, LA22 0NG
015394 36347
www.drunkenduckinn.co.uk

An incredibly popular up market pub restaurant, whose indoor seating is cosy and contemporary and outdoor tables boast priceless views of the surrounding fells. Lunch choices include doorstep sandwiches (from £4.50) and dinner highlights are fine meats such as Goosnargh duck (two courses £22). The wine menu is extensive and bookings are essential.

EATING OUT

The Queens Head
Townhead, Troutbeack, Windermere, LA23 1PW
015394 32174
www.queensheadhotel.com

The Queens Head is one of the friendliest places to eat in the Ambleside area and a big hit with locals and visitors alike. The menu is an appealing blend of traditional Cumbrian foods transformed into contemporary dishes. A set menu of three courses is a steal for £18 and à la carte is also available.

CAFÉ
Pippins Café Bar
Lake Road, Ambleside, LA22 0AD
015394 31338
www.pippinscafebar.co.uk

Decorated in warm yellow, this friendly café bar is a recommended choice for veggies. Pippins opens at 8.30am when you can start the day with Belgian waffles and serves dishes including pizzas (under £10) and tabbouleh (£6) until late. Takeaway available.

 ## Drinking

Barngates Brewery (www.barngatesbrewery.co.uk) in the grounds of the Drunken Duck near Hawkshead brews a growing range of beers using its own water supply from a nearby tarn. You can sink a pint of their distinctive ales – Tag Lag, Catnap, Chesters Strong and Ugly – at this and other pubs in the region. In Hawkshead itself the friendly **Kings Arms** is unmissable with the sign outside declaring 'I wandered lonely as a cloud and then I thought "sod it I'll have a pint instead".' While not far away on the B5285 in Near Sawrey, local favourite the **Tower Bank Arms** (www.towerbankarms.co.uk), next to Beatrix Potter's Hill Top, is the country inn featured in *The Tale of Jemima Puddleduck* and serves a range of local beers and organic wines.

A mile from the Windermere car ferry on the B5285 in Far Sawrey, the **Claife Crier Bar** serves up a local ghost story of a mad medieval monk (often felt following walkers on nearby Claife Heights) along with their local ales. Claife Crier stout brewed by **Cumbrian Legendary Ales** in Hawkshead is just one of their beers named after local legends.

In Troutbeck the **Queen's Head** is a very popular drinking spot for locals and the beer garden at the **Mortal Man** (www.themortalman.co.uk) is the place to sit and take in the views and a cold beer on a summer's afternoon.

For those seeking real ale in a real local in Ambleside, the **Golden Rule** on Smithy Brow is a must, while wine bar lovers should aim for Lucy's 4 (www.lucy4.co.uk) on St Mary's Lane, another incarnation of Lucy's food and drink empire, or sink into comfy sofas at the **Lake Road Café** wine bar.

ℹ Visitor Information

Tourist Information Centres: Market Cross, Ambleside, 015394 32582, www.amblesideonline.co.uk; Lakes Information Centre, Waterhead for guides, maps and walking routes.

Hospitals: Minor Injuries Unit, Westmorland General Hospital, Burton Road, Kendal, LA9 7RG, 01539 732288; Ambleside Health Centre (see below) will also deal with minor injuries; for more serious problems Lancaster Royal Infirmary, Ashton Road, Lancaster, LA1 4RP, 1524 65944; or Furness General Hospital, Dalton Lane, Barrow-in-Furness, LA14 4LF, 01229 870870.

Doctors: Ambleside Health Centre, Rydal Road, LA22 9BP, 015394 32693, www.ambleside healthcentre.co.uk, Mon–Fri 8.30am–6pm.

Pharmacies: Boots, Lake Road, 015394 33355; out of hours Asda Pharmacy, Burton Road, Kendal, LA9 7JA, 01539 731151, Mon–Sat 8am–9pm, Sun 10am–4pm.

Supermarkets: Co-op, Ambleside and Hawkshead.

Internet Access: Ambleside Library, Kelsick Road, 015394 32231.

Bike rental: Biketech, Rydal Road, Ambleside, 015394 31245, www.biketreks.net; Ghyllside Cycles, The Slack, Ambleside, 015394 31245, www.ghyllside.co.uk; Country Lanes, Lakeside Station of Lakeside and Haverthwaite Railway (see p.131); 0845 370 0778, www.countrylanes.co.uk, Easter to October.

Taxis: B Line Taxis; 015394 44644); Kevin's Taxis (015394 3237).

KENDAL AND AROUND

Kendal advertises itself as 'the gateway to the lakes' and whether arriving by bus, train or car, many visitors simply pass through this gateway in their haste to reach nearby Windermere or other more famous regions. If you're not in a rush to reach the National Park, it's well worth pausing in Kendal and finding out what those who travel through miss.

As the largest community in south Cumbria, Kendal comes with all the amenities and attractions you'd expect and some, such as the fine Abbot Hall and unique Quaker Tapestry that you wouldn't. And if you're looking to escape its bustling streets, head to the banks of the River Kent which flows swiftly through the town and is edged by a pleasant riverside walk, or up to the ruins of an old medieval castle which stands on the low hills surrounding the town.

Located close to the A590 to the south of Kendal are two of the finest old houses in south Cumbria – Levens Hall and Sizergh Castle. While strung along the ten miles between Kendal and Windermere to the north-west are a number of small communities of which Staveley, with its fabulous Mill Yard and proximity to Kentdale, is the most worthy of a visit.

Filling the countryside between Kendal and the eastern shores of Windermere are a collection of picturesque valleys and fells whose beauty is much softer than the more mountainous regions of the Lakes but no less attractive for it. This tranquil area contains many scenic walks and a good collection of cracking country pubs.

In this region the Lyth Valley is known for its annual crop of lush, strong damsons and one of the best times to visit is spring when the fells are festooned with frothy damson blossom. Arthur Ransome came to live in the nearby Winster Valley in 1925 and wrote *Swallows and Amazons*, his famous series of children's books, here. The writer's former home is closed to the public, a fact which probably saves this area from the onslaught of tourist coaches that other regions attached to literary figures attract in high season.

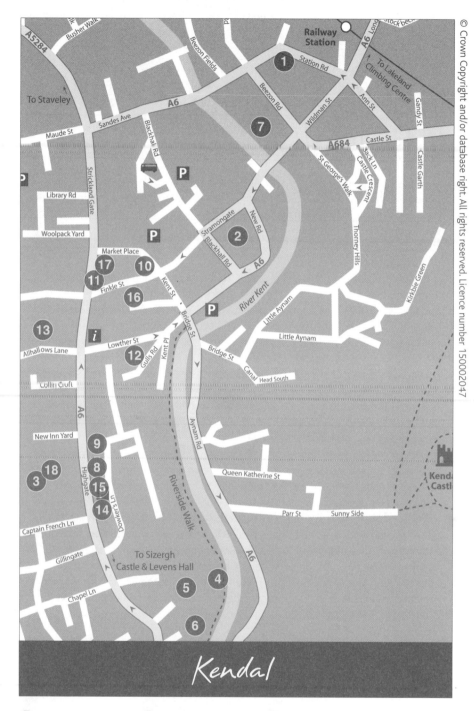

Kendal

1. Kendal Museum
2. Quaker Tapestry
3. Brewery Arts Centre
4. Abbot Hall
5. Museum of Lakeland Life
6. Parish Church
7. Riverside Hotel
8. New Moon
9. Cortez
10. 1657 Chocolate Shop
11. Farrer's of Kendal
12. Burgundys Wine Bar
13. Fellside Wholefoods
14. Fryer Tux Chippy
15. Silver Mountain takeway
16. Staff of Life Bakery
17. Watson & Woollard
18. Vats Bar

Kendal Castle

WHAT TO SEE AND DO

 ## Fair weather

It takes about 15 minutes to walk from Kendal's town centre to the ruins of **Kendal Castle** – follow the signposts from the park adjacent to the Abbot Hall over the river and up Parr Street – and once there you'll be rewarded with 360 degree vistas of Kendal, Kentdale and the surrounding hills. The ruins aren't pristine and require a degree of imagination to recreate their former glory, but they are nonetheless impressive and still exude a palpable sense of history, which a handful of English Heritage interpretive boards help piece together. The castle was built in the early 13th-century and has been in ruins since the Tudor period. It was the second of two castles built in the area, the site of the first and much smaller **Castle Howe**, which was probably constructed in the 11th century, is visible from Kendal Castle and marked by an 18th-century column.

The **Abbot Hall** art gallery is Kendal's finest attraction. The building is an elegant 18th-century villa set on the edge of the River Kent and next door to the town's large parish church (make sure you leave time to pop inside). Its two floors of galleries contain permanent and changing exhibitions of British art from the 18th century to the present day. The house also features period furniture and objets d'art and the programme of work is considered to be one of the finest outside London.

> THE ABBOT HALL, south Kendal, next door to the parish church off Kirkland, LA9 5AL; 01539 722464; www.abbothall.org.uk; £5 adults, £4 children, £14 families; open Mon–Sat 10.30am–5pm Apr–Oct; 10.30am–4pm Nov–Mar.

Sizergh Castle

Gifted to the National Trust in 1950, the Strickland family has inhabited **Sizergh Castle** since it was constructed in the Middle Ages. The oldest part of the building is a medieval pele tower which was built in the 14th century and significantly expanded on during the Elizabethan era. The house features elaborate oak panelling (once sold to, and now on long-term loan from, the Victoria and Albert Museum) and a collection of fine paintings and period furniture. Sizergh's large estate gardens are as lovely as the house and contain two lakes, a splendid rock garden and walking paths that lead to good views over the surrounding fells and nearby Morecambe Bay. Numerous themed events such as Halloween activities are held throughout the year.

Although open to the public, the hugely haunted (see box) **Levens Hall and Gardens** is the private home of the Bagot family. As such it's hardly surprising that the grandeur of this charming Elizabethan house (also built around a medieval pele tower) maintains an intimate feel in the midst of all its intricate oak panelling, Jacobean furniture, family portraits and the earliest English tapestry (dated c.1708). The topiary gardens with their

SIZERGH CASTLE, 4 miles south of Kendal off the A590, LA8 8AE; 015395 60951; www.nationaltrust.org.uk; £6.70 adults, £3.30 children, £16.70 families; castle open 1pm–5pm, gardens and shop open 10am–5pm, Sun–Thur, Easter–October.

LEVENS HALL AND GARDENS, off the A590 6 miles south of Kendal, LA8 0PD; 015395 60321; www.levenshall.co.uk; admission gardens £7 adults, £3.50 children, £19 families; house and gardens £10 adults, £4.50 children, £25 families; open Sun–Thur Easter–October, gardens and café 10am–5pm; house noon–5pm. Last admission 4.30pm.

Local legends: ghosts of Levens

Like many old houses Levens Hall is haunted. However, there are so many ghosts in the house that the owner's son was once told he has to pass seven spirits on the way to his bedroom. The creepy corridor he has to walk down each night is one of the busiest in the house for paranormal activity. Footsteps walking along it, scratches at the doors and a woman's laughter have all been heard in this area and apparitions of a tall man and an old woman have appeared.

Levens most frequently spied spectre is a destitute looking lady in grey who regularly floats through the grounds close to the bridge over the River Kent. Legend claims she is the restless soul of a gypsy who came to the hall one cold winter's night seeking charity. She was turned away and as she lay dying in the snow, too weak with hunger to walk any further, the gypsy cursed Levens, declaring no male heir would inherit until the River Kent stopped flowing and a white fawn was born. Even if the curse is nothing more than a good story, the estate did pass through the female line for generations, until 1896 when the River Kent froze, a white fawn was born in the surrounding park and a male heir, Alan Desmond Bagot, was born. The white fawn's ears survive to this day, carefully pressed into a family scrapbook and every male heir since then has been born when it's freezing cold outside.

Animal spirits also haunt Levens. The ghost of a little black dog has been seen scampering up the stairs and at the feet of both the present owner's wife and mother. And living dogs are unable to settle in the little drawing room located below a large bedroom known as the Bellingham Room (a ley line is said to run underneath both of these rooms). A visiting faith healer claimed to have experienced a horrible feeling in the Bellingham bedroom, where fires keep going out and the owner's mother-in-law once woke in the middle of the night to see three, what she described as, 'muddy coloured figures', standing in the room. The three consisted of a man in a stove-pipe hat holding a walking stick, a woman in a bonnet and a little child who, after standing in the room for a while, gradually faded away.

Perhaps the oddest story attached to Levens is that of an apparition of a living person. During a power cut, a visiting priest saw a man playing the harpsichord in the house. Later he discovered the man he'd seen was the then owner, Robin Bagot, an accomplished harpsichord player, who'd been away in the Lakes the night the vicar saw him playing at Levens.

If you fail to see any of the ghosts of Levens during your visit, get hold of a DVD of the first series of *Most Haunted* and watch the night that Yvette Fielding spent in the house.

The Bellingham Room, Levens Hall

giant sculpted beech hedges are world famous as they continue to grow within the original 17th-century design. They, along with the house, were transformed into the Hamley's family home for the BBC TV series *Wives and Daughters*. No visit to Levens is complete without lunch at the Bellingham Buttery café, which uses produce from the family's estate and other local providers. The food is prepared by a woman whose mother and grandmother were also cooks at Levens, and a splash of spiced Morocco Ale – a beer which originated at the hall in Elizabethan times – is still known to make its way into some dishes.

Walking

Kentmere is one of the best places in the countryside around Kendal to take to the hills for a good walk. This region is easy to reach, just head off the A591 at Staveley and follow the signs through town to the small road that weaves its way up the wide valley alongside the River Kent. Evidence suggests a long history of occupation in this pretty region, including Celtic and Norse settlements – you can find out more about the ancient history of this region at Kendal Museum (see p.109).

About half way along the valley between Staveley and Kentmere, a left turn leads to a narrow lane signposted to the **Kentmere Studio Pottery** (01539 821621 www.kentmerepottery.com) where you can visit the fine ceramics shop of local potter Gordon Fox, housed in an old sawmill.

Once you've reached the tiny community of Kentmere, head to the parish church of **St Cuthbert's**, which once stood near the crossroads of two pack horse routes and today is close to public footpaths that lead practically from its doorstep into the surrounding fells. A popular path for the not so serious walker leads from the church to the Kentmere reservoir approximately 2 miles to the north.

Take time to peek inside the church itself. Although little is known about its early history, it's thought that the yew tree standing in its grounds is nearly 1,000 years old. Today the church's whitewashed interior, plain wooden pews, stone altar and clear glass windows which gaze onto Green Quarter Fell exude a simple, peaceful beauty.

If none of the walks leading from the church inspires you, head to **Maggs Howe** half a mile to the east, which is sometimes open for afternoon tea. The public footpaths that lead from this area include a 2-mile walk to Longsleddale. If you do undertake this walk and the whole area suddenly starts to look very familiar it might be because the children's author John Cunliffe based the countryside setting of his much loved *Postman Pat* series on the Kentmere and Longsleddale valleys.

There's limited parking in Kentmere with only a handful of spaces around the church and nearby hall. If you're visiting on a Sunday in summer it's worth considering catching the Kentmere Rambler bus (service 519) which runs on a fairly frequent basis between the Mill Yard in Staveley (where there's plenty of parking) and Kentmere on Sundays and Bank Holiday Mondays from the end of May until mid-September.

 ## Wet weather

Next door to the Abbot Hall the **Museum of Lakeland Life** takes visitors on a trip back in time through the history of the region. From the beautiful old Columbian printing press in the lobby used in the 19th century to publish the local rag, to the re-creation of an Edwardian street, there's plenty of tangible history to get up close to plus displays on the Arts and Crafts movement. Look out for changing exhibitions from the museum's extensive costume collection and shop for traditional toys and local crafts in the gift shop.

Kendal Museum in the north of town houses an array of static and changing exhibits dedicated to the archaeological finds and geology of the region. It's well worth exploring, especially if you're a Wainwright devotee as the man himself was curator for 30 years and a number of his personal artefacts – including his walking socks – are now on display. See Local Heroes (p.65) for more information on Wainwright.

MUSEUM OF LAKELAND LIFE, off Kirkland, LA9 5AL; 01539 722464; www.lakelandmuseum.org.uk; £3.75 adults, £2.75 children, £11 families; open Mon–Sat 10.30am–5pm Apr–Oct, 10.30am–4pm Nov–Mar.

KENDAL MUSEUM, Station Road, Kendal – opposite Kendal railway station – LA9 6BT; 01539 721374; www.kendalmuseum.org.uk; £2.80 adults, children free; open Thur–Sat noon–5pm.

The Quaker Tapestry in Kendal

THE QUAKER TAPESTRY, access available from either Stramongate or New Road, LA9 4BH; 01539 722975; www.quaker-tapestry.co.uk; £4.90 adults, £2 children, £11 families; open Mon–Fri 10am–5pm Apr–Dec.

The **Quaker Tapestry** and its fabulous vegetarian tearooms are an unexpected gem in the middle of town. The tapestry consists of 77 intricate panels that form a stunning visual history of the Quaker movement. The whole piece took 4,000 people from 15 countries 15 years to create and visitors can learn all about the making of the tapestry and the social history that surrounds it, as well as gaze at its beauty.

What to do with children...

THE LAKELAND CLIMBING CENTRE, Lake District Business Park, opposite Morrisons supermarket off the A685, LA9 6NH; 01539 721766; www.kendalwall.co.uk; £7.50/£6.50 peak/off peak adults, £6.50/£5.50 children for a session on the climbing walls, or £12 a place on a taster session; instructors £25 per hour; open Tues–Fri 10am–10pm, Sat and Sun 10am–5pm May–Aug, closing 7pm the rest of the year, also open Mondays 4pm–10pm in winter.

In Kendal
The **Lakeland Climbing Centre** is a brilliant place for active kids to have fun and learn how to rock climb. During the school holidays the centre runs 90-minute taster sessions on indoor climbing for both junior and adult beginners, which are very popular with visitors. Alternatively, you pay by the hour for training from an instructor (plus entry fee into the centre) and they'll teach a group of up to nine people at any one time the basics of climbing.

The Lakeland Maize Maze

Further afield

The **Lakeland Maize Maze** is what it says on the packet, a maze made out of maize. You can wander around its twists and turns for as long as you like or follow the entertaining quiz trail through this leafy labyrinth. Maps can be bought if you're afraid of getting lost and there's a whole host of other activities to keep children entertained including trampolines, tractor rides, outdoor draughts and indoor go-carts if the weather turns.

> LAKELAND MAIZE MAZE, Sedgwick off the A591 at the roundabout junction with the A590, south of Kendal, LA8 0JH; 015395 61760; www.lakelandmaze.co.uk; £4.75 adults, £3.75 children, £16 families; open daily 10am–6pm July–Sept.

Entertainment

Kendal is also the cultural hub of the south Lakes. The Brewery Arts Centre, with its varied programme of theatre, cinema, dance and art exhibitions, stands at the centre of regional cultural life and the town also boasts a small but thriving music scene.

Theatre and cinema

Kendal's **Brewery Arts Centre** (01539 795090 www.breweryarts.co.uk) on Highgate is housed inside a Grade III listed old brewery and contains a modern cinema, theatre, galleries, restaurant and bars.

Special events

Every April **Damson Day** is celebrated at Low Farm on the A5075 off the A590 in the Lyth Valley (www.lythdamsons.org.uk). This day of celebration coincides with the annual picturesque display of damson blossoms and includes craft demonstrations, children's activities, live entertainment and more food and drink made from damsons than you could possibly imagine.

The annual **Lake District Sheepdog Trials** is a popular all-day event held on the first Thursday in August at Hill Farm in Ings. This is a not-to-be-missed opportunity to watch some the Lake District's many working sheepdogs in action.

In November Kendal's Brewery Arts Centre hosts the renowned **Kendal Mountain Film Festival** (www.mountainfilm.co.uk) and associated **Mountain Book Festival**, which attracts hordes of outdoor enthusiasts and film buffs from around the country.

Shopping

Expect to find an eclectic mix of chain and local stores lining Kendal's bustling streets. However, for a top selection of regional arts, crafts and food shops head to the ever growing **Mill Yard** in Staveley. Just some of the outlets you'll find here are **Out of the Woods** (01539 822033 www.outofthewoodsinteriors.co.uk) a local furniture maker, a fine collection of artists' work at the **Mill Yard Studios** (01539 721836 www.millyardstudio.co.uk), **Myrtle and Mace** a quirky gardening shop (01539 822022 www.myrtleandmace.com) and **Cumbria Herdwick Woollies** (01539 822288 www.cumbrianherdwickwoollies.co.uk) who sell goods made from Herdwick wool such as picnic rugs, skipping ropes and teddy bears.

 The best... PLACES TO STAY

BOUTIQUE

The Punch Bowl
Crosthwaite, Lyth Valley, LA8 8HR
015395 68337
www.the-punchbowl.co.uk

The individually designed rooms of this fabulous inn are all named after past vicars of the adjacent (and rather lovely) parish church of St Mary's. Perched on a hillside in Crosthwaite overlooking the peaceful Lyth Valley, the Punch Bowl is tucked well away from the crowds and offers contemporary luxury in a traditional setting.

Price: B&B and afternoon tea from £110–£280 per room per night.

HOTEL

Riverside Hotel
Beezen Road, Stramongate Bridge, Kendal, LA9 6EL
01539 734861
www.riversidekendal.co.uk

Set in the heart of Kendal on the banks of the River Kent, the Riverside is the town's smartest hotel and includes superb leisure facilities complete with a swish swimming pool. The restaurant uses organic produce from its own kitchen garden and locally reared free-range meat.

Price: B&B from £69 per room per night, midweek and weekend breaks available.

The best... PLACES TO STAY

INN

Eagle and Child 🛒 🍴

Kendal Road, Staveley, LA8 9LP
01539 821 320
www.eaglechildinn.co.uk

A fabulous and friendly country pub in the heart of picturesque Staveley. The riverside gardens are gorgeous in summer and the real fires are the place to sit with a pint of real ale in the winter. The famous Cumbrian breakfast is not to be missed all year round.

Price: B&B £60–£70 per room per night. Special deals available.

B&B

Lapwings Barn 🛒

Howestone Barn, Whinfell, Kendal LA8 9EQ
01539 824373
www.lapwingsbarn.co.uk

Located in a rural setting close to Kendal, this is a good choice for those wanting proximity to a busy town and good walking on their doorstep. One suite in this rustic barn conversion contains it own woodburner and you can expect home-made bread for breakfast.

Price: B&B £32–£35 pppn.

B&B/CAMPING

Maggs Howe 🛒 🏠 🍴

Kentmere, Nr Kendal LA8 9PJ
01539 821 689
www.a1tourism.com/uk/maggs.html

This old (no longer working) farm in the Kentmere hills is a local institution. Choose between B&B in the farmhouse or camping in the converted barn that comes with its own fully equipped kitchen and showers. Evening meals available on request and their Sunday lunch with all the trimmings is popular with walkers and locals.

Price: B&B from £25–£54 per night per room. Camping barn £9 per person.

SELF-CATERING

The Mount 🛒

Lock Bank Farm, Sedbergh LA10 5HE
015396 20252
www.holidaysedbergh.co.uk

West of Kendal and on the edge of the Lakes, this four-bedroom spacious 1920s house is good for families or more than one couple holidaying together. There's a large, private garden and open fires, and a local farm will deliver fresh produce to the door.

Price: £380–£950 per week. Sleeps eight.

The best... FOOD AND DRINK

Kendal and its surrounds are a definite hot spot for buying local food and drink. The town has a Fairtrade status and although associated with the ubiquitous Kendal Mint Cake, this region is fast establishing itself as a place famous for some of the best farm shops and local food shopping in the region. This area is also home to **Strawberry Bank Liqueurs** (www.strawberrybankliqueurs.co.uk) who produce a range of liqueurs and beers made from damsons grown in the Lyth Valley and other soft fruits. The business started in the Mason's Arms in Cartmel Fell and has now moved to Plumgarths on the outskirts of Kendal, but you'll see their products, which include sloe gin, damson beer and strawberry vodka, for sale all over Cumbria. If you do indulge, check out the great cocktails and recipes on the company's website.

▶ Staying in

Market days in Kendal are Wednesdays and Saturdays when you'll find a number of local produce stalls in the town centre – get there early to get the pick of the crop. Also in Kendal, **Watson and Woollard** (01539 720198) are a traditional butcher specialising in wildfowl and rabbit and the **Staff of Life Bakery** (01539 738606) in Berry's Yard off Finkle Street, sells its own artisan breads and the best flapjacks in Cumbria. Chocolate lovers will follow their noses to the quirky **1657 Chocolate House** on Branthwaite Brow (01539 740702 www.chocolatehouse1657.co.uk) and discover chocolate heaven and a tiny café selling 18 different chocolate drinks.

Kendal can also boast two excellent farm shops on its doorstep. **Plumgarths** (01539 736300 www.plumgarths.co.uk) on Crook Road on the outskirts of town sells a large selection of locally sourced meats including seasonal game, local condiments, fresh baked goods, free-range eggs and regional beers and liqueurs, and also runs a home delivery service. Just 4 miles south of Kendal at Alison Park, the award-winning **Low Sizergh Barn** (015395 60426 www.lowsizerghbarn.co.uk) is a food lovers' Aladdin's cave. Every inch of this 18th-century stone barn is crammed with all kinds of local produce including their own organic veg grown under the Growing Well scheme (www.growingwell.co.uk), while in the basement old cattle stalls are filled with local arts and crafts. There's also a farm trail to explore and an excellent upstairs café with a prime view into the milking shed.

Also on the outskirts of Kendal at Staveley's Mill Yard, the **Munx Lakeland Bakery** (01539 822102 www.munx.co.uk) has won two North West Fine Foods Awards including the best bread award for its delicious Cumbrian honey bread with fig.

For takeaways in Kendal you can pick up sandwiches, pies, and prepared organic meals at **Fellside Wholefoods** (01539 722344) on Allhallows Lane, grab fish and chips or Cumberland sausages and haggis at **Fryer Tux Chippy** on Highgate (closed Sundays), or for a Chinese takeaway try the **Silver Mountain** also on Highgate (01539 729911, closed Mondays except Bank Holidays).

EATING OUT

FINE DINING
New Moon
29 Highgate, Kendal, LA9 4EN
01539 729254
www.newmoonrestaurant.co.uk

This swish modern restaurant in the heart of Kendal is dedicated to the 'Best of British' philosophy. Main courses include braised local lamb and cost around £12, or take advantage of the early supper two courses for £9.95 deal – but always leave room for dessert.

RESTAURANT
Cortez
101 Highgate, Kendal, LA9 4EN
01539 723123
www.cortezkendal.co.uk

The colourful mix of tapas, Basque style food and paellas are all made with ingredients from local and Spanish suppliers. There's a wide choice of veggie options including paella mediterràneo made with almond pesto (£10.50). Lunch and early evening specials available.

GASTRO PUB
Strickland Arms
Sizergh, Kendal, LA8 8DZ
015395 61010

Situated near Sizergh Castle, the Strickland Arms has high ceilings, flagstone floors, large fireplaces and scrubbed wooden tables inside, and an attractive terrace and garden outside. The varied menu features local meats such as mixed game casserole (mains £10–£15) and evening entertainment includes jazz and pub quiz nights.

Mason's Arms
Strawberry Bank, Cartmel Fell, LA11 6NW
015395 68486
www.masonsarmsstrawberrybank.co.uk

The pretty flagstone terrace of this popular local pub peers over the beautiful Winster Valley. Expect far better than average pub grub (light meals £5–£8, mains £10–£14), accompanied by a good wine list, fine ales and real fires when it's too chilly to sit outside.

The Brown Horse
Winster, off the A5074 (Lyth Valley Road), LA23 3NR
015394 43443
www.thebrownhorseinn.co.uk

A comfortable olde-worlde style pub situated between Kendal and Windermere whose menu features dishes cooked with organic ingredients from its own estate – which are also for sale in its farm shop. Expect to pay around £13 for a main course and enjoy local ales and fine wines with your food.

EATING OUT

CAFÉ

Farrer's of Kendal

13 Stricklandgate, Kendal. LA9 4LY
01539 731 707
www.farrers.com

Farrer's is a fabulous tea and coffee merchant whose shop and excellent café is housed in a creaking Grade II listed, eight story 17th-century (possibly haunted) building. Inhale the pungent aroma of good coffee and fine tea that you can sip in or take away.

Wilf's

Mill Yard, Back Lane, Staveley LA8 9LR
01539 822329
www.wilfs-café.co.uk

An essential stop for lunch or a Fairtrade coffee and home-made cake, this fabulous rustic riverside café is famed throughout the region for its hearty and inexpensive chillis, butties, rarebits and jacket spuds. Look out for Speciality Nights when you can indulge in four courses of cuisine from around the world for a mere £20.

 ## Drinking

This region is as good for drink as it is for food. In Kendal the **Vats Bar** at the Brewery Arts Centre (see p.111) is a popular local hang out (which also serves top notch pizzas for around £7) and **Burgundys Wine Bar** on Lowther Street (01539 733803) is a pleasant place to enjoy an ale or glass of vino. Outside Kendal the pick of the best drinking places include the **Hawkshead Brewery's Beer Hall** (01539 822644 www.hawksheadbrewery.co.uk) at Mill Yard in Staveley where large glass windows look into the brewery itself and you can lounge in deep sofas or sit at scrubbed wooden tables and sample their superb ales (daytimes only). Also in Staveley, the **Eagle and Child** (see p.113) was voted Westmorland's pub of the year 2007 by CAMRA and is famous for its cask ales and friendly welcome. However, the regional Mecca for real ales lovers is the **Watermill Inn** at Ings (01539 821309 www.watermillinn.co.uk) where 16 ales are available on tap, three of which travel a mere 12 and half yards from their own brewery to the bar.

ⓘ Visitor Information

Tourist Information Centres: Tourist Information Centre, Town Hall, Highgate, Kendal, 01539 725758; Visit Cumbria, Windermere Road, Staveley, 01539 822222, www.golakes.co.uk.

Hospitals: Minor Injuries Unit, Westmorland General Hospital, Burton Road, Kendal, LA9 7RG, 01539 732288; for more serious problems, Lancaster Royal Infirmary, Ashton Road, Lancaster LA1 4RP, 01524 65944.

Doctors: Captain French Lane Surgery, Captain French Lane, Kendal, 01539 720 241, www.cfls.org.uk, Mon–Fri 8.30am–6pm.

Pharmacies: Boots, Elephant Yard, off Stricklandgate, Kendal, 01539 720461; out of hours Asda Pharmacy, Burton Road, Kendal LA9 7JA, 01539 731151, Mon–Sat 8am–9pm, Sun 10am–4pm.

Police: Busher Walk, Kendal, 0845 330 0247.

Supermarkets: Boothes, Wainright's Yard, off Stricklandgate, Kendal (which features an Artisan – a specialist food store); Asda, Burton Road, south Kendal; Morrisons, Queen Katherines Avenue, Kendal, 2 miles north of the town centre.

Parking: Kendal's largest car park, Westmorland Shopping Centre, Blackhall Road, near the bus station; Wainright's Yard, off Stricklandgate; the Brewery Arts Centre has its own small customers' car park.

Internet Access: Kendal Public Library, Stricklandgate, 01539 773520.

Car Hire: Westmorland Vehicle Hire, Westmorland Business Park, off the A6 in north Kendal, 01539 728 532, www.carhirecumbria.co.uk.

Bike Rental: Budgie Bike, Highgate, Kendal (next door to the Brewery Arts Centre), 0870 770 5892); Wheelbase, Staveley's Mill Yard, Kendal, 01539 821443, www.wheelbase.co.uk.

Taxis: ABC Cumbria Taxis, 01539 720620; Blue Star Taxis, 01539 723670.

FURTHER AFIELD

Sedbergh

Located 5 miles from junction 37 of the M6 and 11 miles east of Kendal, the small market town of Sedbergh is still part of Cumbria but also lies just within the border of the Yorkshire Dales National Park. The town is an easy drive from the Lake District or non-drivers can catch the rural bus service no. 564 that runs Mon–Sat from Kendal bus station to Sedbergh via Oxenholme train station.

The town is framed by the imposing **Howgill Fells**, large pear-shaped hills that rise to over 2,200ft and loom over Sedbergh's narrow streets. The Howgills, with their smooth grassy slopes have all the feel of Yorkshire and the famous **Dales Way** walk (www.thedalesway.co.uk) passes through the town en route between Ilkley and Bowness-on-Windermere. It's therefore no surprise that many travel here to walk and you can pick up tips on routes at the Tourist Information Centre based inside the Dales and Lakes Book Centre on Main Street (015396 20125 www.sedbergh.org.uk). However, if the pathways leading into the Howgills feel too imposing, head to the River Rawthey which runs through the south of Sedbergh where you can stroll along the river bank instead.

Situated on the banks of the river on the outskirts of Sedbergh is **Farfield Mill Arts and Heritage Centre**. This beautifully restored old woollen mill now houses a number of arts and crafts studios where visitors can watch painters, weavers, woodworkers, jewellers, ceramicists and textiles artists at work. Farfield Mill also exhibits the work of local artists and contains a heritage exhibition that details the history of the rise and fall of the region's textile industry. And the riverside tea rooms are a good place to stop for lunch.

FARFIELD MILL, 015396 21958; www.farfieldmill.org; £2.50 adults, children free; open daily 10am–5pm Feb–Dec.

In 2006 Sedbergh became '**England's Book Town**', joining ranks with Hay-on-Wye in Wales and Wigtown in Scotland. Book Town means bookshops and there's no shortage of these in Sedbergh to browse around. At Westward Books (015396 21233) to the east end of Main Street you can sip coffee and sink into comfy sofas while choosing some holiday reading. While the Sleepy Elephant (015396 21770 www.sleepyelephant.net) on Main Street, which once featured in an episode of BBC's *House Detectives*, combines Sedbergh's past life as a woollen town with its new life as a Book Town and sells a colourful range of textiles and jewellery as well as a good selection of art and design books. And each September Sedbergh hosts a **Festival of Books and Drama** which includes a lively range of talks, readings and performances and sees the town come alive in a celebration of language and literature.

Sedbergh School, (www.sedberghschool.org) a prestigious public school where Wordsworth sent his son to study and Coleridge's son once taught, dominates the town centre. Adjacent to the school stands **St Andrew's parish church**, scene of one of George Fox's sermons and approximately two miles south of Sedbergh at Brigflatts stands the oldest **Quaker Meeting House** in the north of England (open daily 11am–6pm Easter–September, 11am–dusk November–Easter). Built in 1675, this simple whitewashed building with oak interior has changed little since it first opened for worship.

Kirkby Lonsdale

Kirkby Lonsdale is an old Cumbrian market town, 20 miles south-east of Windermere off the A65, on the banks of the River Lune.

The town itself consists of mainly 17th- and 18th-century buildings and in the summer its jumbled collection of narrow streets and two market squares are adorned with colourful hanging baskets. Although small, the town centre contains around sixty shops, some housed behind listed shop fronts, and spending time browsing through arts, crafts, clothes and antiques is reason enough to visit. This is also a good place to shop for food and gastronomic retail highlights include **Church Mouse Cheeses** (015242 73005 www.churchmousecheeses.com) on Market Street, which was officially voted Britain's Best Independent Cheese Shop and stocks an amazing array of local, British and Continental gourmet cheeses.

Exploring the banks of the River Lune as it crashes past Kirkby Lonsdale is another fine reason to visit the town. On seeing a Turner painting of the view of the river and surrounding meadows, woods and hills from the town, Ruskin claimed that 'the Valley of the Lune at Kirkby Lonsdale is one of the loveliest scenes in England'. Today the view that so inspired him, aptly named **Ruskin's View**, is one of the most romantic nooks in all of Cumbria and to reach it follow the marked footpath from St Mary's churchyard.

Kirkby Lonsdale is also famous for the **Devil's Bridge**, which spans the River Lune on the outskirts of town and dates from the 14th century. According to legend the devil himself appeared to an old woman at this spot and promised to build her a bridge in exchange for the first soul to cross it. However, the wise old woman outwitted the devil by throwing bread across the bridge when it was finished which her dog ran across to retrieve, thus denying the devil a human soul. Anyone visiting on a Sunday will see a line of motorbikes along Devil's Bridge as the tea wagon at this spot is a popular refreshment stop for local bikers.

Visitors are spoiled for choice for places to lunch in town and highlights include **The Lunesdale Bakery and Tearooms** (www.lunesdale-bakery.co.uk) on Main Street which dates back to 1812 and sells locally cured meats, jams, chutneys, bread and cakes and is famous for its speciality breakfasts. Also on Main Street, **Avanti** is a

Kirkby Lonsdale

stylish restaurant, bar and crêperie that serves moderately priced paninis, soups and pizzas, and the **Snooty Fox Hotel** (www.snootyfoxhotel.co.uk) is a CAMRA award-winning traditional inn, famous throughout the region for its good food.

There are two excellent farm shops near Kirkby Lonsdale: **Kitridding Farm Shop** (open 10am–6pm Fri and 10am–5pm Sat, 015395 67484 www.kitridding.co.uk), located off the A65 at Lupton between Kirkby Lonsdale and Kendal and the organic **Mansergh Hall Farm Shop** (open 9am–5pm Tues–Fri and 9am–1.30pm Sat, 015242 71397 www.manserghhall.co.uk) off the B6254 north of Kirkby Lonsdale. Both stock local meats and other produce and will also deliver.

2

ConistonWater
&theSouthWest

a. Coniston and around

b. Furness and Cartmel peninsulas

Unmissable highlights

01 Walking across Morecambe Bay in the summer on a guided walk with Cedric Robinson, Queen's Guide to the Sands, p.145

02 Testing your nerve and fear of heights on Go Ape in the heart of Grizedale Forest, p.132

03 Sailing over Coniston Water on either a solar powered launch or steam powered gondola, p.126

04 Finding out more about the life and work of Ruskin at his lakeside former home Brantwood, p.131

05 Taking in the views at Tarn Hows beauty spot, p,127

06 Discovering art in the forest on the Sculpture Trail in Grizedale Forest, p.125

07 Indulging in a portion of lip smackingly good Cartmel Sticky Toffee Pudding, p.153

08 Standing in the centre of the ancient stone circle on Birkrigg Common, p.144

09 Wandering around the grand ruins of Furness Abbey, p.142

10 Witnessing feeding time at the South Lakes Wild Animal Park, p.148

CONISTON WATER AND THE SOUTH-WEST

Coniston Water and the south-west region of Cumbria form two distinct areas. The first section is the lake itself, the only one in this part of the National Park, which, although easily accessible by road, has the feel of somewhere much more remote. Most activities for visitors are to be found at the north end of the lake, just a few miles south of Hawkshead and the most popular spot for tourists in the area. Visitors travel here to take a trip on the lake, visit Ruskin's former home, Brantwood, or to potter around Coniston village, which is not as picturesque as many Lake District villages but is still surrounded by stunning scenery.

Many travel to this region to spend a day in Grizedale Forest, the largest forest in the Lake District, whose 6,000 acres of woodland are filled with all kinds of activities and trails. The forest attracts a large number of visitors in the summer, but is also a good destination in cold and even wet weather when the smells of the forest come alive.

Good food lovers, especially those that are self-catering, will find plenty to keep their taste buds happy in the south-west of Cumbria as the region contains many fabulous farm shops, and well-stocked stores selling local foods and produce.

To the south of Coniston Water lie the Furness and Cartmel peninsulas, where many of the region's attractions, facilities and working population can be found. This area is surrounded by the sea and, like the west coast of Cumbria, you won't find a traditional seaside here. What you will find is good, and often quiet, walking and cycling terrain and numerous attractions that link into the area's rich history – all surrounded by never ending views of Morecambe Bay.

CONISTON AND AROUND

Coniston Water lies to the west of lake Windermere and is separated from its more famous neighbour by the wilds of Grizedale Forest. This much quieter lake is 5 miles long and, as with Windermere, both sides are very different. The east side runs along the edge of the forest and is dotted with numerous car parks from where visitors can hike into Grizedale or access the lake itself. This side of the lake is popular with locals who travel here in summer to swim and kayak or enjoy a picnic on the edge of these surprisingly quiet shores.

The west side of Coniston Water is traversed by a busy A road that links the communities along this side of the lake with Ambleside in the north. This area is dominated by the brooding Old Man of Coniston, which at 2,635ft is a small mountain by Lake District standards and was the inspiration for Arthur Ransome's fictional Kanchenjunga.

The main community in this area is Coniston, whose surrounding copper mines once transformed the village into a busy industrial centre – the 'Old Man' is riddled with abandoned mine shafts and old potholes. Today Coniston is popular with outdoors folk and is the final resting place of Donald Campbell, the British car and motorboat racer, whose remains were controversially retrieved from the depths of Coniston Water where he died after crashing his *Bluebird* in 1967.

Coniston is also home to the grave of Ruskin which can be found in St Andrew's churchyard, and his former home, Brantwood, on the north-east side of Coniston Water is one of the area's finest of its few attractions. For ultimately this region is all about the outdoors, and destinations such as Grizedale Forest and Tarn Hows beauty spot to the north of Coniston are places where all ages and all abilities come to hike, cycle or simply take in fine views and the scent of the forest.

Donald Campbell's grave, Coniston

WHAT TO SEE AND DO

 Fair weather

In the forest

Grizedale Forest, which sits between lake Windermere and Coniston Water, is an excellent day out for all ages. Many come to this working forest to walk and there are a number of excellent trails to choose from. The most popular and entertaining for children is the Sculpture Trail, on which you encounter many works of art integrated into the forest environment. Grizedale is also a prime cycling destination and you can see far more of it by bike, which are available to hire (see p.138) if you don't bring your own. The exhilarating but tough North Face Trail is a must for serious mountain bikers. Adults and older children can face their fear of heights with **Go Ape** (see p.132) and there's a fabulous adventure playground for younger children near the Visitor Centre. You can pick up walking and cycling maps at the Forest Shop and a nice but pricey café sells home-made cakes and big sandwiches (no credit or debit cards). There are plenty of picnic spots for those who bring their own food, or alternatively pop into either the Eagle's Head pub at Satterthwaite, a tiny village inside the forest, or the White Hart at Bouth to the south of Grizedale for a pub lunch.

Parking is available at various spots in the forest so drive around if the one near the main Visitor Centre is full, or catch the seasonal Cross Lakes shuttle. (p.21)

GRIZEDALE FOREST PARK, main Visitor Centre 2.5 miles south of Hawkshead, LA22 0QJ; 01229 860010; www.forestry.gov.uk/northwestengland; admission free; visitor Centre open Mar–Nov 10am–5pm, Dec–Feb 10am–4pm daily.

Public art sculpture at Grizedale Forest

CONISTON BOATING CENTRE, LA21 8AN; 015394 41366; motor boats £18 per hour for two people, rowing boats £9 per hour for two people, canoes £18 per hour for two people; open daily 10am–4.30pm.

CONISTON LAUNCHES, 015394 36216; www.conistonlaunch.co.uk; round trip £5.60–£8 for adults depending on route, children half price; north route which stops at Coniston and Brantwood runs an hourly daily service in good weather throughout year except Dec–February when launches only run at weekends; routes which include stops at points to the middle and south of the lake less frequent.

STEAM YACHT GONDOLA CONISTON PIER LA21 8AN; 015394 41288; www.nationaltrust.org.uk; round trips £6.50 adults, £3.30 children, £16.30 families; weather permitting a daily hourly service operates from 11am–4pm Apr–Oct.

Steam yacht gondola

On the water

To get out onto Coniston Water head along Lake Road, which leads off the A593 to the south of Coniston – it's a ten-minute walk from the village to the edge of the lake. There's a small café and free parking at this scenic spot, which is also a popular picnic and play area for families in the summer.

Here you can hire a range of different crafts including motor boats, rowing boats and canoes from the **Coniston Boating Centre** or arrange a sailing lesson or two.

This is also a main pick-up point for the **Coniston Launches**, solar powered passenger ferries that ply the waters of Coniston with various other stops, including the Waterhead Hotel, Brantwood and Torver. The launches operate a number of routes and are a fun, hassle free and environmentally friendly way of travelling around the Coniston area. Leaflets detailing walking routes from the various stopping points are available to buy on the launch and cycle racks are provided on board.

Alternatively cruise around Coniston Water on the **Steam Yacht Gondola**. Fully restored by the National Trust this plush craft is a mix of Venetian gondola and Victorian engineering and operates hour-long cruises around the lake departing from Coniston Pier. This is the way to take the waters in style and you can break your journey at Brantwood or the jetty at Monk Coniston from where you can walk to Tarn Hows.

Tarn Hows

Walking and cycling

One of the most popular routes for relatively serious walkers is the hike up **The Old Man of Coniston**. Most reasonably fit and able walkers should be able to conquer this peak, for although its ascent is steep in places, you won't have to do any scrambling to get to the top. The route to the summit is signposted from Church Beck and you can expect to get there and back to the village in around four hours and encounter some steep bits and fabulous views along the way.

Outside of Grizedale Forest, the best terrain for not so serious walkers in this region is to be found at the stunning **Tarn Hows**, a spruce tree lined, landscaped artificial tarn and beauty spot a couple of miles north-east of Coniston. A number of well-marked trails lead from the car park around this magnificent spot, including a circular walk of the tarn itself which takes about an hour and a half to complete, and a 2-mile hike to Coniston along a path that is also a designated cycleway.

Cyclists who prefer riding on the road should try the narrow lane that hugs the east side of Coniston Water for 5 miles. This route is relatively quiet, even during peak periods and for a longer ride you can head from Brantwood to Hawkshead 4 miles to the north, or down to Ulverston via Lowick and Gawthwaite, an 8-mile trip south from the bottom of the lake.

A National Cycle Route leads off the A593 just north of Broughton-in-Furness through Broughton Mills to Hall Dunnerdale before veering south to Ulpha and then across high open countryside before dropping down into Eskdale. This glorious ride, which skirts past the Duddon Valley, is not for beginners, and those who do take it should have plenty of water and high energy snacks with them as there is little in the way of facilities on this route.

Abseiling in Coniston

Outdoor activities

Summitreks is based in Coniston and has been organising outdoor activities for around 20 years. It organises all kinds of land and water based pursuits including gorge scrambling, adventure walks, abseiling and Canadian canoeing. Bookings are taken for groups of four or more and the company also hires outdoors kit such as walking boots.

SUMMITREKS, 14 Yewdale Road, Coniston, LA21 8DU; 015394 41212; www.summitreks.co.uk; £27–£36 per person per session.

CELEBRITY CONNECTIONS

The best-known name attached to the south-west region of the Lake District is **Donald Campbell** who died on Coniston Water on 4 January 1967 while attempting to break his own water speed record. His boat *Bluebird K7* flipped and disintegrated at speeds in excess of 300mph and Campbell died instantly. A memorial to Campbell and his chief mechanic, Leo Villa, who died in 1979 is located opposite the main car park in Coniston village. And Campbell's body, which was recovered from the depths of the lake in May 2001, is buried in Coniston's cemetery. For more information on Donald Campbell see Local Heroes p.63.

Anthony Hopkins played Donald Campbell in the made for TV film *Across the Lake* (1988) which was filmed in and around Coniston. Hopkins, like Campbell, stayed at the Black Bull in Coniston village while in the area.

Other film locations in this area include Yew Tree Farm to the north of Coniston, which was the setting for Beatrix Potter's home Hill Top in *Miss Potter*. Ulverston was the birthplace of **Stan Laurel**, the thin half of the comedy duo Laurel and Hardy. Stan was born Arthur Stanley Jefferson on 16 June 1890 at 3 Foundry Cottages, now renamed Argyle Street (a plaque marks the house), and although he did not live in Ulverston long, he is recorded as remembering with fondness the town where he was born. In 1947 Stan Laurel returned to Ulverston with Oliver Hardy and the pair made a joint appearance to the people of the town from the balcony of the Coronation Hall. The Britannia pub on The Ellers in Ulverston was renamed The Stan Laurel when the building was altered and absorbed a sweet shop where Stan used to buy his favourite toffee. For more information on Stan Laurel see Local Heroes p.64.

A more up-to-date celebrity from the world of art is Turner Prize winner **Keith Tyson** who was born in Ulverston in 1969 and worked as a fitter in Barrow-in-Furness's shipyard before attending the College of Art in Carlisle. Tyson has exhibited in various countries around the world and he has earned the nickname 'the mad professor of art' as his work often includes scientific as well artistic thought processes.

The Visitors' Book

Tarn Hows in winter

'I had my first encounters with the Lake District when I was about 10. Those family holidays when we would hire a cottage each year and explore the area, mostly as I recall by car, but on one memorable occasion after what seemed at the time to be a long arduous climb through darkened woods and past magical waterfalls we reached a clearing at the top of our hill and gazed in awe on the small wonder of Tarn Hows.

'I know now that trek must have been no more than a five minute scramble up a path, but that wonder at seeing the beauty of the Lakes has never left.

'Years later, when moving to Lancaster with my family, we arrived on one of those early January days when the sun is bright and the air so clear, the view across Morecambe Bay is full of snow-capped mountains. It struck me that despite all those early family holidays, I had never seen the Lakes in winter. We left the unpacking and immediately headed off in search of snow and to give my own family their first experience of Lakeland.

'That day I walked again around Tarn Hows, stopped in Ambleside for tea and cakes and watched my children throw snowballs on Hardknott Pass as I took in the view with my wife. Lakeland has a special beauty in winter, and I marvel that so many visitors probably never see it and at how lucky we are to have this inspiring landscape on our doorstep.'

Jonathan Bean, Lancaster

Wet weather

Built from local stone and slate, **The Ruskin Museum** in Coniston was established around the turn of the last century as a memorial to John Ruskin – Victorian art and social critic, poet and writer – who died in 1900. The museum houses a large Ruskin collection, but

THE RUSKIN MUSEUM, Yewdale Road, Coniston, LA21 8DU; 015394 41163; www.ruskinmuseum.com; £4.25 adults, £2 children, £11 family; open 10am–5.30pm daily in summer, 10.30am–3.30pm Wed–Sun in winter.

this fascinating attraction also celebrates the surrounding area and contains exhibits detailing the region's geology, history, industry and farming. The Ruskin Museum is also a must for those wanting to find out about Donald Campbell and his world record breaking water speeds on Coniston Water.

Visitors can discover more about Ruskin at his former home, **Brantwood**, which sits on the east side of Coniston Water overlooking the lake, Coniston village and the fells beyond. Historic homes in the Lakes don't come better than Brantwood and visitors are immersed into the life, times and domestic environment of Ruskin who developed the house from a small cottage into the large property it is today.

You can delve into his work and philosophy or simply enjoy wandering around a beautiful old house and its stunning landscaped lakeside gardens. A programme of changing exhibitions and various events such as lectures and craft fairs are organised throughout the year. For more information on Ruskin see p.61.

BRANTWOOD, 2.5 miles from Coniston off the B5285, LA21 8AD; 015394 41396; www.brantwood.org.uk; £5.95 adults, £1.20 children, £11.95 families; open Mar–Nov 11am–5.30pm daily, Nov–Mar 11am–4.30pm Wed–Sun.

Romantic Insights is an environmentally friendly initiative that has been created to help tourists visit Brantwood and Wordsworth's former home Rydal Mount in one day, with lunch at the Jumping Jenny thrown in. For details see p.167.

 What to do with children...

The **Lakeside and Haverthwaite Railway** sits just off the A590 adjacent to roads leading into Grizedale Forest. This old train service is all that remains of a route that once connected the southern tip of Windermere with Barrow-in-Furness, and its 4 miles of track lead visitors through

LAKESIDE AND HAVERTHWAITE RAILWAY, Haverthwaite Station, off the A390 near Ulverston, LA12 8AL; 015395 31594; www.lakesiderailway.co.uk; adult return £5.20, child return £2.60, family ticket £14.20; six trains daily, Easter–Oct.

GO APE, Grizedale Forest, LA22 0QJ; 0870 458 9189 www.goape.co.uk; £25 per person; open daily Feb–Oct, weekends only in Nov; closed Dec/Jan.

soft woodland to Lakeside. Special events such as Thomas the Tank Engine and Easter weekends are laid on and whatever time you travel this entertaining attraction is an enduring reminder of the romance of steam.

Located further north near the main Visitor Centre in Grizedale Forest **Go Ape** is a blood-pumping high-wire treetop assault course for adults and older children. Even if you're not afraid of heights it takes more guts than you might realise to negotiate your precarious way from treetop to treetop – not to mention the occasional jump into thin air. This attraction is very popular so book ahead during busy times and at the weekends.

 ## Entertainment

Special events
The week-long **Coniston Water Festival** (www.conistonwaterfestival.org.uk) is held in July and has roots running back to the mid-19th century. The festival is a mix of arts, sports and local traditions and events including a water parade and the dressing of boats. And in late September Coniston hosts a **Walking Festival** (www.conistonwalkingfestival.org) whose aim is to celebrate the glorious landscape surrounding the town. This festival is a mix of organised walks, film screenings, events and family activities and, like the Water Festival, exact dates and full programme details are available on the Festival's website or from Coniston's Tourist Information Centre.

 ## Shopping

Coniston has a small collection of outdoors stores and gift shops that won't take long to browse around. And in Satterthwaite, a small community in Grizedale Forest, the studio of local wildlife artist Robert Fletcher (01229 860 234 www.robertfletcherwildlifeartist.co.uk) located at his Laburnum Cottage home is open to the public. Here you can pick up cards and prints of the artist's work as well as browse though his original pastel drawings.

The best... **PLACES TO STAY**

HOTEL

Waterhead Hotel

Located on the B5285 at the head of Coniston Water, LA21 8AJ
015394 42144
www.waterhead-hotel.co.uk

Minutes from the centre of Coniston and Brantwood, the Waterhead Hotel is perched at the northern tip of Coniston Water and claims stunning views down the length of the lake. This old hotel provides relaxed luxury, breathtaking scenery, peace and quiet and a restaurant proud to support local cuisine.

Price: B&B £57 pppn, B&B and dinner £75 pppn.

INN

The Old Kings Head

Church Street, Broughton-in-Furness, LA20 6HJ
01229 716 293
www.oldkingshead.co.uk

Legend claims that Charles I once stayed at this historic inn – one of the oldest buildings in Broughton-in-Furness. The bedrooms are comfortable and spacious, and the food is excellent – Prince Phillip once dined here. There's also a residents' bar for those who don't fancy the busy main bar.

Price: B&B from £60 per room per night for a double occupancy.

The Royal Oak

Spark Bridge, just off the A592 Near Ulverston, LA12 8BS
01229 861006
www.royaloaksparkbridge.co.uk

Conveniently located in the heart of this region, the Royal Oak is a classically good Lakeland pub that's as popular with locals as it is visitors. The rooms are comfortable and airy, the food is excellent and a large beer garden stretches to the banks of the River Crake.

Price: B&B £65 per room per night for double occupancy.

FARMSTAY

Yew Tree Farm

Signposted from Coniston, LA21 8DP
015394 41433
www.yewtree-farm.com

Beatrix Potter once owned this wonderful old traditional 17th-century farm. The luxurious rooms maintain many of their original features and visitors can expect to be surrounded by history, gorgeous views and good walking terrain. The guest lounge has its own open fire and the breakfast menu includes seasonal specials.

Price: B&B £50–£57 pppn.

The best... PLACES TO STAY

B&B

Force Mill Guest House

Satterthwaite LA12 8LX. 01229 860205 www.forcemillfarm.co.uk

This idyllic riverside guesthouse is nestled inside Grizedale Forest and close to many of the Lake District's tourist hot spots, but tucked well away in a peaceful off the beaten track setting. The building dates back to the 17th century, and walking and cycling routes unfold from the front door.

Price: B&B £25 pppn. Cash and cheques only.

CAMPSITE

Grizedale Campsite

Bowkerstead Farm, Satterthwaite LA12 8LL 01229 860208 www.grizedale-camping.co.uk

Located just south of the main visitor centre of Grizedale Forest, this campsite is both family and couple friendly and has numerous cycling and walking trails, plus the great outdoors, on its doorstep. Some pitches are available in wooded areas and pony trekking can be arranged with an associated riding farm.

Price: £6 adult, £2.50 children per night.

Coniston Water

The best... FOOD AND DRINK

The best places to eat out in this region are tucked away off the beaten track, bursting with locals and rarely found by many visitors. The only restaurants are in Coniston and the range is fairly limited, and some of the finest places for evening dining are the fabulous country pubs tucked away in and around the smaller communities such as Broughton-in-Furness and Torver. These communities are also the place to shop for regional produce as they still have thriving village stores that are well supported by residents and stocked high with local meat, dairy products, fruit and veg and all kinds of baked goods that will add inches to your waistline.

Staying in

In Coniston, the **Coniston and Torver Dairy Shop** (015394 41609), opposite the cemetery, sells a small range of local produce and will deliver to holiday cottages in the Coniston/Torver area. On the outskirts of Coniston, **Heritage Meats** (www.heritagemeats.co.uk) at Yew Tree Farm is a meat lover's dream come true. Their animals are reared on land managed in an environmentally sensitive way and the resulting meat is much praised by the celebrity chef Hugh Fearnley Whitingstall. If you can't make it to the farm, you can order online and have a sheep fleece lined hamper of meat delivered to your door.

A prime destination for buying local foods is Broughton-in-Furness. **Broughton Village Bakery** (01229 716 824 www.broughtonvillagebakery.co.uk) on Princess Street is committed to Fairtrade and famous throughout the area for its outstandingly good bread, takeaway sandwiches and other baked goods, all made with local organic flour (closed Mondays).

Melville Tyson (01229 716247 www.melvilletyson.co.uk) is one of the best food shopping experiences in the Lakes. This store is for local residents (so none of the jacked up prices for visitors common in many other areas) and is an old-fashioned butchers and grocers selling local produce, home-made chutneys, organic fruit and veg, fresh fish and the best pies in the south lakes.

Takeaways

In Coniston the **Meadowdore Café** (015394 41638 www.meadowdore-cafe.co.uk) on Hawkshead Old Road, sells an inexpensive range of hot and cold takeaway options such as veggie burgers and baguettes and is a good place to stock up on supplies for the hike up The Old Man of Coniston. For evening takeaways try **Bobbins** on Lake Road (015394 41141) which sells home-made pizzas and the usual fish and chips (closed Mondays). In Broughton-in-Furness, the **Black Cock Inn** (01229 716529 www.blackcockinncumbria.com) on Princess Street serves its menu of hearty traditional pub grub and Thai curries as either eat in or takeaway.

EATING OUT

FINE DINING
Beswicks Restaurant

The Square, Broughton-in-Furness, LA20 6JF
01229 716285
www.beswicks.co.uk

Tucked away in a corner of Broughton's quaint village square, Beswicks is one of the finest places to dine in the region. Expect gourmet dining in cosy but plush surroundings and a special midweek bistro menu. Mains average around £13 or indulge in the five course deal for £33.

RESTAURANT
Jumping Jenny

Brantwood, Coniston LA21 8AD
01539 441715
www.jumpingjenny.com

Locals travel to enjoy Jumping Jenny's delicious food even if they're not visiting Brantwood. Choose between light lunches including their famous soups (£4), or larger meals such as casserole of beef in Morocco Ale (£9). The fabulous outdoor terrace overlooks Coniston Water and log fires blaze inside in winter. Open 11am–5pm daily (closed Mon and Tues in winter).

Harry's Restaurant and Wine Bar

4 Yewdale Road, Coniston LA21 8DU
015394 41389

Harry's is a chilled out restaurant with scrubbed wooden floors and a contemporary feel. It's open daily from 9.30am until late and is good for big breakfasts, coffees or evening meals. The main evening menu is a selection of pasta, pizzas and burgers £6–£10, all supported by a good wine list.

GASTRO PUB
The Blacksmith Arms

Broughton Mills, Nr Broughton-in-Furness LA20 6AX
01229 716824
www.theblacksmitharms.com

The Blacksmiths Arms is one of the hidden gems of the south lakes. This very popular with the locals Lakeland pub dates back to the 16th century, stands in the heart of good walking country and is crammed with character. Its moderately priced menu features traditional pub dishes, many made with local produce.

The Royal Oak

Spark Bridge, off the A5092, LA12 8BS
01229 861006
www.royaloaksparkbridge.co.uk

The Royal Oak is a family friendly pub that's popular with local outdoor enthusiasts and those who enjoy consistently good food. The menu features plenty of local meat and fish (mains £10–£17) plus some unusual specials. 'The Oak' is very busy at peak periods, so weekend bookings are advisable.

EATING OUT

CAFÉ
Yew Tree Farm Tea Rooms
Off the A593 north of Coniston,
LA21 8DP
01539 441433
www.yewtree-farm.com

The delightful tea rooms at Yew Tree Farm were furnished by Beatrix Potter in the 1930s and do a roaring trade with walkers and cyclists. Enjoy reasonably priced home-made food on the lawn in summer or around the open fire in winter. Open daily 11am–4pm in summer, weather dependent in winter.

The Bluebird Café
Lake Road, Coniston LA21 8AN
01539 44164
www.thebluebirdcafe.co.uk

Located right on the edge of Coniston Water, near the lakeside piers, the Bluebird Café is housed in an old Furness Railway Company building and has superb views over the lake and surrounding countryside. This licensed café sells moderately priced hot snacks and sandwiches and tons of Donald Campbell memorabilia.

Drinking

The best known pub in Coniston is the **Black Bull Inn** (015394 41335) on Coppermines Road, favourite haunt of Donald Campbell when he was in town and home of the Coniston Brewery (www.conistonbrewery.com) whose Bluebird Bitter is famed throughout the region.

South of Coniston two good pubs sit on the edge of the A593 at Torver. **The Wilsons Arms** (015394 41237) and **Church House Inn** (015394 41282) are both old-fashioned traditional pubs overlooked by The Old Man of Coniston and known for local ales and a warm welcome.

Further south still, Broughton-in-Furness is famous for its outstanding pubs. Some, including **The Manor Arms** (01229 716286), which has been in the same family for generations and is one of the best real ale pubs in Cumbria, sit around the village's charming Georgian square. And on summer weekends you'll find the square full of locals sitting around the old market cross enjoying a pint. Branwell Bronte would have enjoyed a drink in one of Broughton-in-Furness's pubs when he briefly worked as a private tutor in the area, a position from which he was dismissed, probably for fathering a child with one of the local maidservants.

Real ales lovers should not miss the **Prince of Wales** (01229 716238 www.princeofwalesfoxfield.co.uk) on the A5092 at nearby Foxfield. Voted by CAMRA as the Cumbria Pub of the Year 2007, the Prince of Wales stocks a continually changing range of real ales including those brewed at their own micro brewery plus over 60 whiskies. Look out for themed beer weekends throughout the year and open evenings for local musicians on the second and fourth Wednesdays of the month (closed Mondays and Tuesdays).

ⓘ Visitor information

Tourist Information Centres: Inside main car park, Ruskin Avenue, Coniston, LA21 8EH; 015394 41533; useful website, www.conistonweb.co.uk.

Hospitals: Furness General Hospital, Dalton Lane, Barrow-in-Furness, LA14 4LF, 01229 870870.

Doctors: Wraysdale House Surgery, Wraysdale House, Coniston, LA21 8ES, 015394 41205.

Pharmacies: See Ulverston p.158 or Ambleside p.102.

Supermarkets: A small Co-op in Coniston; larger stores Ulverston (see p.158) or Windermere (see p.84).

Internet Access: Lakeland House Coffee Shop, Tilberthwaite Ave,

Coniston, 015394 41303, www.lakelandhouse.co.uk; Broughton Village Bakery, Princess Street, Broughton-in-Furness, 01229 716824, www.broughtonvillagebakery.co.uk.

Bike Rental: The Mountain Centre, Market Street, Broughton-in-Furness, 01229 716 461, www.mountaincentre.co.uk, £18 full day, £9 half day, maps of cycling routes provided and the owner will personalise routes; Grizedale Mountain Bikes, Grizedale Forest, 01229 860369, www.grizedalemountainbikes.co.uk, off-road adult and children's bikes, plus trailers to tow those too young to peddle around the forest.

Taxis: Coniston Cabs, 015394 41171.

FURTHER AFIELD

Millom

Millom is a small working town situated on the coast 7 miles south of Broughton-in-Furness. The town is perched on the edge of a peninsula overlooking Morecambe Bay and has an isolated feel, but there are a number of attractions in and around Millom that make the journey worthwhile.

MILLOM FOLK MUSEUM, Millom Railway Station, LA18 5AA; 01229 772555; www.millomfolkmuseum.co.uk; £3 adults, 50p children, £6.50 families; open 10.30am–4.30pm Tues–Sat Easter–Oct.

The **Millom Folk Museum** features displays on the life and work of Norman Nicholson, one of the Lakes' best known modern poets, who lived in Millom and left the town only once in his lifetime (see p.57 for more information on Norman Nicholson). The museum also features details on the region's industrial history, exhibits of local archaeological finds, and clothes and artefacts from the town's bygone days. Demonstrations of old local crafts are laid on in the summer.

RAF Millom Aviation and Military Museum on the outskirts of Millom is the place to find out more about the North West's military heritage and aviation history. Displays of artefacts and photographs are housed in various themed zones and it's easy to spend a day exploring the maze of fascinating exhibits.

RAF MILLOM AVIATION AND MILITARY MUSEUM, Bankhead Estate, Haverigg, Millom, LA18 4NA; 01229 777444; www.rafmillom.co.uk; £5 adults, £2.50 children, £10 families; open 10.30am–5pm daily.

This museum is also good for children as they get to touch many of the displays.

RAF Millom is located near **Haverigg Beach** and it's well worth making the short trip to the sands to see the magnificent Josefina De Vasconcellos sculpture *Escape to the Light*, which is located on the beach. The sculpture is dedicated to the UK's Inshore Rescue Teams and features a human form escaping the jaws of the sea.

Silecroft Beach, just a couple of miles north of Haverigg, is home to the **Murthwaite Green Trekking Centre** which organises horse rides and pony treks along this wild stretch of beautiful coastline. Beach rides are available for complete beginners or experienced

MURTHWAITE GREEN TREKKING CENTRE, Silecroft, LA18 5LP; 01229 770876; www.murthwaitegreen.co.uk; beach rides £17 per hour; open daily; call ahead to book a ride.

riders and the centre takes riders aged four and upwards. If you don't fancy galloping along the sands you can choose to head up into the fells instead.

CUMBRIAN HEAVY HORSES, off the
A590, 4 miles from Silecroft, LA18 5LY;
01229 777764;
www.cumbrianheavyhorses.co.uk, from
£40 for farm ride to £130 for a full day
beach or fell riding; call ahead.

If you prefer to ride 'heavy horses', the **Cumbrian Heavy Horses** centre is located a couple of miles north of Millom and is the place to saddle up a Clydesdale or Shire horse and head to the fells. This small equestrian centre offers farm, beach, fell and trail rides for riders of varying abilities. You can also have a go at driving a carriage pulled by these magnificent horses.

Sunset over Coniston Water

FURNESS AND CARTMEL PENINSULAS

The Furness and Cartmel peninsulas hang off the southern border of the Lake District National Park and are much ignored by visitors in their haste to head north to the more well-known regions of Cumbria. The terrain is much softer here than the rugged fells of the central and northern lakes and picturesque countryside rolls gently down to the vast expanse of Morecambe Bay, whose tides disappear far over the horizon only to race back to shore again every day.

Cartmel is the smaller of the two peninsulas and the main tourist draw here is Cartmel village, home of the world famous Cartmel Sticky Toffee Pudding. The focal point of this pretty village is its priory founded by Augustinian monks in 1188. The priory, and the narrow streets surrounding it, are a Conservation Area and contain over a hundred listed buildings, an old Quaker meeting house and many first-class pubs and unusual gift shops.

Further west, the Furness Peninsula is dotted with numerous decent sized communities, all different in character and all places where people live and work, not just visit on holiday. The largest town in this region is Barrow-in-Furness, which advertises itself as the place 'where the lakes meets the sea', and remains very dominated by its working shipyard. All of the region's major facilities and biggest chain stores are in Barrow and the town's best attraction is Furness Abbey, which, despite being in ruins, remains magnificent.

The other main community on the Furness Peninsula is Ulverston, an attractive market town that extends out to the coast and contains some of the best shopping and places for visitors to eat and drink in the region. A selection of diverse attractions from Swarthmoor Hall, birthplace of the Quaker movement, to the South Lakes Wild Animal Park can be found in and around Ulverston, ensuring that there is something in the area to please all ages.

WHAT TO SEE AND DO

 ## Fair weather

FURNESS ABBEY, on a minor road off the A590 1.5 miles north of Barrow-in-Furness, LA13 0PJ; 01229 823420; www.english-heritage.org.uk; £3.50 adult, £1.80 child; open 10am–5pm daily Apr–Sept, 10am–4pm Thur–Mon Oct, 10am–4pm Thur–Sun Nov–Mar.

The impressive red sandstone ruins of **Furness Abbey** are located in the Vale of the Deadly Nightshade on the outskirts of Barrow-in-Furness. The Abbey was once the second richest Cistercian monastery in England and it takes little imagination to envisage how magnificent it must have been prior to the Dissolution of the Monasteries in the 1530s. An adjacent museum and visitor centre explains the history of Furness Abbey as well as exhibiting numerous artefacts from the ruins. Even if history isn't your thing, the abbey is well worth visiting to experience the peace and tranquillity of this pretty spot, whose melancholy woodlands are allegedly haunted by the restless spirit of a former monk.

Local legend claims that an ancient underground tunnel links Furness Abbey with **Piel Castle**, which sits on the tiny Piel Island, located off the south coast of the Furness Peninsula near Barrow-in-Furness. The monks of Furness Abbey once owned the island and used it as a safe harbour and for storage. In the 14th century a large stone castle-like keep was built on the island to defend the Abbey's goods from smugglers –

PIEL CASTLE, 0870 333 1181; www.english-heritage.org.uk; Piel Island is reached by ferry from Roa Island on the mainland; ferry runs at weekends Easter to early autumn (weather depending) from 11am; last ferry returns from Piel Island at 5.30pm; for more information on the ferry call 01229 475770; admission to the castle is free.

although it's believed the monks weren't averse to a bit of smuggling themselves. Today the ruins of this remote castle stand guard over the mouth of Barrow's deep water harbour and are accessible to visitors to the island.

GLEASTON WATER MILL GLEASTON, LA12 0QH; 01229 869244; www.watermill.co.uk; £2 adults, £1 children; open 10.30am–5pm Tues–Sun.

Situated between Barrow-in-Furness and Ulverston in the tiny community of Gleaston is **Gleaston Water Mill**, an old working corn mill near the ruins of Gleaston Castle. The castle is in a deep state of decline and can only be viewed from a nearby road as it stands on private land, however, the restored mill is open to the public. The building dates from 1774 and the large original wooden gearing system, powered by an 18ft water-wheel, is still in full working order and in operation most days. You can find out how wheat and oats were once made into flour and enjoy the delightful surrounding scenery.

Gleaston Water Mill is also home to the Furness Beekeeper's Apiary and every Saturday morning in the summer, weather permitting, visitors are invited to take part in a free beekeeping experience. The sessions last around two hours and you get to don all the beekeeping clothes, find out how honey is made and what goes on inside a hive.

Those who head from Gleaston over Birkrigg Common will pass through Swarthmoor, a tiny community that runs almost seamlessly into Ulverston and is home to **Swarthmoor Hall**. This charming Elizabethan house was, in the 17th-century, the base and powerhouse behind the Quakers and home to Margaret Fell who married the movement's founder, George Fox. Swarthmoor Hall was extensively restored in the 20th-century and features numerous fine pieces of 17th-century furniture and various of Fox's belongings such as his Bible, travelling bed and sea chest. The house and its country garden are infused with history and tranquillity, and only a short walk from Ulverston. For more information on George Fox see Local Heroes p.64.

SWARTHMOOR HALL, Ulverston, LA12 0JQ; 01229 583204; www.swarthmoorhall.co.uk; £3.50 adults, £2.50 children; open for guided tours at 2.30pm Tues–Fri mid-March–mid-Oct.

Over on the Cartmel peninsula, 4 miles west of Grange-over-Sands, stands **Holker Hall**, one of Cumbria's best stately homes. This magnificent estate and related attractions is a good day out for all ages. The hall itself is dates from the 16th-century and underwent a significant rebuild in 1871; although undeniably grand it maintains all the intimacy of a family home. Visitors are allowed admission into part of the house, including a large library containing around 3,000 leather bound volumes and an impressive cantilevered staircase. The surrounding 25 acres of award wining gardens are, for many, Holker's biggest draw and visitors can explore a network of paths through landscaped gardens and natural parklands, home to a roaming herd of fallow deer. The estate also contains a fabulous food hall and excellent gift shop.

HOLKER HALL, Cark-in-Cartmel, LA11 7PL; 015395 58328; www.holker-hall.co.uk; hall and gardens £9.25 adults, £5 children, £25 families; garden only £5.95 adults, £3 children, £15.50 families; hall open noon–4pm Sun–Fri Easter–Oct; gardens open 10.30am–5.30pm Sun–Fri Easter to Oct.

Attached to Holker Hall is the **Lakeland Motor Museum**, a must for any motoring enthusiast. The museum contains an extensive collection of glorious old cars and motorbikes, plus many other related exhibits. The main attraction though is the Donald Campbell exhibition which features a full-scale replica of the Bluebird.

LAKELAND MOTOR MUSEUM, Holker Hall, Cark-in-Cartmel, LA11 7PL; 015395 58509; www.lakelandmotormuseum.co.uk; £7 adults, £4.50 children, £23 families; including Holker Hall and Gardens £11.50 adults, £6.50 children, £32 families; open 10.30am–4.45pm daily mid-Jan–Oct.

Walking and cycling

Some of the best walking in this region is around the Ulverston area. Those looking for a gentle walk can stretch their legs along the town's tiny canal – the shortest in the country. The canal starts just off the A590 near Booths on the east side of town and it's a scenic mile-long stroll to the locks at the end, where you're rewarded with commanding views over Morecambe Bay and an excellent nearby pub – the Bay Horse.

For a longer walk head up **Hoad Hill**, a distinctive 450ft high hill overlooking the town where on Easter Monday locals come to roll pasche eggs down its slopes. The **Sir John Barrow Monument** (www.sirjohnbarowmonument.co.uk), a 110ft tall lighthouse, stands on top of Hoad, and is open at various times during the summer (for more information on Sir John Barrow see Local Heroes p.63). If a flag is flying at the top of Hoad it means the monument is open and you can climb the 112 narrow steps to reach the lantern chamber at the top. It takes around half an hour to climb Hoad and on a clear day you can see many of the Lake District's hills and the three peaks of North Yorkshire from its summit. To reach Hoad from town head along church Street to St Mary's Church from where you can take various routes to the top.

Ulverston is also the start of the **Cumbria Way**, a 70-mile walk to Carlisle that leads through the lakes, and is an access point for the Cumbria Coastal Way, a 45-mile walk around the shores of Morecambe Bay. For details on these walks, or to pick up a selection of free walking guides to the Ulverston area, visit the town's Tourist Information Centre.

To the south of Ulverston is **Birkrigg Common** a wild and craggy limestone common that looks out over Morecambe Bay. The common is popular with local walkers and the network of lanes that lead around it through the small villages of

The Druid's Circle

If you go walking or cycling on Birkrigg look out for the small but impressive stone circle that's located on the coastal side of the common just north of Bardsea. Known as the Druid's Circle or Druid's Temple, Birkrigg's stone circle is in fact two circles. The small inner circle consists of 12 mostly upright stones and is surrounded by the barely visible remains of a larger circle that once consisted of around 20 stones.

Excavations which took place on this spot in 1911 and 1921 revealed a pavement of cobbles inside the inner ring beneath which the cremated remains of five burials from the early Bronze Age were found. A decorated urn (dated between 2000 and 1800BC) from the same period was also found in the circle along with a pear-shaped stone, thought to have been used as a pestle and an oyster-shaped stone, believed to have been used as a palette, and some red ochre. Many believe that these artefacts were once used for ceremonial purposes.

Cross-sands walk over Morecambe Bay

Prior to the coming of the railway in 1857, the quickest way to get from one side of Morecambe Bay to the other was to walk across the sands. However, as the death of eighteen Chinese cockle pickers on Morecambe Bay in 2004 proves, its treacherous sands regularly claim lives and no one should venture even a short distance onto them without a local guide.

This walk has always been dangerous, for dotted throughout the sands, hidden just below the surface, are patches of treacherous quicksands which continually shift position as the rivers that feed the bay change their route to the sea. Swift tides add to the danger, as they come in so fast it's impossible to outrun them. These dangers, plus the ever-changing weather, have shaped the history of the oversands walk into the stuff of legend.

Tacitus first recorded the shifting sands of Morecambe Bay, but it's believed people walked the route long before the Romans. Robert the Bruce's troops are thought to have marched over the sands and the monks of Furness Abbey are known to have made regular crossings.

Walkers have always needed a guide to advise them on the safest route and the history of the men who have undertaken the job is as rich as that of the walk itself. In 1548, the then guide Thomas Hodeson was accused of being a drunken gambler, who watched travellers drown while in her journal of 1909, a Miss AM Wakefield described the guide she encountered as 'a strange wild looking figure with masses of long unkempt hair'. In contrast other guides are recorded as putting the safety of travellers above their own, even to the extent of losing their own lives while saving others.

Hazards of the job include the constant threat of drowning and often miserable weather. John Carter, the guide in 1715, also records the dangers of 'happenings of the mists'. These mysterious 'happenings' can only be speculated upon as over the centuries hundreds have drowned while trying to cross Morecambe Bay and their bones, and perhaps their spirits, still lie out there somewhere.

Although the opening of the railway brought decline to the oversands route for trade purposes, many still undertake the walk for pleasure. However, even today, anyone wanting to walk across the sands needs a guide. The current Queens Guide to the Sands is Cedric Robinson. Cedric comes from a family of Flookburgh fishermen and organises a number of walks across Morecambe Bay each summer, which leave from either Hest Bank or Arnside on the east side and end at Kents Bank on the west side, all of which are connected by a regular train service. To book a place on a walk contact the Grange-over-Sands Tourist Office (015395 34026) and never venture out onto the sands without a recognised guide.

Little and Great Urswick, Scales and Gleaston are fabulous cycling terrain. And for those who don't mind roads with a bit more traffic, the A5087, which leads south from Ulverston along the edge of the coast to Rampside, is a great ride with superb coastal views for confident cyclists.

CONISHEAD PRIORY, off the A5087, Ulverston, LA12 9QQ; 01229 584029; www.manjushri.org; £2.50 adults, £1.50 children; open for house/temple tours weekends/bank holidays Easter–Oct; tours depart 2.15pm and 3.30pm; gardens open all year dawn to dusk.

Cartmel Priory

Ancient priories

The south Lakes contain two wonderful old priories. In Ulverston the **Conishead Priory** was originally founded in 1160 by Augustinian monks and after extensive rebuilding in the 19th century was reborn as an outstanding example of Gothic revival architecture. The Priory has a remarkable history that's seen it being used as a hotel and hospital and its present incarnation is as the home of the Manjushri Kadampa Buddhist meditation centre. The new owners have extensively restored the once crumbling building and built a stunning World Peace Temple in the grounds. Visitors are taken on guided tours of the old Priory and new Buddhist temple and are then free to discover the picturesque surrounding woodlands and gardens for themselves.

Cartmel Priory, or the church of St Mary and St Michael, sits in the centre of Cartmel village. Like Conishead, Cartmel was founded in the 12th century but has remained a centre for Christian worship ever since. Following Dissolution the Cartmel Priory was ransacked and great chunks of stone were removed to build many of the village's houses. However, the church was restored, although the National Trust now owns the former gatehouse, and remains a working church where visitors are welcome to marvel at its solid splendour. Look out for Cromwell's door in the south-west of the church where it is believed local parishioners fired at Parliamentarian soldiers through holes in the door.

CARTMEL PRIORY, Cartmel LA11 6PU; www.cartmelpriory.org.uk; £2.50 adults; open 9am–5.30pm daily Easter–Oct; 9am–3.30pm daily Nov–Easter.

Wet weather

Museums

The **Dock Museum** at Barrow-in-Furness is one of the most interesting and newest museums in the region and it effectively brings to life the history of Barrow and its shipbuilding trade, which boomed then bust in the later part of the 20th century. The museum is built over

THE DOCK MUSEUM, North Road, Barrow-in-Furness, LA14 2PW; 01229 894444; www.dockmuseum.org.uk; free entry; open 10am–5pm Tues–Fri, 11am–5pm Sat and Sun Easter–Oct, 10.30am–4pm Wed–Fri and 11am–4.30pm Sat and Sun Nov–Easter.

an old Victorian dry dock and visitors are taken right down to the bottom of the dock in this multi-levelled attraction. A visit includes watching a film on Barrow, playing with interactive computers and there are often events and exhibitions laid on. The waterfront area, with its playground and walkways, is great for children.

In Ulverston the **Laurel and Hardy Museum** is the most bizarre museum in Cumbria. Don't expect any sense of order or an aura of reverence when visiting this loving tribute to one of the town's most famous sons, Stan Laurel

LAUREL AND HARDY MUSEUM, Upper Brook Street, Ulverston, LA12 7BH; 01229 582292; £2 adults, £1 children, £4 families; open 10am–4pm daily Feb–Dec.

(otherwise known as Arthur Stanley Jefferson), and his comedy partner Oliver Hardy. This ramshackle, higgledy piggledy collection of all things Laurel and Hardy, from one of their few remaining bowler hats to old curtains from a former home, might appear to some as a 'right mess'. However, to most it's a refreshing alternative to sleek museums and a fitting tribute to one of cinema's finest comedy double acts.

What to do with children...

For first time visitors it comes as a surprise when driving along the main A590 between Barrow-in-Furness and Ulverston to see a giraffe or rhino staring over a major roundabout. However, just off this roundabout is the **South Lakes Wild Animal Park**, one of the best places for children and animal lovers in the South Lakes. This attraction is home to a vast array of animals from around the world,

SOUTH LAKES WILD ANIMAL PARK, off the A590 at Dalton-in-Furness, LA15 8RJ; 01229 466086; www.wildanimalpark.co.uk; £10.50 adults, £7 children; open 10am–5pm daily Easter–Oct, 10am–4.30pm Nov–Easter.

including the Sumatran tiger, a large collection of kangaroos, pandas, wolves, tapirs and meerkats. The park, which is committed to animal conservation and protection, also features a Safari Railway and numerous picnic spots.

Local legends: the mysterious lantern of Plumpton Hall

Sitting on the edge of the sea on the outskirts of Ulverston where the Levens estuary pours in Morecambe Bay is Plumpton Hall – if you are arriving into Ulverston by train look out for this large old building on the left-hand side of the train tracks near the edge of the shore as you cross over the Levens viaduct. Parts of this private residence are thought to date from the 12th century although a significant section of the hall was built in 1636. However, what really interests most people about Plumpton Hall is its mysterious lantern.

According to local folklore a centuries-old brass lantern decorated with astrological symbols was washed up by the tide just outside the hall hundreds of years ago. Some believe it came from a ship that sunk during the Spanish Armada, others claim its origins run back as far back as the Crusades. The lantern is too large and heavy to be easily carried around by hand, and the present owner believes it was once used as a ship's riding light – lit when a vessel was at anchor.

Local accounts of the lantern say that it was once lit at night and hung in the Hall as a guide to travellers crossing the sands of Morecambe Bay. However, folklore states that the lantern must never leave Plumpton. Former residents have claimed to have made repeated attempts to get rid of the lantern including sinking it at sea, but it always mysteriously reappeared hanging from its spot inside Plumpton Hall. They also claimed that 'much annoyance at night' was the result of interfering with the lantern in any way.

Plumpton's famous brass lantern, which is coated in the remains of a horn glazing, still hangs in the hall, and the present owners took it to the Antiques Roadshow to have some light thrown upon its origins. According to the show's experts, the lantern was made in the Orient, probably for a Dutch market and was given a date of the early 19th century.

Local Knowledge

Nicknamed the 'Al Gore of Cumbria', **Kate Rawles** lived in Lancaster, Scotland and Colorado before settling in the Ulverston area in 2000. She's a lecturer in Outdoor Studies at the University of Cumbria's Ambleside campus where her teaching focuses on environmental issues. Kate also works as a climate change campaigner and has recently cycled from El Paso to Anchorage engaging North Americans with climate change issues along the way. When she's not on her bike, Kate lives with her partner Chris, and Easter the bunny – who roams free-range on what used to be her lawn.

Favourite takeaway: The consistently delicious Jade Fountain Chinese takeaway on Fountain Street in Ulverston.

Favourite café: Ulverston has great cafes, including Gillam's Organic Cafe and the World Peace Cafe, run by Buddhists from the nearby monastery. Both have lovely, secluded outdoor seating as well as great food.

Favourite pub: The Capitola Wine Bar run by locals Wendy and Vicky who are famous for creating friendly, welcoming bars with a wonderful atmosphere. The Capitola also features excellent coffee and hot chocolate, ideal for those cold, wet afternoons.

Best view: The panoramic views from the top of Birkrigg Common. You can look south over the shining sands of Morecambe Bay, or north to the hills and mountains.

Best walk: The walk up Ulverston's Hoad hill. It's well used by local dog walkers and each Christmas an unknown walker decorates a holly tree en route to the top.

Best kept secret: Ulverston's International Music Festival. Thanks to local lad Anthony Hewitt, aka international concert pianist, Ulverston hosts the most fantastic classical music festival in its Coronation Hall for a week in June – with a bit of jazz thrown in for good measure.

Favourite treat: Smoked brie from the Ulverston deli along with a bottle of organic champagne from Booths.

Best thing about living here: The great biking and walking country right on your doorstep, with countless places to stop for a good pint on the way home.

149

Entertainment

Theatre and cinema

The main cinema in this region is a large **Apollo** multiplex (0871 220 6000 www.apollocinemas.co.uk), on the northern outskirts of Barrow-in-Furness off the A590. There's a smaller cinema in Ulverston, the **Roxy** (01229 582340 www.nm-cinemas.co.uk) on Brogden Street, which shows mostly mainstream films but also has a well-supported regular film club that screens non-mainstream world cinema.

Forum Twenty Eight (01229 820000 www.barrowbc.gov.uk/forum28) on Duke Street in Barrow-in-Furness is the south Lakes' largest theatre and arts centre. Its programme includes a mix of touring and local theatre, music, comedy and dance shows. Ulverston the Coronation Hall (01229 587140 www.corohall.co.uk) on County Square hosts regular evening events and concerts, plus a number of the town's many festivals.

Special events

Ulverston has earned the nickname 'Festival Town' due to the sheer number of festivals it hosts every year and no matter when you visit, don't be surprised to see flags flying and some kind of festival taking place. One of the highlights of the town's busy festival calendar is the **Dickensian Christmas Festival** (01229 580640 www.dickensianfestival.co.uk), which takes place on the last weekend in November. Many residents dress up in Victorian costumes for this popular event, which includes local craft stalls, a 'Made in Cumbria' food market, street entertainment and evening ghost walks. The **Ulverston International Music**

The Dickensian Christmas Festival

Festival (www.ulverstonmusicfestival.co.uk) is a week-long programme of top classical music events in late May/early June and May's **Printfest** (www.printfest.org.uk) is an exceptional weekend arts festival for such a small town. It sees the Coronation Hall transformed by the work of leading print makers from around the country. For details on Ulverston's other many festivals contact the town's Tourist Information Centre.

One of the best events in the South Lakes' calendar is the **Cartmel Races** that take place at the village's small race track, the smallest National Hunt course in

England, over Spring and August Bank Holiday weekends (www.cartmel-steeplechases.co.uk). The races are fantastic for families as there's a small fairground and lots to keep children entertained, while adults can enjoy the beer tent and place the odd bet or two. Thousands descend on Cartmel for the races and the country lanes are always chocked with traffic, so if you can arrive by train into the Cark and Cartmel station, which is on the main Lancaster to Barrow-in-Furness line, from where coaches are laid on to transport visitors to the track.

Shopping

Both Ulverston and Cartmel are charming places for visitors to shop. Ulverston is the larger of the two communities and has plenty of unusual shops to choose from – most independently owned and well supported by locals. Highlights include the **Tinner's Rabbit** fine arts and crafts shop (01229 588808 www.tinnersrabbit .co.uk) on Market Street and the adjoining **Bookshop at the Tinner's Rabbit** (01229 588858 www.ulverstonbookshops.co.uk) which stocks a good range of titles by local authors and has an extensive children's section.

Cartmel is also home to a number of local craft and gift shops including a **Made in Cumbria** shop opposite the Priory that opens daily from 11am and sells a selection of work by local artists, including paintings and woodcrafts.

Just off the A590 in Lindal-in-Furness, five miles south of Ulverston, is a large store attached to the **Colony Candle** factory (www.colony.com). The store sells all of Colony's products and has a bargain section where you can save a fortune, and children can try their hand at candle dipping. You can also peek into the factory through a plate glass window to catch a glimpse of how candles are made en masse.

South of Lindal-in-Furness and adjacent to the Gleaston Water Mill is the fabulously quirky **Pig's Whisper** (01229 869764 www.pigswhisper.com), a shop dedicated to all things pig where you can pick up everything from cuddly pigs to pig teapots. The shop has roots in the area's history as pigs were kept by the corn millers of old and archaeological digs have unearthed the bones of centuries old pigs. The proprietors of the Pig's Whisper also own a nearby ancient Grade II listed pigsty that's been converted into a delightful self-catering cottage for one couple.

The best... PLACES TO STAY

HOTEL

Clarence House Country Hotel

Skelgate, Dalton-in-Furness, LA15 8BQ
01229 462508
www.clarencehouse-hotel.co.uk

This luxurious, richly decorated hotel is one of the finest places to stay in the region. It's easy to reach many Lake District attractions from this off the beaten track location, or relax inside with a good book on wet days. The on-site restaurant is superb.

Price: B&B £110 per room per night based on double occupancy. Special weekend breaks available.

The Lymehurst Hotel

Kents Bank Road, Grange-over-Sands, LA11 7EY
015395 33076
www.lymehurst.co.uk

Situated in the centre of Grange-over-Sands, this elegant Victorian hotel is convenient for much of the Lakes and considerably cheaper than its equivalents in the tourist hot spots. The rooms are spacious and the dining is first class.

Price: B&B £33–£45 pppn, special deals available.

INN

The Royal Oak

The Square, Cartmel, LA11 6QB
015395 36259
www.royaloakcartmel.co.uk

This friendly old coaching inn in the heart of Cartmel comes complete with low beamed ceilings, a large 15th-century fireplace and picturesque riverside beer garden. The comfortable rooms are all en suite and traditional, locally sourced pub food is served in the bar.

Price: B&B £65–£70 per room per night.

The Bay Horse Hotel

Canal Foot, Ulverston, LA12 9EL
01229 580502
www.thebayhorsehotel.co.uk

This atmospheric inn stands at the end of Ulverston canal and has wide views of Morecambe Bay and the surrounding hills. The inn was once a staging post for the horse-drawn carriages that crossed the sands and today is popular with business folk and visitors, all drawn to the location and reputation for fine dining.

Price: B&B from £85–£120 per room per night.

The best... PLACES TO STAY

B & B

Hill Farm

Cartmel, LA11 7SS
015395 32576
www.hillfarmbb.co.uk

Located on the outskirts of Cartmel in idyllic surroundings this large 16th-century farmhouse sits in beautiful countryside overlooking Morecambe Bay. This award winning B&B is full of character and the excellent breakfasts include home-made breads, local sausages and farm eggs.

Price: B&B £40–£50 pppn.

HOSTEL

The Duddon Sands Hostel

The Ship Inn, Askewgate Brow,
Kirkby-in-Furness, LA17 7TE
01229 889454
www.theship1691.co.uk

This upmarket hostel, attached to a friendly local pub, is a good regional budget option. Rooms sleep between two and eight (bedding provided) and the hostel's lounge looks out over the Duddon Sands. The adjacent pub serves meals Thur–Sun.

Price: Bed only £13 pppn.

The best... FOOD AND DRINK

The Furness and Cartmel peninsulas are home to some of the best places to shop for local foods in Cumbria. Ulverston and Grange-over-Sands both contain fabulous traditional butchers, bakers, greengrocers and more contemporary delicatessens, all of which are heavily supported by the town's residents. First-class farm shops are situated close to both communities.

Cartmel Village Stores is the powerhouse behind the nationally renowned Cartmel Sticky Toffee Pudding (www.stickytoffeepudding.co.uk), a traditional and delicious regional speciality. The pudding is made with

Cartmel sticky toffee pudding

free-range eggs, local cream and butter and is for sale in Cartmel's Village Store, in delis and on dessert menus around Cumbria and as far afield as Harvey Nichols and Fortnum and Mason.

The other regional food speciality is Morecambe Bay shrimps (www.morecambe bayshrimps.com), which have been caught by fishermen local to communities around the bay such as Flookburgh, Bardsea and Rampside for centuries. The shrimps feature heavily on local menus and can be bought in many of the area's delicatessens.

▶ Staying in

In Grange-over-Sands, **Higginsons** (015395 34367) on Main Street was voted Britain's best butchers and sells an excellent array of local meats, takeaway pies, pasties and quiches. The **Hazelmere Bakery** is adjacent to its café and bakes all the usual breads and cakes, plus a selection of not so usual hearty pies, including good vegetarian options. Hazelmere also stocks a range of frozen ready meals that have been cooked on-site – perfect for self-caterers who don't want to cook. Also in Grange-over-Sands, **Ainsworths Specialist Grocers** (015395 32946) on Kents Bank Road sell many local specialities such as Morecambe Bay shrimps, Cumbrian bacon and local cheeses.

West of Grange-over-Sands at Holker Hall, the **Holker Food Hall** (015395 59084 www.holkerfoodhall.co.uk) is a sight for those who love good food to behold. This large store sells seasonal produce from the Holker Estate including Saltmarsh lamb and Shorthorn beef, plus an array of other Cumbrian foods and ales. **Howbarrow Organic Farm** (015395 36330 www.howbarroworganic.co.uk) on the outskirts of nearby Cartmel, past the race course, sell organic fruit, vegetables, breads and meats from their farm shop (open 10am–5pm Wed–Sat), or you can order online and have it delivered.

Ulverston's Thursday market is the place to stock up on inexpensive locally grown fruit and veg, fresh fish, meats and dairy products from the stalls that line Market Street. South of town off the A5087 coast road at Goadsbarrow Farm, the **Baycliffe Farm Shop** (01229 869257 www.farmshopbaycliffe.co.uk) is famous for its regional meats including dry cured bacon and sausages made from locally produced beef and lamb, as well as traditionally produced black pudding and home baked pies (open 9am–3pm Tues–Fri and 9am–2pm Sat).

Takeaways

In Ulverston the **Temple Thai** restaurant (0229 58056) on Cavendish Street sells an excellent selection of authentic Thai food to eat in or take away (closed Wednesdays), or for fish and chips head to King Street where you can choose between the ever popular **Chippy Bank** (01229 585907) or **Lakeland Continental** (01229 583506). For out of the ordinary takeaway sandwiches at lunchtime try the **Cumbrian Way** (01229 588906 www.cumbrianway.co.uk) on Brogden Street.

In Grange-over-Sands you can pick up a Chinese takeaway at the **Amber Court** (015395 35830) on Main Street, or fish and chips from **Fish Over Chips** (015395 32277) on Kents Bank Road (closed Sundays and Mondays). During the day the carvery on Kents Bank Road that's attached to Higginsons butchers sells takeaway hot carvery rolls, filled baked potatoes and burgers all made with meats from the butchers.

In the centre of Cartmel on The Square, the **Nazz Indian Restaurant** (015395 36718) is good for either eating in or takeaway.

EATING OUT

FINE DINING
Clarence House Hotel
Skelgate, Dalton in Furness, LA15 8BQ
01229 462508
www.clarencehouse-hotel.co.uk

The elegant Victorian-style orangery of this fine hotel is the place where locals come to dine in style on special occasions. Expect linen tablecloths and fine china and a menu heavy with local meats and fish (mains £17–£23), all complemented by a comprehensive wine list.

RESTAURANT
Rustique
Brogden Street, Ulverston, LA12 7AJ
01229 587373

Tucked away off the main drag, Rustique is one the more

contemporary restaurants in town. The changing menu combines modern British food with traditional dishes such as roast pheasant breast (£18) and asparagus soufflé (£15), which can be rounded off with one of their deliciously unusual deserts.

Amigos
30 Cavendish Street, Ulverston, LA12 7AD
01229 587616
www.amigosmexican.com

Amigos is famous for its generous portions of freshly made Mexican food plus a range of steaks and seafood. Mexican dishes such as fajitas and chilie sombrera average at £11 and the seafood paella is to die for. Reservations recommended for Friday and Saturday nights, closed Mondays.

EATING OUT

GASTRO PUB

The Bay Horse
Canal Foot, Ulverston, LA12 9EL
01229 580502
www.thebayhorsehotel.co.uk

Located at the end of Ulverston's canal, the Bay Horse serves better than average pub food in its cosy bar and conservatory restaurant overlooking the wide expanse of Morecambe Bay. Lunch includes light bites (£5–£7) and the dinner menu, with the likes of Angus Aberdeen steaks (£25), is excellent for meat lovers.

Pig and Whistle
Aynsome Road, Cartmel, LA11 6PL
015395 34433

Parringtons Bistro at the Pig and Whistle pub in Cartmel stands on the outskirts of the village and serves a diverse menu of dishes from around the world. There are some unusual veggie options such as Goan style veg and bean curry (£10) and local Cumbrian sausages for die-hard meat eaters.

CAFÉ

Hazelmere Café
1–2 Yewbarrow Terrace, Grange-over-Sands, LA11 6ED
015395 32972
www.hazelmerecafe.co.uk

Hazelmere is a multi-award winning licensed café and local institution.

The owners travel abroad to source the amazing selection of single estate teas and all of the fabulous food is baked on-site. The regularly changing menu includes a range of traditional afternoons teas from £7–£10.

Gillam's Tearoom
64 Market Street, Ulverston, LA12 7LT
01229 587564

Gillam's is a 100% organic, vegetarian, old-fashioned tea shop housed in a restored 18th-century building. The menu features unusual sandwiches for around a fiver, Cumbrian tea-bread and their very own traditional cream teas, which you can enjoy in a pretty secluded garden in summer.

Dusty Miller's
Gleaston Water Mill, Gleaston, Ulverston, LA12 0QH
01229 869244
www.watermill.co.uk

Dusty Miller's is a charming licensed traditional teas hop attached to Gleaston Water Mill that bakes everything on-site using local produce. The extensive menu features all day Cumbrian breakfast dishes (£2–£6.50) and seasonal specials such as hot stews and comfort puddings in winter and fresh salads in summer. Closed Mondays.

🍺 Drinking

A cluster of good village pubs can be found in around Cartmel's main square including the **King's Arms** and **Royal Oak**, both of which have riverside beer gardens, while the Cavendish Arms is located just off the square.

In Ulverston the **Rose and Crown** on King Street is a good choice for a friendly pint and the **Swan Inn** on Swan Street (just off the A590 as it swings through town) is a Hawkshead Brewery pub and the place for a pint of local cask ales. Although not attached to a pub, the **Ulverston Brewing Company** (www.ulverstonbrewing.co.uk) sells its premium ales, including Another Fine Mess and Lonsome Pine after local lad Stan Laurel, through many of the town's pubs. While the latest edition to the town's nightlife, **Capitola Bar** on Daltongate is a first-class Italian wine bar that serves continental beers and fine wines along with Italian tapas and light jazz.

ℹ️ Visitor Information

Tourist Information Centres: Coronation Hall, County Square, Ulverston, LA12 5AD, 01229 587120, www.ulverston.net; Victoria Hall, Main Street, Grange-over-Sands, LA11 6DP, 015395 34026, daily 10am–5pm mid-March to October.

Hospitals: Furness General Hospital, Dalton Lane, Barrow-in-Furness, LA14 4LF, 01229 870870.

Doctors: Ulverston Community Health Centre, Stanely Street, Ulverston, LA12 7BT, 01229 484050, www.gpsulverston.co.uk, 8.30am–6.30pm Mon–Fri.

Pharmacies: Co-op Pharmacy, Kents Bank Road, Grange-over-Sands, Mon–Fri 9am–5.30pm, Sat 9am–5pm; Boots, Market Street, Ulverston, 9am–5.30pm Mon–Sat; 24-hour Tesco in Barrow-in-Furness.

Police: Barrow Police Station, Market Street, Barrow-in-Furness, 0845 3300247.

Supermarkets: 24-hour Tesco, Hondpool Road (A5087), Barrow-in-Furness; Boothes off the A590 in Ulverston; small Co-op and Spar in Grange-over-Sands.

Internet Access: Public libraries, Kings Road, Ulverston, 01229 894151; public library, Ramsden Square, Barrow-in-Furness, 01229 894370.

Bike Rental: Gill Cycles, The Gill, Ulverston, 01229 581116, www.gillcycles.co.uk, £15 first day, £10 subsequent days.

Taxis: Geoff's Taxis, Ulverston, 01229 586666; Road Runner, Grange-over-Sands, 015395 33792.

157

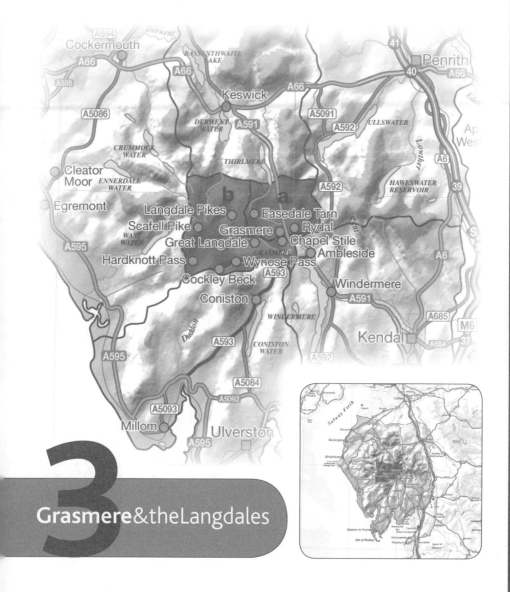

3

Grasmere&theLangdales

a. Grasmere

b. The Langdales

Unmissable highlights

01 Heading up to the heights of **Hardknott Pass** to explore the ruins of a remote Roman fort, p.178

02 Visiting Dove Cottage, the main Lake District destination for Wordsworth lovers, p.166

03 Strolling through the landscaped gardens at Rydal Mount, p.167

04 Enjoying dinner at the unique and quirky Jumble Room restaurant in Grasmere, p.174

05 Sinking a pint of real ale at the Hiker's Bar in the Old Dungeon Ghyll in the heart of Great Langdale, p.182

06 Spending time and far too much money in Chester's Shop and Café by the River, p.183

07 Striding up to Easdale Tarn from the centre of Grasmere, p.164

08 Hiring a rowing boat and paddling across Grasmere lake to its tiny island, p.164

09 Sunbathing on the village green at Elterwater on sunny Sunday afternoons, p.178

10 Visiting the Wordsworths' final resting place in St Oswald's churchyard, Grasmere, p.162

GRASMERE AND THE LANGDALES

Grasmere and the Langdales, a magnificent mountain range, stand at the heart of the Lake District National Park. To the east of this region the A591 – the only main road linking north with south – skirts around Grasmere and connects the wilder fells of the northern lakes with the more docile, tourist friendly landscape of the south. It therefore comes as no surprise that this central region forms an appealing blend of the two.

Grasmere is the main draw to this area and is one of the Lake District's tourist hot spots, mainly because of its association with William Wordsworth and its proximity to two of his former homes open to the public – Dove Cottage and Rydal Mount. In the Langdales to the west of Grasmere, the Lake District scenery becomes seriously dramatic and attracts walkers and outdoor pursuits enthusiasts from around the country to its breathtaking peaks.

To the west of the Langdales is the only quick, but precarious, access to the Western Lakes and north Cumbrian coast. Here Hardknott and Wrynose passes wend their exhilarating but steep way past Scafell Pike, which at 3,210ft above sea level is England's highest mountain, and the remains of a remote Roman fort, before dropping down into Eskdale and the western Lake District.

Although this region is dotted with large mountain tarns reached via well-trodden footpaths, it's home to only to two small lakes – Grasmere and Rydal Water. Grasmere lake is easily reached from the village that shares its name and is well used by day trippers and tourists staying in the region. In contrast, most visitors whizz past Rydal Water, which stands adjacent to the A591 between Grasmere and Ambleside and maintains a moody, somewhat melancholy presence in this area.

The central region's appeal to such a mix of visitors has generated a diverse range of accommodation options to cater for them, and all those wanting to eat out will be delighted with the range and quality of options available.

GRASMERE

Located only 8 miles from Windermere and 13 miles from Keswick, Grasmere is the jewel in the crown of the central Lake District. This picturesque village is surrounded in all directions by stunning scenery and Grasmere itself is closed in by reams of high peaks whose colours and moods change with the seasons and sometimes even by the hour.

It won't take long to explore Grasmere's winding streets, which gather near the banks of the River Rothay, where you'll find some of the region's best shopping and a collection of first-class restaurants.

There's hardly an inch of the village that hasn't been touched by Wordsworth, and his presence alone attracts many tourists to Grasmere, making it one of the most visited villages in the whole Lake District. The main attraction is Wordsworth's early home, Dove Cottage, which stands on the village's southern outskirts. Rydal Mount to the south of Grasmere is the only one of Wordsworth's other homes in this region open to the public and another main draw.

The Wordsworths' graves

Wordsworth often went boating on Grasmere's tiny lake when he lived at Dove Cottage. And today this small body of water – just a mile long and half a mile wide – remains a popular place to hire a rowing boat, or walk and picnic around its shores.

The final stop on the Wordsworth pilgrimage is the graves of William, his wife, Mary, and sister, Dorothy, in the solemn churchyard of St Oswald's parish church. Pop into the church itself, which dates back to the 1300s, to view the poet's old prayer book and see St Oswald's unusual high timbered roof.

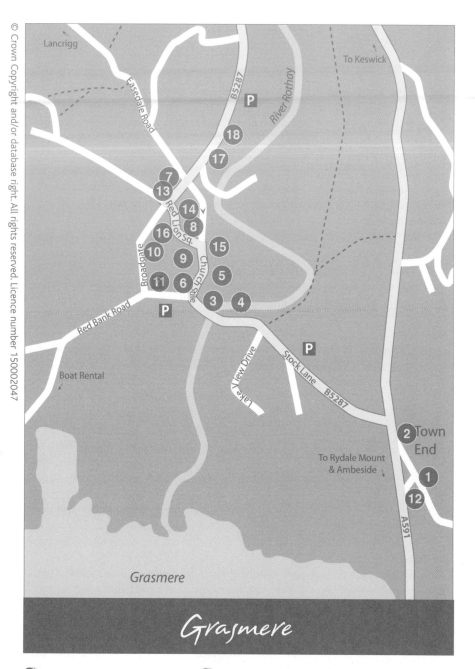

Grasmere

1 Dove Cottage
2 Wordsworth Museum
3 St Oswald's Church
4 The Wordsworths' Graves
5 Sarah Nelson's Gingerbread Shop
6 Story Teller's Garden
7 Heaton Cooper Studio
8 Moss Grove
9 Newby's
10 The Jumble Room

11 Dale Lodge Hotel
12 Dove Cottage Tea Rooms/Villa Colombina
13 Miller's How café
14 Baldry's
15 Dove & Olive Branch
16 Lamb Inn
17 Co-op
18 Grasmere Pharmacy

From the churchyard follow the scent of warm buttery ginger that wafts in through its north entrance to discover Grasmere's other big draw, Sarah Nelson's Gingerbread Shop. Her simply divine gingerbread has been popular with tourists since Victorian times and, although Sarah Nelson is long dead, visitors still queue out the door of her tiny shop to purchase her famous creation.

However, there's far more to Grasmere than old poet laureates and delicious cakes. Despite the tourist onslaught this village maintains a strong sense of community that's cemented by a love of the stunning environment in which Grasmere sits.

WHAT TO SEE AND DO

 ## Fair weather

Boat hire

One of the nicest things to do when the sun shines in Grasmere is to head down to the **Faeryland Tea Garden** on the edge of the lake (about a ten-minute walk from town) and hire a rowing boat. In addition to messing about on the lake itself you can explore a small wooded island. If you believe the tea shop owners, this island is home to a mysterious Faery Oak tree, which marks a secret doorway into the Faery Realm. Unfortunately this magical tree can't be seen by the likes of ordinary human folk, but you can see enchanting views of Grasmere and the fells beyond instead.

> **FAERYLAND TEA GARDEN BOAT HIRE,**
> Red Bank Road, LA22 9PU; 015394
> 35060; 200 yards from the Gold Rill Hotel,
> which is just past the Grasmere Garden
> Centre; boats rented by the hour; £10
> deposit, rates depend on how many people
> share the boat; open daily 10am–6pm
> Mar–Oct.

Walking

Many people come to Grasmere to walk and you don't have to be super-fit or buy tonnes of expensive outdoor gear to enjoy some of the well-trodden paths that lead from the village and its surrounds. Popular low key routes include walking around the lakes of Grasmere and Rydal Water, hiking the old **Coffin Trail** between Ambleside and Grasmere – a path used by medieval coffin bearers carrying the dead to their final resting place from Ambleside to consecrated ground in Grasmere – and striding up to Easdale Tarn, a dramatic and isolated tarn 2 miles above the village.

To reach **Easdale Tarn** head to the car park on Easdale Lane and across Goody Bridge. From here cross Easdale Beck and follow the signposted path to the tarn.

A range of inexpensive walking booklets and guides can be picked up from Sam Read Booksellers on Broadgate (015394 35374 www.samread.co.uk).

The Visitors' Book

A walk around Rydal Water

'This walk is one of my — and Wordsworth's — favourite walks in Lakeland. It's suitable for all ages and has something for everyone: an historic home, a church, a lunchtime pub — and caves thrown in for the younger walker. On its own, it's a walk which can be done in under two hours, or, if you want to take in the sites, it makes a very leisurely day.

'You park the car in the large car park at White Moss Common and then take the track uphill which leads away from the main road. This will take you up onto the old Keswick/Ambleside road. From here follow this old road east towards Rydal, providing spectacular views of Rydal Water to your right and Loughrigg Fell beyond.

'As you approach Rydal at the end of the lake, you will arrive at Rydal Mount and Gardens. By now you will probably want to rest your tired feet and I recommend a lunchtime visit to the Badger Bar in the nearby Glen Rothay Hotel, which is famed for its local produce.

'Then, after lunch, the walk continues over the bridge, where Rydal Water squeezes into the River Rothay, and then along a clear path around the south side of the lake. You can take a higher path here, which takes you past two great caves.

'Across the water, the house nestling on the far shore beyond Heron Island is Nab Cottage, another Lakeland literary landmark. You can look for the path to your right, away from the lake, which takes you down through the wood and over a footbridge, back to the main road and White Moss Common once again.'

Marcus Pugh, London

The Wordsworth Attractions

Dove Cottage, the former home of William Wordsworth, stands on the southern outskirts of Grasmere in a tiny hamlet known as Town End. The Wordsworth Trust owns the cottage and a ticket to this attraction includes entrance to the adjacent Wordsworth Museum (see Wet weather). The Trust also own the striking **Jerwood Centre**, which stands close to Dove Cottage and was opened by Seamus Heaney in 2005. The centre contains a large collection of manuscripts, portraits and books relating to Wordsworth and other figures from the Romantic period plus a major Romantic library, but is not open to the public. However, take time to view the building itself as its simple architecture imaginatively marries contemporary design with that of local traditional buildings and is well worth a view. This area also contains a busy tea room (see p.174) and decent-sized gift shop.

Dove Cottage itself is a small, pretty, whitewashed cottage on the outskirts of Grasmere and the most famous of Wordsworth's Lake District homes. The Wordsworths lived in this former coaching inn for eight years (from December 1799 to May 1808) and it was here that William was inspired to write his best work and Dorothy, 'Wordsworth's exquisite sister' as Coleridge called her, penned her famous Grasmere Journals. These journals are an essential read for anyone seeking an insight into life at Dove Cottage and a wider understanding of Lakeland life in the early 19th century. After marrying Wordsworth in 1802, Mary Hutchinson joined William and Dorothy in Dove Cottage and gave birth to three of their five children while living here.

Frequent visitors included other major figures from the Romantic period such as Samuel Taylor Coleridge, Robert Southey and Thomas de Quince who moved into Dove Cottage when the Wordsworths left – look out for his old opium scales. The cottage is much as it would have looked in the Wordsworths' day, containing some of their old furniture and belongings. Knowledgeable tour guides lead parties around the property and its quaint gardens and it takes some imagining to understand how so many people managed to live in such a tiny place and still find room to be creative. Winter is a surprisingly good time to visit, not only are there fewer tourists but real fires blaze in the hearths.

DOVE COTTAGE AND THE WORDSWORTH MUSEUM, south of Grasmere off the A591, LA22 9SH; 015394 35544; www.wordsworth.org.uk; tickets bought in the gift shop £6.50 adults, £4.10 children, £10.30–£15.20 families – depending of the number of adults; open 9.30am– 5.30pm daily, closed 1 Jan–1 Feb.

The **Wordsworth Museum** is housed in an old coachhouse behind Dove Cottage. It was opened in 1936 by the then Poet Laureate, John Masefield, and is the place to learn about the life and work of Wordsworth. The fascinating permanent exhibition features portraits, manuscripts and memorabilia and there's an accompanying programme of temporary exhibitions and major shows relating to the age of Romanticism and the village of Grasmere.

The Wordsworths moved to **Rydal Mount** in 1813 and, although William died here in 1850, his wife Mary continued to rent this large airy house until her death in 1859. The property is now owned by the poet's descendants and has all the feel of a family home – the latter day Wordsworths come to stay every January and recent family photos

RYDAL MOUNT, off the A591 at Rydal, LA22 9LU; 015394 33002; www.rydalmount.co.uk; £5.50 adults, £2 children, £13 families, £2.50 garden, open daily 9.30am–5pm Mar–Oct, 10am–4pm Nov, Dec and Feb (except Tues), closed Jan.

line the shelves. Visitors are free to wander at will through a number of rooms including William and Mary's old bedroom, Dorothy's room and William's attic study which commands outstanding views over Rydal and beyond. The house is filled with furniture, paintings and belongings from William's time and friendly guides are on hand to answer any questions. Equally worth spending time strolling through are Rydal Mount's large gardens, landscaped by William himself they are a pleasant place to linger in fine weather. Also take time to peek into the tiny St Mary's church close to Rydal Mount where Wordsworth was once churchwarden.

Romantic Insights is an excellent way to visit Rydal Mount and Ruskin's former Coniston home, Brantwood (see p.131), in one day. The package provides you with a ticket to each property plus a ride on a solar powered launch from the Waterhead Hotel in Coniston (see

ROMANTIC INSIGHTS, 015394 33002; www.romanticinsights.org; £17.50 adults, £8.70 children; full details of this package are available at Rydal Mount where pre-bookings can be made.

p.126) to Brantwood and a light meal at the Jumping Jenny restaurant (see p.136). The advised schedule starts at Rydal Mount at 9.30am and encourages visitors to use either car share or public transport to the Waterhead Hotel, although free parking is available at the hotel if you do decide to drive. Details of car-free travel is provided on the website and when making a booking.

Wet weather

On rainy days in Grasmere most visitors head to Dove Cottage, the Wordsworth Museum and nearby Rydal Mount as these are the only indoor attractions in the vicinity. That said don't let the odd rain shower deter your from exploring the village itself. Grasmere's eclectic array of shops and the fine Heaton Copper Gallery (see Culture p.60) are a pleasure to explore whatever the weather. St Oswald's church – once Wordsworth's local parish church – feature two striking stained glass windows created by the English Pre- Raphaelite artist Henry Holiday and a striking statue of the Madonna and Child by Ophelia Bell, the late wife of local artist William Heaton Cooper.

CELEBRITY CONNECTIONS

Many well-known celebrities make their way to this region of the Lakes for a holiday. **Jude and Sadie Law** have been spied in the area and **Sting**, real name Gordon Sumner, is known to have a holiday cottage near Grasmere.

Although the film director **Ken Russell** is more associated with Keswick and Borrowdale to the north, he used a disused slate quarry near Rydal caves as a location in his 1988 film adaptation of Bram Stoker's *The Lair of the White Worm*.

 ## What to do with children...

Right in the middle of this mainly adult orientated village is the **Story Teller's Garden**, one of the Lake District's most delightful attractions for children. The garden is home to Tales in Trust, a centre for storytelling in northern England, and is used as a venue for a

THE STORY TELLER'S GARDEN, opposite St Oswald's church, LA22 9SW; 015394 35641; www.taffythomas.co.uk; £5 adult, £3 children, £12 families; various events throughout the year. (Storytelling with Taffy Thomas also on first Tues of the month 7.30pm at the Watermill Inn at Ings) see p.116.

Taffy Thomas, resident storyteller

programme of family storytelling events that take place throughout the year. A list of events is available on the website of Taffy Thomas, the resident storyteller, or posted in the window of his fairy-tale cottage located next door to the garden. The Halloween and Christmas events are especially magical and even if there's no storytelling session on when you're visiting, make sure your children take a peek into this enchanting garden.

Dove Cottage and the Wordsworth Museum (see p.166) organise family activities such as painting, treasure hunts and story and poem writing, during the school holidays (except Christmas). Written children's guides to the museum are also available.

Entertainment

Literary events

The Wordsworth Trust (www.wordsworth.org.uk) runs a regular programme of evening poetry readings by top name poets – described by Andrew Motion as 'the best poetry programme in Britain' – and daytime lectures. Full details are available on the Trust's website or you can pick up a brochure at Dove Cottage. Pre-booking is essential as all of these events are very popular.

Special events

From the end of July until the beginning of September the Lake Artists Society (www.lakeartists.org.uk) – a society of fine artists based in the Lake District – hold their popular annual exhibition in Grasmere's Village Hall. Many of the 300 exhibits of paintings and sculpture are inspired by the Cumbrian landscape, but expect to see work on other subjects as well.

The annual **Grasmere Sports and Show** (www.grasmeresportsandshow.co.uk) has been running since 1852 and is held on the August Bank Holiday Sunday in a showground at the junction of the A591 and Stock Lane. Watch traditional Lakeland sports such as Cumberland wrestling and modern outdoor pursuits including mountain bike races, plus a range of fell races such as the infamous 'Guides Race' which involves a near vertical hillside and some very fit runners. Additional entertainment includes racing pigs and dancing dogs! Tickets £7.20 adults and £2.50 children.

Grasmere's rushbearing is an ancient ceremony held at St Oswald's church on the nearest Saturday to St Oswald's Day (5 August). The ceremony dates back to a time when church floors were mere earth and rushes were strewn on them for warmth and as a means of purifying the air. After church floors became flagged most rushbearing ceremonies died out and St Oswald's is one of only five Cumbrian churches who carry on the tradition. Today a procession bearing rushes and flowers and starring six maids of honour, makes its way through the village to the church. Following a special rushbearing service, people head for the grounds of Grasmere School where local gingerbread is dished out and children's sports take place.

Shopping

Grasmere is one of the best places to shop in the South Lakes. The **Heaton Cooper Studios** (see p.6) is the place to pick up regional fine art – you can get everything from original work to postcard reproductions – and budding artists can choose from a selection of fine artists' materials. The pick of Grasmere's other stores includes **Elk Home** on College Street (015394 35154 www.elkhome.co.uk)

The Visitors' Book

The perfect day in Grasmere

'It would be rude to visit the Grasmere area and not visit Dove Cottage. The guided tours run every half hour and if you arrive early you may be lucky enough to be the only person on the tour; avoid the middle of the day when the bulk of the tourist traffic arrives. If you get a chance, see the garden — the view from the top is stunningly beautiful.

'Grasmere village itself is picturesque and worth exploring. Be sure to pick up some of the famous gingerbread from Sarah Nelson's shop. For lunch one of the best ideas is to make a picnic and head out up the Coffin Trail that runs uphill past Dove Cottage. Either follow the path for a couple of miles through to Rydal (where you can also visit Rydal Mount) or branch off left from the Coffin Trail and head up to Alcock Tarn. The walk is steep and about 4 miles, but it has rewarding views.

'After lunch I'd head out as quickly as possible on your main walk. A walk that is (relatively) easy to accomplish is up to Easedale Tarn. Follow the signs out from Easedale Road in Grasmere and you'll reach the tarn. On the way up make sure that you stop to admire the view from the Sour Milk Gill waterfall. Back in Grasmere reward yourself with an ice cream/hot drink/stiff whisky — all are to be found in walking/hobbling distance when you arrive back.'

Lexi Drayton, Hampshire

which sells funky gifts and homeware, **Mother Earth** on Church Bridge (015394 35166 www.motherearth.co.uk) which makes and sells a range of sensuous natural skincare products and Barney's Newsbox (015394 35627 www.barneys-newsbox.co.uk) a jigsaw specialist where you can choose from hundreds of different sized puzzles.

Grasmere is also home to the **English Lakes Perfumery** (www.purelakes.co.uk) and **Beck Steps Gift Shop** on College Street (015394 35820) stocks their range of natural and organic fragrances and skin and haircare products. You can also pick up their wares at local festivals and fairs.

 The best... PLACES TO STAY

HOTEL

Lancrigg

Easedale, Grasmere, LA22 9QN
015394 35317
www.lancrigg.co.uk

Lancrigg is a luxurious vegetarian country house hotel in peaceful settings on the outskirts of Grasmere. The rambling building is a former home of the playwright and feminist Eliza Fletcher and boasts many other literary connections. The hotel's excellent organic vegetarian restaurant is famous throughout the Lakes.

Price: B&B and evening meal from £65–£95 pppn.

HOTEL/ORGANIC

Moss Grove

Located just past Grasmere Church,
LA22 9SW
015394 35251
www.mossgrove.co.uk

A completely organic, environmentally conscious hotel – even the paint is organic – in the heart of Grasmere. All rooms and suites are individually decorated and embody the principles of simple luxury. The Mediterranean breakfast is served buffet style in a farmhouse kitchen and organic wine is available.

Price: B&B £125–£250 per room per night.

The best... PLACES TO STAY

R&B/ORGANIC

Cote How

Located just off the A591 at Pelter Bridge near Rydal, LA22 9LW
015394 32765
www.cotehow.co.uk

The oldest part of this luxury, environmentally friendly guest house dates back to medieval times. There's no TV but plenty of games, books and organic beer and wine to enjoy instead and the organic tea rooms serve delicious lunches. Those wanting an active holiday have plenty of outdoor activities to choose from.

Price: B&B £45–£65 pppn.

B & B

Nab Cottage

Located two miles south of Grasmere off the A591, LA22 9SD.
015394 35311
www.rydalwater.com

Built in 1565 and extended in 1702, Nab Cottage sits on the edge of Rydal Water and is the former family home of de Quincey's wife (the poet's opium room is still here) and Coleridge's son, Hartley. A relaxing lounge overlooking the lake is a perfect reading spot and good walking spreads out in all directions.

Price: B&B £26–£29 pppn.

SELF-CATERING

Howthwaite

Grasmere
01628 82529
www.landmarktrust.co.uk

Howthwaite is an airy 1920s house with a large, wild garden standing directly behind Dove Cottage and owned by the Landmark Trust. Dorothy Wordsworth records her brother walking and writing in the countryside around this cottage and fabulous lake views abound. Full address and postcode is supplied after booking.

Price: £683–£2,219 per week, shorter booking available. Sleeps up to seven.

Hollens Farm Cottage

Grasmere, LA22 9QZ
015394 36088
www.grasmereholidaycottage.co.uk

Owned by a family who have lived in Grasmere for 400 years and situated in a quiet spot on the outskirts of town, this delightful property was once a dairyman's cottage. Natural pine features throughout and the flagstone kitchen comes complete with a Rayburn cooker. Rent includes membership to a nearby leisure club.

Price: £395–£595 per week. Sleeps four.

The best... FOOD AND DRINK

Grasmere is famous for its delicious gingerbread but it also has a regional reputation for its fine restaurants and whether you're meat eaters or committed vegetarians you'll find first-class places to eat out in the village.

▶ Staying in

Sarah Nelson's Gingerbread Shop

Sarah Nelson's Gingerbread Shop (01539 35428 www.grasmereginger bread.co.uk) next door to St Oswald's churchyard is famed throughout the land for its hearty, spicy gingerbread. The shop is housed in the old village school which opened in 1630 and is where Wordsworth, his wife and sister all taught – you can still see the old school coat pegs. Gingerbread has been made here since the mid-19th century and bakers still follow an old secret recipe that's locked away in a nearby bank vault for safe keeping. Jamie Oliver has been known to sing the praises of Grasmere's gingerbread and customers have included actors, celebrities and politicians. The gingerbread is certainly sturdy stuff and a perfect snack to sustain you on a long walk in the fells. However, for more healthy picnic food aim for **Newby's Delicatessen and Bakery** on Red Lion Square for a range of gourmet sandwiches, local cheeses, chutneys and jams and freshly baked pies.

For takeaway head to **Tweedies** (015394 35300) inside the **Dale Lodge Hotel** which does takeaway pizzas in the evening, but call ahead in the day if possible as they sometimes run out of pizza dough.

🍸 Drinking

Tweedies bar inside the **Dale Lodge Hotel**, with its flagstone floors, wood-burning stove, range of real ales and fine wine, is all you can wish for in a good Lakeland pub. If you want to sample a range of local beers ask for a bat of ale, which is literally a bat containing three third of a pint glasses which you can ask to be filled with different ales. Tweedies is also the place to catch live music. Other popular drinking spots in Grasmere itself are the **Dove and Olive Branch** at the Wordsworth Hotel in the centre of the village and the **Lamb Inn** on Red Lion Square. On the outskirts of town the **Traveller's Rest** off the A591 is popular with both locals and visitors and the **Badger Bar** at the Glen Rothay hotel near Rydal Mount is an old 17th-century coaching inn that's full of character and fine ales.

EATING OUT

RESTAURANT
The Jumble Room
Langdale Road, Grasmere, LA22 9SU
015394 35188
www.thejumbleroom.co.uk

This funky and friendly restaurant in the heart of Grasmere, with a focus on world cuisine and local meats (dinner mains £13–£20), is a must for a meal out. The eclectic décor includes large oil paintings of cows and old album covers line the toilet walls. Open for lunch from noon and dinner from 6pm. Evening reservations recommended.

The Lodge
Dale Lodge Hotel, Grasmere, LA22 9SW
015394 35300
www.dalelodgehotel.co.uk

Choose between the intimate surroundings of the hotel restaurant or their busy bar, Tweedies – both serve the same food. The menu includes plenty of meat and Mexican dishes plus veggie and fish options. Evening mains cost £10–£15 and the wine list is excellent.

RESTAURANT/CAFÉ
Dove Cottage Tea Rooms/Villa Colombina
Off A591, near Dove Cottage, LA22 9SH
015394 35268

This popular establishment is a busy tea room by day (10am–5pm) and popular licensed restaurant (Villa Colombina) serving a combination of moderately priced traditional English and Italian cuisine by night (from 5.30pm). The décor is warm and inviting and evening reservations are recommended.

VEGETARIAN
Lancrigg
Easedale, Grasmere, LA22 9QN
015394 35317
www.lancrigg.co.uk

Open to non-residents, Lancrigg serves excellent vegetarian cuisine in the elegant setting of its Georgian dining room. Organic beers and wines are available and vegans and other special diets catered for. Open all day from 8.30am for breakfast, lunch, afternoon tea and dinner

CAFÉ
Miller's Howe Café
Red Lion Square, Grasmere, LA22 9SX
015394 35234

This licensed café near the village green is a good fair weather option as it makes for a pleasant place to sit outside on a summer's day. Open for lunch only and serving a range of meals such as homity pie for around £7 and lighter options including cream cheese toasted muffins.

Baldry's
Red Lion Square, Grasmere, LA22 9SP
015394 35301

Baldry's, hugely popular with the locals, is an inexpensive café that serves a hearty range of home-made food. It's located right in the centre of the village and is a perfect spot from which to watch the world go by while you eat.

Local Knowledge

Rebecca Heaton Cooper is the fourth generation of artists from the Heaton Cooper family. Brought up in Ambleside and Grasmere, she left the Lakes to study fashion and textiles at the University of Northumbria and worked for various designers including designing clothes for Marks and Spencer. After growing tired of living away from the Lakes, Becky moved back to Grasmere and today creates her own art while also helping to manage the family studio. As someone who appreciates good food, Becky knows all the best places to eat in the area.

Favourite restaurant: The Jumble Room. There's always a warm atmosphere with great music and the puddings are to die for.

Favourite café: Baldrey's – lovely home-made everything!

Secret tip for lunch: Take a picnic up to a quiet spot on Silver How.

Favourite takeaway: Doi Ithanon in Ambleside, truly authentic Thai food. I love going to eat in, but it's such a treat to take it home.

Best view: When I come round Penny Rock corner on the A591, I get a view of Grasmere and Helm Crag and a feeling of coming home. My grandfather painted this view many times and sometimes customers in the studio see his paintings and claim the view doesn't ever look that way. But I've seen it in many different moods, just as he captured it.

Best walk: Silver Howe overlooking Grasmere. There are many ways to get there, but my favourite is past Score Crag. Turn up the road to Allen Bank, make the steep ascent past the lovely juniper bushes. From here you can decide whether to carry on up to the summit or walk along the ridge towards Langdale. Silver Howe rewards walkers with beautiful views without having to make too much effort. You can walk all day or for just a couple of hours. You might even see the deer if you're lucky.

Favourite treat: Having friends to stay and going for a good long walk that ends with a beer at Tweedies in Grasmere.

175

ⓘ Visitor Information

Tourist Information Centres:
No tourist information centre in
Grasmere; Tourist Board Visitor
Information Point inside the lobby of
the Dale Lodge Hotel; also see
www.grasmere-village.com for
information on the village, its history
and places to visit, eat and stay.

Hospitals: Minor Injuries Unit,
Keswick Cottage Hospital, Crosthwaite
Road, CA12 5PH, 017687 67000;
Ambleside Health Centre (see p.102)
will also deal with minor injuries; for
more serious problems Lancaster
Royal Infirmary, Ashton Road,
Lancaster, LA1 4RP, 01524 65944; or
Furness General Hospital, Dalton
Lane, Barrow-in-Furness, LA14 4LF,
01229 870870.

Doctors: Ambleside Health Centre,
see p.102.

Pharmacies: Grasmere Pharmacy,
Oakbank, Broadgate LA22 9TA,
015394 3553, www.grasmere
pharmacy.com, 9am–5.30pm
Mon–Fri, Sat 9am–1pm.

Police: PC Malcolm MacLennan,
015397 22611.

Supermarkets: There's a small Co-op
in Grasmere.

Parking: closest to Dove Cottage,
Stock Lane off the A591; a left turn at
the end of Stock Lane leads to Red
Bank Road; Swan Lane, off the A591
just past the garden centre;
Broadgate, to the north of the village
just past a children's play area; for
walking around Rydal Water car parks
on either side of the A591 between
Rydal Mount and Nab Cottage.

Cashpoint: The only cashpoint in
Grasmere is inside the Post Office,
which charges a fee for use; some
banks supply cash over the counter
for no charge; the local Co-op does
cashback.

Internet Access: At the time of writing
the Faeryland Tea Garden (see p.164)
is planning to install internet access.

Bike Rental: Ambleside, see p.102.

Taxis: Grasmere Taxis, 015394
35506.

The best of... THE FELLS AND PEAKS

THE LAKE DISTRICT CONTAINS OVER 200 DRAMATIC FELLS, ALL OF WHICH HAVE BEEN WALKED, DRAWN AND MADE MADE FAMOUS BY WAINWRIGHT. THIS IS ENGLAND'S ONLY MOUNTAINOUS REGION AND ITS DRAMATIC PEAKS ARE PARADISE TO MANY WALKERS, CLIMBERS AND THOSE WHO SIMPLY WANT TO ENJOY VIEWS OF THE ENGLISH COUNTRYSIDE AT ITS MOST STUNNING.

Top: Striding Edge; Middle: Fell ponies; Bottom: Great Langdale

Top: Ascent of Skiddaw; Middle: Lords Rake; Bottom: The ruins of Sleddale Hall

Top: Walkers climb Helvellyn from the Thirlmere side; Middle: The Topiary Garden at Levens Hall;
Bottom: Ewes and their lambs on a quiet lane in the Northern Fells

Top: The view down Borrowdale from Castle Crag; Middle: Cald Beck flows through a sandstone gorge at Watersmeet;
Bottom: The hamlet of Hartsop

THE LANGDALES

The area to the south-west of Grasmere is known generically as 'the Langdales' and consists of two Langdales – Great Langdale and Little Langdale. By far the more popular and easier to access is Great Langdale whose wide valley opens out after the B5343 the only road into the dale – past the tiny community of Chapel Stile. Great Langdale is walled in by the heights of the Langdale Pikes and some of the great names in Lake District peaks such as Crinkle Craggs and Bowfell and is one of the most impressive sights in the Lake District. This is for serious walkers, climbers and fell runners territory and a string of good pubs and hotels caters for them and less energetic visitors.

Little Langdale runs parallel with, and to the south of, Great Langdale and with its lower hills makes for picturesque rather than dramatic terrain. The road through Little Langdale is narrow and far less travelled by visitors making this dale a good option for those seeking some off the beaten track peace and quiet.

At the western end of Little Langdale a narrow road twists and turns over Wrynose Pass whose name means 'pass of the stallion', warning travellers that only fit horses were suitable for this old packhorse trail. At the top of this exhilarating pass is the Three Shires Stone that marks the meeting point of the three old counties of Westmorland, Cumberland and Lancashire, which existed before the 1974 county changes created Cumbria.

Above Bad Step on Crinkle Craggs

At Cockley Beck just past Wrynose you can either head south towards Broughton-in-Furness or brave England's steepest and scariest road over Hardkott Pass to the impressive remains of a Roman fort and onto Eskdale in the Western Lakes – expect an overall gradient of 1 in 3 or 33% that rises to 1 in 2.5 in places. This ancient and remote link with the coast was well used by smugglers and tales of their illicit trade are rife along Wrynose Pass and into Little Langdale.

Located between the two Langdales and to the south of Chapel Stile is Elterwater, a tiny community popular with self caterers and youth hostellers and those seeking to chill out on its village green in summer. At the turning into Great Langdale off the main A593 is Skelwith Bridge, you'll find the excellent Chesters shop and café and a cluster of unusual slate picnic tables overlooking the River Brathay.

All of this makes the Langdales an excellent choice for those seeking to escape, get stuck into some good walking or just relax in the region's welcoming hotels or pretty self-catering cottages and drink in some of the finest views the Lake District has to offer.

WHAT TO SEE AND DO

Fair weather

There are numerous Roman remains scattered throughout the Lakes but the ruins of their remote fort at **Hardknott Pass** are by far the most evocative and best preserved. Built between AD120 and AD138 under the rule of Emperor Hadrian and called Mediobogdum by the Romans, Hardknott was designed to house 500 soldiers and formed part of the defence of their road from Ravenglass to Ambleside. The fort is thought to have been destroyed by local tribes in AD197 and today the partially reconstructed ruins cover 3 acres and include remains of the old commandant's house, a bath house and parade ground. The commanding views over Hardknott Pass and into nearby Eskdale prove the point of building the fort in the first place, although there's no denying that life at 853ft above sea level must have been pretty bleak when winter closed in.

This most spectacular of Lake District attractions is also one of the hardest to reach as you have to negotiate the scary road from Little Langdale which leads over both Wrynose and Hardknott Passes – don't expect a bus service up here. If you're also planning to spend time in the Western Lakes, visit this attraction via the road from Eskdale, which leads through Boot to Hardknott. Although still narrow and steep, it's an easier drive.

HARDKNOTT ROMAN FORT, on the west side of Hardknott Pass; www.english-heritage.org.uk; open all the time and access is free.

Walking

The Langdales is one of the most popular areas for walkers in the Lakes and countless routes for all abilities lead from the car parks along the B5343. However, there are few gentle strolls here and only those with a reasonable degree of fitness and good pair of walking shoes should venture too far in this terrain.

A good place for beginners to start is the Stickle Ghyll car park next door to the Sticklebarn Tavern. Here you'll find some National Trust information boards detailing the geology of the area and the starting points for a number of low-level and more challenging walks. Those seeking altogether more gentle terrain can walk along a marked footpath by the side of the River Brathay from **Skelwith Bridge** to **Elterwater**. The walk begins opposite the car park just past the Talbot Bar off the B5343.

If you're not driving, catch the Langdale bus (service 516) that runs between Ambleside and the end of the B5343 at the Old Dungeon Ghyll Hotel. This service also travels to Kendal Bus Station and Windermere Railway Station at weekends and public holidays. Pick up a timetable from Tourist Information or contact Stagecoach (0871 200 2233 www.stagecoachbus.com) for further information. Inexpensive walking guides can be picked up at the Co-op in Chapel Stile.

Wet weather

Apart from curling up with a good book, your only real option in the Langdales when wet weather closes in over the fells is to pamper yourself at the **Langdale Estate's** superb leisure club. Facilities include a fabulous indoor heated pool, large spa pool, gym, sauna and Jacuzzi. You can also indulge in beauty treatments and various therapies.

THE LANGDALE ESTATE, off the B5343, Great Langdale, nr Grasmere LA22 9JD; 015394 37302; www.langdale.co.uk; day pass £9.50, can be used all day except between 4pm–6.30pm (residents only); twilight pass £7 admits non-residents after 7pm; no prior booking required.

Entertainment

Special events

The Langdale Gala takes place every year on the first Sunday in July at Walthwaite Meadow in Chapel Stile off the B5343. This large fête, set against the stunning backdrop of the Langdales, includes a host of traditional events such as Cumberland and Westmorland wrestling, stick making, fell running and slate-riving. It is an entertaining day out for locals and visitors alike.

Shopping

In Elterwater you'll find the studio of traditional Lakeland artist Judy Boyes (07071 780533 www.judyboyes.co.uk). Located close to the Britannia Inn, the studio is open Easter–October, Wednesday to Saturday 10am–5.15pm, November–Christmas; Thursday–Saturday, 10am–4pm and all bank holidays.

 # *The best...* PLACES TO STAY

HOTEL

New Dungeon Ghyll

Located off the B5343, Great Langdale, nr Grasmere, LA22 9JX
015394 37213
www.dungeon-ghyll.com

Located at the head of the Langdale Valley, the New Dungeon Ghyll dates back to medieval times and is crammed with character. Walk up the Langdale Pikes from the doorstep, or admire the views from the cosy lounge.

Price: B&B £47–£60 pppn, special deals available.

Old Dungeon Ghyll

Located off the B5343, Great Langdale, nr Grasmere, LA22 9JY
015394 37272
www.odg.co.uk

The Old Dungeon Ghyll stands at the end of the B5343 – there's nothing but fells after this – and is seriously popular with walkers, climbers and locals. The restaurant serves hearty home-made meals and what the hotel lacks in glamour, it more than makes up for in history, character and a warm welcome.

Price: B&B £50–£53 pppn, special deals available.

INN

The Three Shires Inn

Little Langdale, just west of the A593, near Grasmere LA22 9NZ.
015394 37215
www.threeshiresinn.co.uk

This charming inn stands in a peaceful spot in the middle of Little Langdale. A pretty veranda overlooks the Tilberthwaite fells and open fires crackle in the lounge in winter. Walking, photography and painting holidays are also on offer.

Price: B&B £37–£51 pppn.

The best... PLACES TO STAY

Britannia Inn

**Elterwater, south of the B5343 near
Grasmere, LA22 9HP**
015394 37210
www.britinn.co.uk

Standing in the heart of the tiny
community of Elterwater, the Britannia
is an old oak-beamed pub famous for
real ales and value-for-money food.
The refurbished rooms are
comfortable but small – the inn is 500
years old – and the outdoor terrace is
the place to sit on a sunny afternoon.

Price: £44–£57 pppn.

CAMPSITE

Great Langdale

**Off the B5343 near the Old Dungeon
Ghyll, LA22 9JY**
015394 37668
www.ntlakescampsites.org.uk

A very popular National Trust
campsite surrounded by stunning
countryside and within walking
distance of three great pubs – the
New and Old Dungeon Ghylls and
Sticklebarn Tavern. The site accepts
tents and camper vans and there's a
well-stocked on-site shop plus a
laundry and children's playground.
Advance booking advised in summer.

Price: Nightly rates £4.50–£4.80 per
adult, £2 per child, £3 per vehicle.

SELF-CATERING

Greenbank Holiday Apartments

**Greenbank, Skelworth Bridge, off the
A593 nr Grasmere, LA22 9NW**
015394 33236
www.visitgreenbank.co.uk

Two attractive and cosy holiday
apartments each set up for one couple
and with their own private gardens.
This is a convenient spot for the
Langdales, Grasmere, Ambleside and
Hawkshead and close to numerous
fine pubs, first-class restaurants and
plenty of good walking.

Price: £200–£380 per week. Both
cottages sleep two.

Descent by the side of Dungeon Ghyll

181

The best... FOOD AND DRINK

The Langdales has a generous sprinkling of fine pubs, all of which come with stunning views and serve good food and fine beers and wines. Some are perfect places to head if you're still muddy from walking the fells and gasping for a pint, while others are more suited to fine dining. Those seeking the latter will also find more upmarket restaurants in the limited number of hotels in this area.

▶ Staying in

Sign outside Chapel Stile Co-op

The only place to buy in food in the Langdales is the small local **Co-op** in Chapel Stile which sells a range of local produce including regional beers, Hawkshead relishes and local jams. Above the Co-op, **Brambles Café** (015394 37500) is open daily from 9am to 5pm and sells takeaway picnics of rolls and cakes for £5.60 and fills up flasks – £1.80 for tea and £2.50 for coffee.

For farm shops head to **Millbeck Farm** off the B5343 in Great Langdale (015394 37364 www.millbeckfarm .co.uk) which sells its own home-produced Herdwick lamb and Angus beef which you can pick up at the farm or arrange to be delivered.

🍸 Drinking

All of the pubs featured in the Where to Stay and Eating Out sections are also fine places to drink in the evenings. Pick of them all is the **Hiker's Bar** at the Old Dungeon Ghyll with its worn flagstone floors, battered old tables and atmosphere thick with the tales of walkers and climbers. **The Talbot Bar**, located inside the Skelworth Bridge Hotel off the A593 at Skelworth Bridge, is also worth a try if you want somewhere closer to a main road.

EATING OUT

All of the hotels and inns featured in the Places to Stay section are also good places to eat. Listed below are a few more.

FINE DINING
Purdey's Restaurant
The Langdale Estate, off the B5343, Great Langdale, LA22 9JD
015394 37394
www.langdale.co.uk

One of the restaurants attached to the luxurious but low key Langdale Estate, Purdey's is the place to head if you fancy sophisticated dining off the beaten track. Expect to pay around £23 for two courses of contemporary cuisine served in upmarket rustic surroundings and accompanied by a fine wine list.

PUB
The Wainwright's Inn
Chapel Stile off the B5343, Great Langdale, LA22 9JD
015394 38088

The Wainwright's Inn is far enough off the main road to provide spectacular views but close enough to be easy to reach. The food is traditional pub fare (mains under £10) with veggie options and a range of salads and jacket spuds. The outside terrace is fab and real ale free flowing.

Sticklebarn Tavern
Located off the B5343, Great Langdale, Grasmere, LA22 9JX
015394 37356

Neighbours with the New Dungeon Ghyll (see p.180), the Sticklebarn Tavern is yet another fine pub in the Langdales with an outdoor terrace offering diners unbelievably good views. This popular flagstone pub serves hearty pub grub for around £8 and offers a good selection for vegetarians and children.

CAFÉ
Chesters by the River
Skelwith Bridge, off the A593, LA22 9NN
015394 32553
www.chesters-cafebyteriver.co.uk

Chesters is a fabulous and extremely popular licensed riverside café. Open for drinks and delicious home-made cakes in the morning and simple but stylish lunches (£8–£13) from noon. The outdoor terrace overlooking the River Brathay is a perfect spot for summer dining, or relaxing on a sofa by the wood-burning stove in winter.

ⓘ Visitor Information

Tourist Information Centres:
There are no tourist offices
in the Langdales; see
www.langdaleweb.co.uk for
useful information for visitors.

Supermarkets: A small, well-stocked
Co-op in Chapel Stile, open daily
9am–5pm.

Parking: Parking is not permitted on
the B5343 in Great Langdale – walkers
or those visiting the pubs along this
road should park in one of the pay and
display car parks next to the Old
Dungeon Ghyll and Sticklebarn Tavern
and opposite the entrance to the New
Dungeon Ghyll; in Little Langdale at
Blea Tarn; in Elterwater parking
available near the village green.

See also Visitor Information in the
Grasmere section, p.176.

Skelworth Bridge

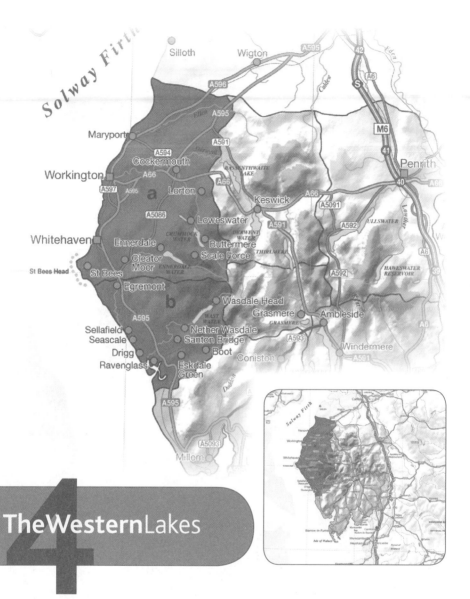

TheWestern**Lakes**

4

a. The north-western Lakes

b. The south-western Lakes

Unmissable highlights

01 Gazing at Britain's Favourite View over West Water in the Wasdale Valley, p.211

02 Muncaster Castle near Ravenglass has numerous attractions and is an entertaining day out for the whole family, p.214

03 A walk around Lake Buttermere is good for all ages and levels of fitness and provides classically picture-perfect Lake District views, p.193

04 The Ravenglass and Eskdale Railway is a fun way to reach amazing scenery and its stations are good starting points for numerous walks and cycle rides, p.212

05 St Bees Head is an easy to reach place from which to view the north Cumbrian coast and its diverse birdlife, p.195

06 The Sellafield Visitor's Centre is the place to learn about and engage with the production of energy in Cumbria, p.216

07 The Rum Story immerses visitors in Whitehaven life during the slave-trade era and other regions associated with its triangular route, p.200

08 Wordsworth House in Cockermouth provides visitors with a sense of 18th-century town life and the childhoods of William and Dorothy, p.189

09 Whitehaven's harbour is steeped in maritime and industrial history and you can still take a trip onto the ocean from its slipway with Whitehaven Marine Adventures, p.190

10 The annual World's Biggest Liar Competition is an entertaining and uniquely Cumbrian night out, p.221

THE WESTERN LAKES

The western region of the Lake District starts at the end of a number of passes – Whinlatter, Honister and Hardknott – which thread their often precarious way through the mountain peaks that separate this area from the central fells and more well-known areas of the National Park. Few first time visitors venture this far away from either the M6 or West Coast Mainline and many of the families and couples that do travel here often come from neighbouring areas of the north, and have been visiting the region for years and know that this west side is one of the Lake District's best-kept secrets.

The lakes that populate the inland regions are uncommercialised and unspoilt, the most famous of which is Wast Water, voted Britain's Favourite View in a recent ITV poll. Many travel to these lakes, and the countryside that surrounds them, to walk, climb or cycle, while others come to simply enjoy the views and renowned local pubs.

The Western Lakes are a good choice for those on a limited budget. On the whole accommodation is cheaper here than in the busier parts of the National Park and there are some surprisingly luxurious and often quirky options to choose from.

The other main draw to this area is the Cumbrian coast, which is filled with a wide variety of family orientated attractions, industrial heritage, wildlife and areas of outstanding natural beauty. However, don't travel here expecting to find traditional bucket and spade British seaside. This is a working coastline dotted with maritime communities and underpinned with a seafaring history rich with stories of the Romans, the slave-trade and the smuggling of illegally imported goods into the region from the Isle of Man and Ireland.

Cumbria's coast is also a major provider of energy. In the middle of it stands Sellafield, on the site of the world's first commercial nuclear power station, while further north between Maryport and Workington you can practically touch the wind turbines that line the coast road. This road, which becomes the A595 at Whitehaven, marks the dividing point between coast and countryside and is the only major route through the region. If you can, drive it as the sun is setting over the Irish Sea on one side and the western peaks of the Lake District are shining in its fading light on the other.

THE NORTH-WESTERN LAKES

This diverse region of Cumbria is split into two distinct areas – the collection of inland lakes that make up the far north-west corner of the Lake District and the busy communities, some coastal, that sit outside the National Park's boundaries.

The inland Lakes are split into two further areas. The first contains the three lakes of Buttermere, Crummock Water and Loweswater, all of which are easily reached from Keswick and popular with day trippers, especially in the summer and on fine weather weekends. The countryside surrounding these lakes, and the terrain around Ennerdale Water to the south, is laced with many walking and cycling routes which cater for all levels of experience and fitness, and are as popular with Sunday afternoon strollers, as they are with serious outdoor enthusiasts.

Ennerdale Water, the second inland area of this region, is about as far off the beaten track as you can reach by car in the Lake District. There's little in the way of facilities around the shores of this little-known lake and no quick route from other areas of the National Park, only minor roads leading from the coast. All of which makes this an excellent choice for those wanting to get away from the tourist crowds and enjoy a day of walking, cycling or picnicking around its shores.

Of the communities outside of the National Park, Cockermouth is the most popular with visitors. It's located on the main A66, which leads from the M6 junction at Penrith to the coast at Workington, and is well worth a day trip or longer stay. There are a number of attractions and fine restaurants in the town itself, plus some first-class accommodation options in its vicinity, making Cockermouth a good base for those who want to be close to all that the north-west has to offer visitors – lively communities, wild countryside and rugged coastline.

Situated on the coast is Whitehaven, the other main community in this region, which hit national headlines in October 2007 when it became the first place in Britain to have its analogue television signal cut off and go entirely digital – just one of this town's often surprising claims to fame. There are a number of excellent attractions in and around Whitehaven's large harbour, most of which appeal to all ages, making this town one of the best places in the north-west region to visit with children.

Most other visitor attractions along the coast are in Maryport, a small community that teeters around a tiny harbour, which was once an important Roman port. However, the coastline itself, and the wildlife that lives along it, is also one of this area's biggest draws and the best place to see it from is St Bees Head, to the south of Whitehaven. This dramatic cliff provides stunning views along the north Cumbrian coast and out to the Irish Sea where, if you're lucky, you'll spot porpoises, basking sharks, dolphins and seals, all of which frequent the waters around this area.

WHAT TO SEE AND DO

Fair weather

Cockermouth

Cockermouth sits on the outskirts of the north-west border of the Lake District National Park, just 14 miles from Keswick. The town is named after the River Cocker which pours into the River Derwent to the north of Main Street and its wide, tree-lined roads are a refreshing alternative to the narrow lanes that characterise many Lakeland communities.

Its proximity to Scotland once made Cockermouth vulnerable to border raids and Robert the Bruce attacked the town in 1315. However, don't expect to be able to visit the castle that took the brunt of this, and other attacks, as Cockermouth's Norman, partly ruined castle remains a private residence which only throws open its ancient doors to the public during the town's summer festival.

The main attraction in Cockermouth is Wordsworth's birthplace. Built in 1745, the house is a fine example of the town's predominantly Georgian architecture and is as worthy of a visit as their more famous residences – Dove Cottage and Rydal Mount (see p.166–167). **Wordsworth House**, a large distinguished Georgian building in the centre of town that offers visitors the chance to delve deep into the world of William's and Dorothy's childhoods. The house has been fastidiously restored to its 18th-century glory and provides a real insight into the Wordsworth household of the time. In some rooms visitors are allowed to touch exhibits making this a good attraction to visit with children and make sure you leave time to enjoy the walled riverside kitchen garden which changes with the seasons.

> **WORDSWORTH HOUSE**, Main Street at the point where it meets the A5086 (Crown Street) CA13 9RX; 01900 824805; www.wordsworthhouse.org.uk; £4.90 adults, £2.60 children, £13.50 families; open 11am–4.30pm Mon–Sat Easter to Oct.

Also worth a visit in Cockermouth is the **Castlegate House Gallery**, a contemporary art gallery that specialises in the work of northern English and Scottish artists, particularly Cumbrian painters, but also exhibits paintings,

> **CASTLEGATE HOUSE GALLERY**, opposite the entrance to Cockermouth Castle, Castlegate Drive CA13 9HA; 01900 822149; www.castlegate house.co.uk; admission free; open 10am–5pm Fri, Sat and Mon, 2.30pm–4.30pm Sun.

sculptures, ceramics, prints and jewellery from artists around the world. There's a varied programme of changing exhibitions and the gallery's outdoor walled secret garden displays large sculptures.

Whitehaven

Situated 14 miles south-west of Cockermouth off the main A595 coast road, Whitehaven is a longer journey for day trippers from other regions of the Lake District, but quick and easy to reach for those staying in the western reaches of the National Park.

Whitehaven's wide harbour has recently been treated to a smart multimillion-pound renovation and on a fine day there's no better place to breathe in the fresh sea air and panoramic views of the Solway Firth, and get up close to the maritime history this stretch of coast is famous for.

Whitehaven harbour

The slave-trade forms a prominent part of this history and Whitehaven prospered so much during this era that for a brief period in the 18th century its harbour was the third busiest in Britain after London and Bristol. The place to learn all about this era is the Rum Story, an entertaining and educational attraction that's one of the best places in town to visit with children (see below).

You can follow a footpath that leads up and along the cliff from behind the Beacon to the **Haig Colliery Mining Museum**. This fascinating attraction provides visitors with an in-depth insight into the history of the mining industry that grew around this area's small coalfield and the harsh reality of life for those who worked in the pits. The Haig Colliery closed in 1986 making it the last of Cumbria's deep coalmines and its pits included the world's first undersea pit which extended out underneath the Solway Firth. Ongoing restoration work is steadily breathing new life into the workings of the mine after they fell into a state of disrepair following closure. Old photographs and documents in the museum chart the history of the mine and its many disasters.

HAIG COLLIERY MINING MUSEUM, half a mile south of the centre of Whitehaven on Solway Road, CA28 9BG; 01946 599949; www.haigpit.com; admission free; open daily 9am–4.30pm.

Also overlooking the harbour is Jonathan Swift's house (not open to the public) a former inn where the famous author lived for a short period of time as a young boy. Local legend claims that the view from his window of Whitehaven's bustling harbour below inspired Swift's most famous novel, *Gulliver's Travels*.

Like Cockermouth, the architecture of Whitehaven's bustling town centre is mainly Georgian and its grid system layout, with the large St Nicholas Church at its centre, is considered to be the first post-Renaissance planned town in Britain – some historians even believe it formed a blueprint for New York's grid system.

As interesting as it is to wander around Whitehaven's wide straight streets, the real draw to the town is the harbour and coastline it sits on. Get out onto the water itself if you can and view the town as hundreds of sailors of old would have done on arrival from all over the world. Or stride out along the coastal walk that leads from Whitehaven to St Bees approximately 4 miles to the south and threads through magnificent terrain that was once the haunt of smugglers and pirates.

Walking and cycling

The most remote destination in this area is **Ennerdale Water** (www.wildennerdale.co.uk), as it's the only lake in the National Park that doesn't have a road running alongside it, which means most of its shores are accessible only to walkers. There's a car park at the western end of the lake near Ennerdale Bridge village – home to a couple of good walkers' pubs – or try Bowness Knott car park, located halfway along the lake's north shore, from where a number of paths snake into

The Americans are coming!

The only ever unfriendly invasion of Britain by the USA occurred in Whitehaven on 23 April 1778 and was lead by John Paul Jones.

Jones was born in Scotland and trained as a seaman in Whitehaven – an apprenticeship that provided him with an intimate knowledge of the workings of the town's busy harbour. After being accused of murdering a sailor under his command, Jones fled to join his brother in Virginia and the year before his hostile return to Whitehaven he was given command of the USS Ranger under orders to aid the American War of Independence (1775–1783) wherever possible.

Initially Jones sailed to France where his ship became the first American naval vessel to be saluted by the French following France's signing of the Treaty of Alliance which recognised America as an independent nation.

Jones then turned his attention to Britain and, after a spate of attacking British merchant ships in the Irish Sea, hatched a plan to destroy a large number of wooden vessels and their cargo packed tightly into Whitehaven's busy harbour.

The Ranger anchored 2 miles offshore on 22 April and, shortly after midnight in difficult conditions, two rowing boats and 30 men set off from the ship. Jones managed to successfully disable the guns in a fort defending Whitehaven's harbour, which meant that his ship couldn't be attacked as it retreated following their invasion. However, this was the only part of his scheme that did go according to plan.

After being sent to a public house to find a light when their candles went out, a number of Jones's men stopped to get drunk and the night was nearly over by the time they returned.

With daylight fast approaching Jones decided to just burn one ship loaded with coal in the hope that the flames would spread to the rest of the vessels. However, one crew member took it upon himself to warn Whitehaven's residents that their town was soon to go up in flames, calling them to get out of bed and put the fire out.

Although Jones's daring attack ended in failure it did send shock waves through the nation and led to improvements to Britain's coastal defences. Jones himself returned to France and died in Paris in 1792 where he was buried. In 1913 his remains were re-interred in the United States Naval Academy Chapel where he is credited as being the 'Father of the American Navy'.

Ennerdale Forest. The walk around the lake itself is 8 miles long and takes approximately 4 hours to complete, and cyclists can whiz along a gravel road that leads from Bowness Knott car park to Blacksail – a return journey of around 14 miles.

In the summer the Ennerdale Rambler 263 bus service runs on Sundays and bank holidays between Cockermouth and Bowness Knot car park.

Lake Buttermere sits at the foot of Honister Pass, a steep B road that leads along the edge of Derwent Water from Keswick and into the western fells. Buttermere and Crummock Water to the north were once one large lake and between the two sits the tiny village of Buttermere, home to a couple of good pubs and a farm tea shop. Surrounded on all sides by some of the Lake District's most dramatic peaks, Lake Buttermere is one of the undisputed gems of the Western Lakes and the easy walk around its shores provides visitors with what many consider to be some of the best views in the National Park. The walk is about 4 miles long and won't take more than a couple of hours to complete. Many walkers park in the small car park behind the Fish Hotel (see p.194) where a bridleway marked 'lake shore path' leads to the lake itself. Alternatively park in the car park on the western outskirts of Buttermere where a marked path leads to Scale Force, the Lake District's highest waterfall, which tumbles 170ft down a tree-lined gorge and is particularly dramatic after heavy rain. A footpath to nearby Crummock Water also leads from this car park.

While in Buttermere, take time to look inside the tiny parish church of St James whose Wainwright window looks out over the crinkly top of Haystacks – this famous walker's favourite peak and final resting place. Directly behind Haystacks is the smooth top of Great Gable where every Remembrance Day a service is held

Fish Hotel, Buttermere

The Maid of Buttermere

In the centre of the tiny community of Buttermere stands the Fish Hotel (www.fishhotel.com), which in the 1790s was run by the Robinson family. This decade saw the number of tourists travelling to the Lakes rise sharply, an increase aided by Romantic poetry preaching the virtues and beauty of the region, and the production of guidebooks. One such guidebook, *A Fortnight's Ramble In the Lake District*, written by Joseph Budworth (alias Palmer) in 1792, recounts his meeting Mary Robinson, the 15-year-old daughter of the landlord of the Fish Hotel or, as he called her, 'the fair maid of Buttermere'. Palmer described the unmarried Mary as having thick long hair, a fine oval face, full eyes and 'lips as red as vermillion' and stories of her beauty spread fast. In 1802 a gentleman who went by the name of Colonel Alexander Hope came to stay at the Fish Hotel and wasted no time in wooing Mary with his charms and ingratiating himself with her parents. He eventually married Mary in a nearby church later the same year.

However, a London newspaper soon got wind of the marriage of the 'Maid of Buttermere' and exposed her new husband as a charlatan and bigamist. The real Colonel Hope was in fact abroad at the time and Mary's new husband was the bankrupt John Hatfield who was already married to a lady in Devon.

The exposed Hatfield fled fast and was eventually arrested in Swansea, tried in Carlisle and sentenced to death by hanging.

The story of Mary's plight spread throughout the country and fuelled a brisk trade to the inn. Eventually the Maid of Buttermere married a local farmer and ran the inn herself when her parents became infirm.

Mary died in nearby Caldbeck in 1837 and is immortalised in Book VII of Wordsworth's *The Prelude* in which he describes her as the 'artless daughter of the hills' who lived 'without contamination', thus placing her firmly on the Romantic heroine pedestal. Melvyn Bragg has also been inspired by the life of Mary Robinson and those wanting to read more about her should pick up a copy of his best-selling historical novel, *The Maid of Buttermere*.

on its peak. Also look out for the two wooden angels that guard the church's alter, which were carved by a local farmer when the church's original old painted angels were stolen.

A dial-a-ride 949 bus service operates three times a day between Cockermouth and Buttermere, with stops at Lorton and Loweswater. Those wishing to use it should call 01900 822795 before 10pm on the day before they wish to travel. A return adult fare to Buttermere is £3.30, which makes it cheaper than many of the car parks around the north-western Lakes and you won't have to battle to find a parking spot in high season.

St Bees Head

St Bees Head is a spectacular 100ft cliff situated on the coast between Whitehaven and Egremont and is one of the finest places along the north-west Cumbrian coast to walk or mess about on its fine pebble and sand beach. The community grew up around a 12th-century Benedictine Priory, which is still a place of worship and open to visitors. In 1981 a group of archaeological students unearthed an almost perfectly preserved body of a medieval man in grounds near the priory and you can learn all about 'St Bees Man' from displays inside the church.

St Bees is the starting point of Wainwright's famous Coast to Coast walk (www.coast2coast.co.uk) which travels 190 miles across England to Robin's Hood Bay on the east coast. A much shorter walk, which is perfect for day trippers, is the 3-mile-long nature trail which leads along the cliff-top and adjacent to the largest seabird colony on the western coast of England. To access the path head over the metal footbridge at the north end of the promenade, but be warned the path is fairly steep and uneven in places. At various times of the year you'll encounter the likes of black guillemot, spotting razorbills, peregrines, kittiwake, fumars and herring-gull and three viewing platforms along the cliff path provide views into the colony.

St Bees is a stop on the west coast railway line and there's plenty of parking in a large car park by St Bees beach, adjacent to a beach shop and tea rooms whose plate glass windows look far out over the Irish Sea.

West Cumbrian coast looking south from St Bees

The Visitors' Book

Following in Wainwright's footsteps

'The last time I spent time in the Western Lakes it was on a sort of homage to the memory of Alfred Wainwright.

'It was Wainwright's dying wish for his ashes to be scattered at his favourite spot of all: Innominate Tarn on Haystacks above Buttermere in the Western Lakes and it was this walk my partner and I decided to do. You can find this route in his book 'The Western Fells'.

'It's an easy climb, only about 1,900ft and suitable for families — though of course there are a few awkward bits here and there. The path follows the east side of Buttermere lake. Keeping Buttermere to your right, you simply make for the path that winds to the left up the flank of the ridge of hills in front of you. The climb took us perhaps an hour and a half, and for the effort we were rewarded with some of the most dramatic scenery on offer in this part of the world. I could see why Wainwright loved the place so much.

'We made our way to Innominate Tarn, which was an unassuming pool bronzed by peat. Beyond this rocky basin many of the Lakes' most famous peaks could be seen: Green Gable and Great Gable to the east, Kirk Fell and Pillar to the west, and the placid waters of Buttermere and Crummock Water stretching away to the north.

'We ambled back down a lazy route through the valley above Warnscale Bottom. The whole thing took us around five hours.'

Dave Hall, London

Kirk Fell

Wildlife

Like St Bees Head, **Linskeldfield Tarn** nature reserve on the outskirts of Cockermouth is an excellent place to get up close to, and learn all about, Cumbria's rich birdlife. The reserve is set amongst picturesque farmland overlooked by Skiddaw mountain and a wide range of birds including cormorants, curlews, lapwings and whooper swans can be viewed from its hide. Also expect to encounter other Lake District wildlife such as otters and red squirrels.

LINSKELDFIELD TARN NATURE RESERVE, Linskeldfield Farm, Isle, Cockermouth, CA13 9SR; 01900 822136; www.linskeldfieldtarn.co.uk; admission free – donations welcome; open daily all year.

Water tours

The best way to appreciate the impressive beauty of north Cumbria's coast is to get out onto the sea itself. **Whitehaven Marine Adventures** operates 75-minute-long ecotours which, in calm conditions, take visitors along the coast and share with visitors both the secrets of its myths and legends, and facts about its marine wildlife. You'll be able to view bird colonies on St Bees Head and, if you're lucky, you'll spot the likes of grey seals and dolphins in their natural habitat. Tours run at various times during the day, including a sunset tour and warm clothing and life jackets are provided.

Fleswick Bay

WHITEHAVEN MARINE ADVENTURES, 07967 967038; www.whitehavenmarine adventures.co.uk; boats depart from slipway at Whitehaven Harbour; £20 adults, £10 children; weather permitting, daily year-round; call in advance for sailing times and availability.

Wet weather

Cockermouth

The **Printing House Museum** in Cockermouth is one of Cumbria's more specialist attractions. At this working museum you can view a unique collection of beautiful old printing presses of all ages from around Britain. This attraction also details the history of printing from its invention in the 15th century and its collection includes old iron presses, treadle machines and hot metal casts. You can see how type was once set by hand and have your name printed in this traditional style, and learn how newspaper headlines were set in the days before computer design software.

THE PRINTING HOUSE MUSEUM, 102 Main Street, Cockermouth CA13 9LX; 01900 824984; www.printinghouse.co.uk; admission £2.75; open 10am–4pm Mon–Sat.

Also in town, on the banks of the River Cocker where it meets the River Derwent, is one of Cumbria's best-known traditional breweries – **Jennings** – whose regular tours are well worth taking even if real ale isn't your favourite tipple. Famous for beers such as Cocker Hoop, Sneck Lifter and Cumberland Ale, the company has been brewing ale from this site since 1874. **Jennings brewery tours** provide visitors with an insight into the art of brewing and the opportunity to sample some of their Lakeland ales.

JENNINGS BREWERY TOURS, Castle Brewery, Brewery Lane off Castlegate CA13 9NE; 0845 129 7190; www.jenningsbrewery.co.uk; £4.95 adults, £2 children (only over-12s); tours at 11am and 2pm Mon–Sat during high season, 2pm only during low season.

Whitehaven

The Beacon overlooks Whitehaven's harbour and is one of the town's most distinctive landmarks. The five floors of this lighthouse-shaped building include a museum detailing the history of the area from pre-Roman times to the regeneration of Whitehaven's harbour, and a large art gallery which hosts a programme of regularly changing exhibitions. Best of all is the top floor where panoramic sea views can be enhanced by peering through powerful telescopes and you can interact with a wind turbine and present the forecast in the weather zone.

THE BEACON, West Strand, Whitehaven Harbour CA28 7LY; (01946 592302; www.thebeacon-whitehaven.co.uk; admission to the art gallery free; tickets to the rest of the attraction £4.60 adults, children under 16 free with a paying adult; open 10am–4.30pm Tues–Sun/bank holiday Mon.

Maryport

Further afield

Maryport, to the north of Workington, is the only other town in this region with attractions to keep you occupied on wet weather days – although its small harbour is best viewed in the sunshine.

Maryport's **Maritime Museum** is a small facility detailing the town's maritime and shipbuilding history. All kinds of model ships and paintings are on view but the most interesting section is the room dedicated to Fletcher

> **MARYPORT MARITIME MUSEUM,**
> 1 Senhouse Street, Maryport CA15 6AB;
> 01900 813738; admission free; open
> 10am–4pm Mon–Sat.

Christian's mutiny which includes a facsimile of the HMS *Bounty* logbook. Christian was born near Cockermouth and was distantly related to Wordsworth. The top floor provides wide views over the town's small harbour, the Solway Firth and not so distant Scottish coast.

High on the cliffs to the north of Maryport is the **Senhouse Roman Museum** which sits adjacent to a fort built during the reign of Emperor Hadrian (AD76–138) and forms part of the Hadrian's Wall World Heritage Site (www.hadrians-wall.org). The museum houses a collection of Roman artefacts

> **SENHOUSE ROMAN MUSEUM,**
> The Battery, Sea Brows, Maryport
> CA15 6JD; 01900 816168;
> www.senhousemuseum.co.uk; £2.50
> adults, 75p children; open 10am–5pm
> Tues, Thur–Sun April–June.

– most notably a large collection of Roman altars – and you can view the extent of the remains and scale of the fort from the top of an observation tower. Children are encouraged to get into the spirit of the times by dressing up as a Roman and a programme of regular events and lectures are organised for those who want to find out more about this era.

What to do with children...

LAKELAND SHEEP AND WOOL CENTRE, a mile south of Cockermouth off the Egremont Road at the A66/A5086 roundabout, CA13 0QX; 01900 82273; www.sheep-woolcentre.co.uk; admission charged only to see a show £4.50 adults, £3.50 children; open daily 9am–5.30pm except for two weeks in January; sheep show runs four times a day, Sun–Thur Mar–Oct.

THE RUM STORY, Lowther Street, CA28 7DN; 01946 592933; www.rumstory.co.uk; £5.45 adults, £3.45 children, £16.45 families; open 10am–4pm daily.

The Rum Story

The **Lakeland Sheep and Wool Centre** is the place to get up close to Cumbrian farm life and livestock. The free visitors centre is open all year and is the place to learn all about the 19 breeds of sheep that live in the Lakes – pay a visit between March and October when the centre programmes a series of live shows including sheep shearing and indoor sheepdog trials. Woolly gifts galore are for sale in the centre's shop and the café is a good place to stop for a coffee even if you're not interested in any of the shows.

Housed in an 18th-century shop, courtyard and warehouse that once belonged to the Jefferson family, **The Rum Story** tells the story of the UK rum trade. Expect to spend an hour at this indoor attraction learning how slaves were transported from African villages in appalling conditions to the Caribbean to work on the sugar plantations that produced the rum and hear tales from Whitehaven's maritime history.

Standing on the southern side of Maryport's small harbour is the **Lake District Coast Aquarium** one of the region's best places to bring young children. The aquarium takes visitors through the different aquatic environments of the Lake District from streams to oceans and brings you right up close to the plants and animals that call them home. Outside the aquarium is the fabulous 'Shiver Me Timbers' play area where young children can let off steam on a sunny day. And if you don't want to eat in the aquarium's café, why not pick up one of their takeaway sandwiches and enjoy lunch sitting on the harbour wall instead.

The **St Bees Maize Maze** to the south of Whitehaven is one of the few places in the Lake District where you can actually encourage your children to get lost. The large maze, made entirely from maize plants is just one of the activities set up to entertain children. Young visitors can also feed the farm animals, take a tractor ride, collect eggs from the hen-house and race around on mini-tractors. Don't leave without watching the pigs race.

THE LAKE COAST AQUARIUM, South Quay, Maryport CA15 8AB; 01900 817760; www.lakedistrictcoast aquarium.co.uk; £5 adults, £3.25 children; open 10am–5pm daily.

ST BEES MAIZE MAZE, north of St Bees on the Byresteads Road which runs adjacent to the B5345, CA28 9UF; 01946 823706; www.stbees-maizemaze.co.uk; £4.50 adults, £3.50 children, £14 families; open 10am–6pm Thur–Sun July to Sept.

 ## Entertainment

Theatre and cinema

Cockermouth's **Kirkgate Centre** (01900 826448 www.thekirkgate.com) on Kirkgate is a former school that's been transformed into a small community feel arts centre which screens mainly non-mainstream films and hosts small-scale theatre events and live music. A mile north of Whitehaven off the A595, the **Rosehill Theatre** (01946 692422 www.rosehilltheatre.co.uk) programmes a range of theatre and music events plus children's shows. And for mainstream films head to Workington's six-screen multiplex cinema (01900 87001 www.workington-plaza.co.uk) in Dunmail Park.

Special events

Maryport's annual **Blues Festival** (01900 817200 www.maryportblues.com) takes place on the last weekend in July and is recognised as one of the top five Blues festivals in the country. Previous headline acts have included Van Morrison and Gary Moore and special public transport from Carlisle, Whitehaven and Keswick is laid on for the festival.

Throughout June and July Cockermouth organises a **Summer Festival** during which locals and visitors can enjoy a number of events including Saturday Showtime street entertainment, regular children's events and the annual Cockermouth Children's Carnival. During this time the town's castle throws open its door to the public. Check www.cockermouth.org.uk for dates and a programme of what's on.

Nightlife

The Vagabond on Marlborough Street in Whitehaven is a warm and friendly restaurant and pub that hosts regular live music events. While in Cockermouth, **Neo's** (see p.206) organises a series of evening events including open poetry nights and **Merienda** (www.merienda.co.uk) on Station Street is the place for live jazz and tapas on Friday nights.

Shopping

Cockermouth's mix of small branches of some high street chains and individually owned stores makes it the best place in the north-west Lakes to shop. Art and crafts lovers should head for the large **Percy House Gallery** (www.percey house.co.uk) on Market Place. Housed in Cockermouth's oldest town house, which dates back to the 14th century, Percy House is crammed with textiles, paintings, jewellery, sculpture and ceramics, and exhibits the work of local artists. Also on Market Place, the **Bitter Beck Pottery** (www.bitterbeck.co.uk) sells and exhibits the work of local potter Joan Hardie whose intricate work is inspired by the natural world.

Also expect to find well-known chains lining the streets of Whitehaven. More unexpected, however, is **Michael Moon's Bookshop** on Lowther Street (not far from The Rum Story see p.200) – a book lover's delight. This massive antiquarian bookshop sells a vast range of second-hand books, local history titles and old prints, and is the perfect place to pick up some holiday reading or just spend time browsing.

The best... PLACES TO STAY

HOTEL

Bridge Hotel 🏊 🍴

Buttermere, CA13 9UZ
017687 70252
www.bridge-hotel.com

The Bridge is a traditional old Lakeland hotel surrounded by stunning scenery and within easy walking distance of Lake Buttermere. Several of the attractive rooms feature four-poster beds and you can choose between bar meals or fine dining in the evening – both accompanied by a long wine list. Self-catering apartments and a farm cottage are also available to hire.

Price: B&B and evening meal £70–£100 or £25 less for B&B only. Apartments £225–£695 per week, farm cottage £305–£605.

New House Farm 🏊 🍴

Lorton, CA13 9UU (on the B5289 one mile south of Low Lorton)
01900 85404
www.newhouse-farm.co.uk

Housed in a Grade II 17th-century building, this fine country house hotel successfully marries traditional comforts with contemporary luxury. Many original features are in place and the 15 acres of rambling grounds include a hot spa for guests' use. The on-site restaurant is renowned for first-class traditional English fare.

Price: B&B £75 pppn.

INN

Kirkstile Inn 🏊 🍴

Loweswater, CA13 0RU
01900 85219
www.kirkstile.com

Located in the heart of the north-western fells, the Kirkstile Inn is an old 16th-century riverside inn, crammed with character and history. The meals make full use of local produce and the refurbished bedrooms offer smart, comfortable accommodation and fabulous countryside rolls out in all directions.

Price: B&B from £42–£58 pppn, family suite £130–£154 per suite per night.

B & B

Six Castle Gate 🏊

6 Castlegate, Cockermouth, CA13 9EU
01900 826786
www.sixcastlegate.co.uk

Six Castle Gate is a contemporary B&B housed in an elegant Georgian property in the heart of Cockermouth. Many original Georgian features remain and sit comfortably with modern refurbishments that include flat screen TVs and Internet access in all rooms. Full Cumbrian breakfasts available.

Price: B&B from £35–£75 per room per night.

The best... **PLACES TO STAY**

SELF-CATERING

Anns Hill Cottage 🍴

**Bridekirk, Cockermouth, CA13 0NY
(2 miles north of Cockermouth)
01900 388180
www.annshill.co.uk**

This five-star self-catering oak-beamed cottage comes with open fires and a Victorian bathroom. A luxury hamper and bottle of chilled champagne greets all guests and breakfast in bed and evening meals can be arranged.

Price: range from £560–£625 per week or £118–£131 per night. Sleeps four.

The Lazy Fish 🍴 🌿

**Brook House, Embleton,
Cockermouth, CA13 9TN (10 minute
drive from Cockermouth and Keswick)
017687 76179
www.thelazyfish.co.uk**

Self-catering doesn't come better than this luxury, eco-friendly barn conversion. A hamper crammed with breakfast food awaits your arrival and dinner and complimentary champagne can be delivered to the door. Added extras include an outdoor spa pool and wood-burning stoves.

Price: Weekly rates £690–£980, short breaks £450–£650. The two bedrooms sleep two each and there is an additional double sofa bed.

The best... FOOD AND DRINK

All of the small communities around this region's lakes boast excellent rural pubs, many serving good food and local ales. All are popular haunts for walkers, visitors and locals.

Expect to find fewer farm shops in this area, but the towns of Cockermouth and, to a lesser extent, Whitehaven, make up for this gap with their diverse range of restaurants and cafés that serve everything from local fare to world cuisine.

▶ Staying in

Local produce can be picked up at **Cockermouth's Food and Craft Fair**, which is held on the first Saturday of the month 9.30am–1.30pm in the Town Hall off Market Place. **Wellington Farm** (01900 822777 www.wellingtonjerseys.co.uk) on the outskirts of Cockermouth (from the Egremont roundabout at the junction of the A66 and A5086 take the exit signposted to Mitchells Agricultural Market) makes it's own award winning ice-cream with milk fresh from its pedigree Jersey cows – whisky and marmalade is the most popular flavour. A larger selection of dairy foods and preserves is for sale in its small farm shop and the excellent adjacent tea room exhibits the work of local artists.

For an Indian takeaway try **The Spice Club Island** (01900 828288 www.thespiceclubcockermouth.co.uk), in Cockermouth on Main Street or the **Akash Tandoori Restaurant** (01946 691171) in Whitehaven on Tangier Street. In Maryport you can pick fish and chips to munch on the quayside from the **Cross Quays Fish 'n' Chip Shop** (01900 815956) on King Street. **Casa Romana** (01946 591901 www.casaromanauk.com), an Italian restaurant on Queen Street in Whitehaven, serves good pizzas and a selection of other Italian food to eat in or take away.

Also in Whitehaven on Lowther Street next door to The Rum Story, **Richardson and Sons** wine shop (01946 65334 www.richardsonswines.co.uk) is a fine wine merchant that also stocks many different whiskies and champagne.

 EATING OUT

RESTAURANT

The Front Room
**2 Market Place, Cockermouth,
CA13 9NQ
01900 826655**

This rustic wine bar and bistro is decorated in cheerful yellow and scrubbed pine features throughout. Evening meals are all under £10 and have a distinct Mediterranean flair – try the roasted vegetable and brie hotpot. Local produce is used where possible. Open 5.30–11pm Thur–Sun.

Heaven's Kitchen
**66 Lowther Street, Whitehaven,
CA28 7DG
01946 66066**

Heaven's Kitchen is a colourful, busy restaurant in the centre of town. The menu mixes international cuisine with steaks and seafood – expect to pay around £6 for lunch and from £9 for an evening main course – and the jazzy yellow and purple décor blends well with the restaurant's lively atmosphere.

Platform 9
**The Old Station House, Main Street,
St Bees, CA27 0DE
01946 822600
www.platform9.co.uk**

Standing next to the railway tracks in St Bees, Platform 9 is a railway themed restaurant that opens daily for lunch and dinner. The menu is a mix of English and Mediterranean dishes and makes full use of local produce. Choose between à la carte (mains £13–£18) mains or bar meals (£4–£8).

EATING OUT

GASTROPUB
The Kirkstile Inn
Loweswater, CA13 0RU
01900 85219
www.kirkstile.com

Nestled in the heart of the stunning scenery around Loweswater and Crummock Water, the Kirkstile Inn has a well-deserved reputation for first-class food made with an emphasis on local produce and traditional Cumberland dishes. Open for lunch (£4–£9), evening meals (mains £8–£11), the Kirkstile is also good for morning coffee or afternoon tea.

VEGETARIAN
Quince and Medlar
13 Castlegate, Cockermouth, CA13 9EU
01900 823579
www.quinceandmedlar.co.uk

This gourmet vegetarian restaurant attracts custom from across Cumbria. The dining room is oak panelled and candle lit and the menu features unusual world cuisine such as Lebanese pancakes. All mains (£14) served with seasonal vegetables and dinner is rounded off with delicious deserts (£5) and home-made chocolates. Open Tues–Sat from 7pm. Booking advisable.

CAFÉ
Neo's
25–31 Market Place, Cockermouth, Bookshop Café and Gallery
01900 829900
www.neo-bookshop.co.uk

A small, funky café that started life as an art gallery and has grown to include a bookshop specialising in art and design and works by Cumbrian authors. The inexpensive menu is heavy with organic and local products and includes unusual brunch and lunch dishes. Neo's is as bohemian as the Lake District gets.

Courtyard Café
The Rum Story, Lowther Street, Whitehaven, CA28 7DN
01946 592933
www.rumstory.co.uk

This inexpensive café is particularly recommended for families, as children love its themed décor and large kinetic clock. Midday meals include Cumberland sausage and Shepherd's pie and are all under a fiver and you can pick a two-course Sunday lunch for £7.

Syke House Farm Café
Buttermere, CA13 9XA
017687 70277

This small farm café is famous for its home-made Ayrshire ice-cream – the perfect summer treat – or choose from a range of hearty cakes and scones. The café also sells a select range of locally made gifts and jewellery.

🍷 Drinking

A collection of excellent rural pubs are dotted around the lanes surrounding the north-western Lakes. **The Kirkstile Inn** at Loweswater (see p.206) has its own on-site micro brewery whose Melbreak Bitter, Grasmoor Dark Ale and Kirkstile Gold are all served from its busy bar. **The Wheatsheaf Inn** in Low Lorton (www.wheatshefinnlorton.co.uk) is popular with locals and serves a range of Jennings beers. Its Wednesday night quiz is open to all.

In Buttermere you can choose between the walkers' bar at the **Bridge Hotel** (see p.203) whose outdoor terrace has superb views over the western fells and the legendary **Fish Hotel** (www.fish-hotel.co.uk) where the Maid of Buttermere herself once pulled pints (see p.194).

In Cockermouth the **Bitter End** on Kirkgate (www.bitterend.co.uk) is home to Cumbria's smallest brewery, which can be viewed through a plate glass window in one of the pub's three bars. Or try **1761** (www.bar1761.co.uk) on Market Place, which serves local ales and fine wines in more contemporary surroundings, plus a range of hot drinks. A selection of card and board games are also on hand in case you run out of conversation.

Cockermouth's Beer Festival is held every December in the town's Kirkgate Centre (p.201). At this popular event you can sample a large range of local ales and listen to the live jazz, which is laid on to support the festival. Check www.cockermouth.org.uk for exact dates.

St James Church, Buttermere

ⓘ Visitor Information

Tourist Information Centres:
Town Hall, off Market Street,
Cockermouth, 01900 822 634;
www.cockermouth.org.uk; Market Hall,
Market Place, Whitehaven, 01946
59894, www.rediscoverwhitehaven.com;
website packed with visitor
information www.western-
lakedistrict.co.uk.

Hospitals: West Cumberland Hospital,
Homewood Road, Hensingham,
Whitehaven, CA28 8JG, 01946 93181.

Doctors: Lowther Medical Centre, 1
Castle Meadows, Whitehaven, CA28
7RG, 01946 692241,
www.lowthermedical.co.uk,
8.30am–6pm Mon–Fri, call 01946
67401 in an emergency; North
Cumbria also served by Cuedoc,
01228 401999, an out-of-hours
emergency doctor service based in
Carlisle but also serves much of the
west coast as far south as
Whitehaven.

Pharmacies: Tesco Pharmacy, Bransty
Row, Whitehaven, 01946 852449,
8.30am–7pm Mon–Sat, 10am–4pm
Sun; Morrisons Pharmacy, Flatt Walks,

Whitehaven, 01946 599811,
8.30am–7pm Mon–Fri, 8am–6pm Sat,
10am–4pm Sun; Boots, Main Street,
Cockermouth, 01900 823160.

Police: Main Street, Cockermouth,
0845 330 0247; Scotch Street,
Whitehaven, 01946 692616.

Supermarkets: Tesco, Bransty Row,
Whitehaven; Morrisons, Flatt Walks,
Whitehaven; Sainsbury's, Station
Road, Cockermouth.

Internet Access: Public library,
Lowther Street, Whitehaven, 01946
852900; public library, Main Street,
Cockermouth, 01900 325990.

Bike Rental: Ainfield Cycle Centre,
Jack Trees Road, Cleator, Whitehaven,
CA23 3DW, 01946 812 427, £12 per
day; 4 Play Cycles, Market Place,
Cockermouth, CA13 1NH, 01900
823377, £14 per day with weekly
rates available.

Taxis: L&G Taxis, Whitehaven, 01946
66644; Cockermouth Taxis, 01900
825339.

FURTHER AFIELD

Silloth

Silloth is a small, charming coastal community and old port situated approximately 18 miles from Cockermouth on the far north Cumbrian coast. Once a bustling Victorian seaside resort, Silloth remains a popular place to breathe sea air and visitors and locals alike enjoy strolling along its 2 miles of promenade to take in views of southern Galloway and sunsets over the Solway Firth. The two main attractions in Silloth are the Solway Coast Discovery Centre, which is also home to the town's Tourist Information Centre (016973 31944 www.sillothonsolway.free-online.co.uk) and the Gincase Farm Park. And every September a lively beer festival (www.sillothbeerfestival.co.uk) is held in a giant marquee on The Green – a large grassy area between the seafront and town.

The Solway Coast Discovery Centre is the place to find out just how this Area of Outstanding Natural Beauty was formed during the Ice Age. Visitors are then led through the history of human occupation of the coast and discover how the Romans, Vikings and medieval monks all influenced its development. Before you leave you can get to choose which future you'd like to see for this unique environment and its diverse wildlife.

> **THE SOLWAY COAST DISCOVERY CENTRE,** Liddell Street, Solway, CA7 4DD; 016973 33055; www.solwaycoast aonb.org.uk; £2 adults, £1 children; open 10am–4.30pm daily.

The Gincase on the outskirts of Silloth is a great place for animal-loving children as they can get up close to numerous friendly farm animals and their young in this attraction's rare breeds farm animal park. An indoor playbarn and go-kart track keep children who are animal-shy occupied instead. Adults can browse around a craft barn and art gallery where visitors can buy Cumbrian crafts and view changing exhibitions of local artists' work. The tea room, which features an old cooking range dating back to 1760, serves local food made from traditional recipes and, if the weather is good, you can eat in an orchard garden.

> **THE GINCASE,** on the B5300 between Mawbray and Beckfoot (turn for Newton and then follow the signs), CA7 4LL; 016973 32020; www.gincase.co.uk; admission to tea room, craft barn and gallery free; small fee admission to farm park and playground; open Easter–Oct 10.30am–4.30pm daily, Nov–Easter 10.30am–4.30pm Tues–Sun; farm park open only Easter–Oct.

THE SOUTH-WESTERN LAKES

The part of Cumbria that stretches down the coast, from Egremont in the north to Ravenglass in the south and into the Lake District National Park as far east as Wasdale Head and Boot is a remarkable area and one much neglected by many visitors who aren't serious walkers, climbers or campers. This relatively small region is overlooked by Scafell Pike, England's highest mountain and also claims England's deepest lake, smallest church, biggest liar and Britain's Favourite View – all of which are steeped in a raft of folklore, ghost stories and bizarre local traditions.

The only lake in this area is the stunning Wast Water and even though images of this remote body of water were splashed across national media when it officially became Britain's Favourite View, no photograph can ever capture its full magnificence. The experience of standing on its shores, in the shadow of some of the finest peaks in the Lakes, is reason enough to travel to this area.

In contrast Eskdale, the valley that runs south of and adjacent to Wasdale – home of Wast Water – is less dramatic terrain and its softer fells are popular with campers. Here, and throughout the inland area of this region, you'll find numerous excellent pubs, that are good places to stay, eat and enjoy a pint of real, often locally brewed ale.

The road through Eskdale narrows as it leads east from Boot towards the heights of Hardknott Pass. This is the only direct route into the Lake District's central fells and forms an ancient link with Ravenglass on the coast, an old fishing village and former Roman naval base. Some link the town with sites from Arthurian legends and claim that the ruins of a large Roman bathhouse in the village are in fact Lyons Garde – one-time home of Morgan le Fay. The ruins are managed by English Heritage and access is free, but the main draw here is the old narrow gauge railway, known locally as La'al Ratty, that operates a regular service of steam trains from Ravenglass into Eskdale.

WHAT TO SEE AND DO

 ### Fair weather

With a depth of 258 feet, **Wast Water** is England's deepest lake and the valley it sits in – Wasdale – rewards visitors with the most awe-inspiring views the Lake District can provide. Generally speaking this region attracts mainly experienced walkers, but even if you're not interested in either walking or cycling, it's worth coming here in fair weather just to experience the spectacular views firsthand. Wast Water is approximately 3 miles long by half a mile wide and is lined with steep scree slopes on its south-eastern shores that plummet dramatically into the lake. These slopes are responsible for the lake's great depth as they continue their steep descent far under water.

What's hidden in Wast Water?

The icy depths of England's deepest lake is about the last place you'd expect to find a **garden of gnomes**. However, an unknown diver or divers had, at some point created a garden of gnomes at a depth of 48ft complete with its own picket fence. The garden was well known in the diving community, but following a series of fatalities, believed to have been caused because divers were spending too long in deep water searching for the garden, the National Park Authority asked the police to remove the ornaments. Rumour has it that a new gnome garden has since appeared at a depth below 50ft – the deepest level that police divers are legally allowed to go.

In March 1984 a diver in Wast Water spied what he initially thought was a rolled up piece of old carpet lodged on a shelf of rock 110ft underwater. On retrieval the carpet, which had been weighed down by a concrete block, was found to contain the body of Margaret Hogg, the wife of airline pilot Peter Hogg who had disappeared eight years earlier. Margaret's body had been perfectly preserved due to a lack of oxygen in the water and following identification her husband was found guilty of her manslaughter. If Peter Hogg had rowed just a few yards further out on the night he disposed of his wife's body in the lake, it would have sunk much deeper and probably never have been found.

A narrow road clings to the south-western shore of Wast Water and although most drive along it to reach the remote **Wasdale Head**, a tiny community a mile from the northern tip of Wast Water, it makes for a good and relatively flat cycle ride through Britain's Favourite View. There are car parks at the north end of Wast Water and at Wasdale Head, or for a longer ride, park in the car park on the east side of Gosforth village just off the A595, from where the trip to Wasdale Head and back is 18 miles.

Wasdale Head is surrounded by some of the highest peaks in the Lake District including Great Gable and Scafell Pike, which at 3,210ft is England's highest mountain. This small settlement is home to the famous Wasdale Head Inn (see p.217), a National Trust campsite, outdoors store and St Olaf's – England's smallest church – and lies at the foot of some of the Lakes' most serious walking and climbing terrain. The majority of the walks that lead into the mountains from this region aren't recommended for beginners, but most should be able to manage the easy walk to Wast Water itself, which is just a mile away.

Wasdale Head

For those without a car, a taxibus service operates on Thursdays, Saturdays and Sundays, between Seascale railway station and Wasdale Head, stopping at Gosforth and Nether Wasdale along the way. The service is operated by Gosforth Taxis (019467 25308) and must be pre-booked by 6pm the day before you plan travel.

The Ravenglass and Eskdale Railway

RAVENGLASS AND ESKDALE RAILWAY, Ravenglass Station, off the A595 at Ravenglass, CA18 1SW, 01229 717171; www.ravenglass-railway.co.uk; return tickets £9.60 adults, £4.80 children, £24.90 families; frequent trains daily Mar–Oct; less frequent service operates at weekends/half-terms.

Trains have steamed along the **Ravenglass and Eskdale Railway** for around 130 years, originally carrying iron ore from Eskdale's mines to the coast at Ravenglass, and today transporting visitors along the same scenic route. The 7-mile-long journey takes the tiny narrow gauge train around 40 minutes to complete and you can choose between doing it in one go or jumping on and off at the various stations along the way. Bikes are allowed on the trains (pre-booking required) and can be hired at Dalegarth station at the end of the route (see p.222) where details of various cycling routes are available. Wainwright himself created a series of walks from stations along the route and a booklet detailing his walks titled *Walks From Ratty* is available to buy on board for £2.50.

Various special trains are laid on throughout the year including one at Halloween and Mince Pie specials at pre-Christmas weekends. You can discover more about the history of the railway at the Railway Museum located in the Ravenglass Station car park.

The Gosforth Cross

Gosforth is a small village 7 miles south of Egremont off the A595 that contains a number of pubs, café and gift shop. But for many visitors the main attraction to this ancient community is a remarkable old stone cross in the churchyard of St Mary's, which stands next to Gosforth Hall Hotel (p.217). This cross, known as the 'Viking Cross', is nearly 15 feet tall, dates back to the late 900s and is believed to be one of the finest surviving Viking relics in the region. The intricate carvings that grace this remarkable red sandstone structure are very worn and thought to represent scenes from Norse mythology including Yggdrasil, the World Ash Tree, which Vikings believed held up the universe. The cross also contains Christian symbolism such as Christ's crucifixion, indicating a marrying of cultures in the generation prior to the Norman Conquest.

Further Viking relics can be found inside the church itself including two 10th-century 'hogback' tombstones. Also in the church on its north side are doors known as 'devil doors'. These ominous doors are a feature of numerous Cumbrian churches and according to ancient tradition they are to be opened during a baptism, thus allowing any evil spirits inside the church to exit and return home to the dark north.

Eskdale Mill

Eskdale Mill is one of England's oldest working mills and is reached by crossing an old 17th-century packhorse bridge. The mill's two waterwheels have ground cereals since 1578 and the original grinding machinery is still in place and in working order, powered by water from Whillan Beck which streams down the

ESKDALE MILL, at the end of Boot village alongside Whillan Beck and a short walk from the Boot station of the Ravenglass and Eskdale Railway; 019467 23335; admission £1.50; open Apr–Sept 11.30am–5.30pm 5 days a week – call to check which days.

mountains from the nearby Scafell range. A small exhibition details the history of the mill and its picturesque grounds make for a perfect picnic spot.

CELEBRITY CONNECTIONS

Wast Water was championed as Britain's Favourite View by actress **Sally Whittaker** who has played Sally Webster in Coronation Street since 1986. Sally was born near Rochdale and trained at the Oldham Repertory Theatre, and has a holiday home in the western Lakes. Comedian **Harry Enfield** also has a holiday home in this region and visitors to Muncaster Castle can hear him at the MeadowVole Maze attraction in the castle where he provides all the narration. The other comedian attached to this area is Rowan Atkinson, better known as Mr Bean. Although not born in the area, Rowan was educated at St Bees School. A hero for many Whitehaven residents is England goalkeeper **Scott Carson** who was born in Whitehaven and played for the local amateur side Cleator Moor Celtic before debuting for Leeds in a schoolboy tournament in 2000. And well-known film locations in this area include Ennerdale, where the final scenes from Danny Boyle's *28 Days Later* were shot and Mr Jefferson's office in The Rum Story was used as a set in *Miss Potter*.

Muncaster Castle

Wet weather

Muncaster Castle is a fascinating 13th-century castle and estate that's crammed with things to do for all ages. A tour of the castle takes in several rooms including the infamous Tapestry Room – reputed to be one of the most haunted rooms in England. The room features distinctive 17th-century Flemish wall hangings and an enormous old fireplace; visitors can pay to spend the night on a 'ghost vigil' in the room if they dare. Surrounding the castle are its magnificent gardens, which claim stunning views of Eskdale and can be explored via a number of marked trails. In winter the gardens stay open some evenings after dusk to allow visitors to experience **Darkest Muncaster**, a spectacle of lights, music and special effects that transforms the grounds after dark (call ahead for times and dates).

Muncaster is also the unlikely home of the headquarters of the **World Owl Trust** and visitors can view around 45 different species at what is one of the largest collections of owls in the world. Young visitors are catered for at the **MeadowVole Maze**, where they can experience the world from a vole's eye view and help Max MeadowVole escape being eaten by an owl. Various interactive computers are dotted around the castle and its grounds offer the added attraction of interactive games, tours and quizzes. A large plant centre sells a wide variety of shrubs, vegetable plants and herbs that can also be found growing in the castle's estate.

MUNCASTER CASTLE, off the A595 near Ravenglass, CA18 1RQ; 01229 717614; www.muncaster.co.uk; £7 adults, £5 children, castle costs an extra £2.50 adults and £1.50 children; darkest Muncaster £5 adults, £2.50 children; Feb–Oct, all attractions open daily 10.30am–6pm/dusk, castle closed on Saturdays, Nov–Feb all attractions, except the castle, open 11am–4pm, castle open Sun, Nov/Dec; all closed during Jan.

Local Knowledge

Local writer, **Tom Fletcher** knows every nook and cranny of the Western Lakes having lived in most of the region, including Gosforth, Drigg, Holmrook and Whitehaven. Although university dragged Tom away at 18, he returned to the west coast and the remote fells of this side of the Lake District, which he spends his time hiking through when not busy writing. Look out for Tom's short stories or the novel he's currently working on which is set deep in the Cumbrian mountains and draws on the folklore and supernatural tales this region is famous for.

Secret tip for lunch: Pies from Gosforth Bakery. They're huge!

Favourite pub: The Lutwidge Arms, in Holmrook. Good beer, good pool table, and a leafy, open beer garden with a view down the fields to the river.

Favourite activity: One of the best things about Cumbria is the lack of light pollution. Going outside at night and looking up at the sky is utterly awe-inspiring.

Best walk: Drigg beach. It's maybe not what you'd call a nice place, it's just completely unlike anywhere else, and has a peaceful sense of desolation that stays with you.

Best view: Wast Water from the pumping station at the very end, so you're looking straight down the lake towards Great Gable and Yewbarrow. That way you can get a real impression of the scale of it. And it's better in bad weather.

Favourite haunt: The end of the harbour wall at Whitehaven. It's not too safe in the wind or rain, but it's good to walk out there and you can sit by the lighthouse with the seagulls and the fisher-people and be surrounded by the sea.

Favourite treat: Hartley's ice-cream, from Egremont. Although the ice-cream van parks on Whitehaven harbour sometimes. It's the best ice-cream ever.

Best thing to do on a rainy day: If you live in this part of Cumbria, you just get used to the rain. You carry on as if it doesn't make a difference. And, by and large, it doesn't.

215

What to do with children...

Sellafield is a large nuclear reprocessing plant just north of Seascale and its **Visitor Centre** is one of the few places in Cumbria where children can engage with science. There are various sections to explore including Live Labs where you get to learn all about gravity, a Thinking Lounge complete with electronic newspapers and The Core which details where electricity comes from and the issues surrounding its generation. The centre also contains an Immersion Cinema where visitors take charge of the country's energy crisis – just one way that the centre encourages visitors to engage with the debate on how we should be providing energy in the decades to come.

SELLAFIELD VISITOR'S CENTRE, off the A595 near Calder Bridge, CA20 1PG; 01946 727027; www.go-experimental.com; admission free; open 10am–5pm daily Apr–Oct, 10am–4pm Nov–Mar; sometimes closed to the public for events; call in advance.

 ## Entertainment

Special events
Gurning is the art of pulling ugly faces and on the third Saturday of September Egremont hosts the **World Gurning Championship** (www.gurning.co.uk) as part of its annual crab fair. The competition to find the world's ugliest man and woman is open to all and visitors are encouraged to take part as well as watch this bizarre ancient tradition that dates back to the 13th century. Contact the Egremont Tourist Information Centre (see p.222) for more details.

The **Boot Beer Festival** (www.bootbeer.co.uk) takes place every June and is hosted by the Brook House Inn, the Boot Inn and the Woolpack. All pubs are within easy walking distance of each other and the Boot station of the Ravenglass and Eskdale Railway. In addition to a fine selection of ales, Cumbrian food and local Morris dancing are also laid on. Check the website for exact dates each year.

 ## Shopping

The largest community in the south-western Lakes region is Egremont and one of the best shops for visitors here is the **Lowes Court Gallery** (01946 820693 www.lowescourtgallery.co.uk), which exhibits the work of local artists and sells a range of Made in Cumbria crafts.

Other outlets dotted around the small communities south of Egremont include the **Gosforth Pottery** (019467 25296 www.gosforth-pottery.co.uk) located to the north of Gosforth; this traditional working pottery sells a range of hand-thrown work and canvas-mounted local photographs. You can also have a go on the potter's wheel or paint your own pot – pre-booking required.

The best... PLACES TO STAY

HOTEL

Gosforth Hall Hotel 🏊 🦮 🍴

Gosforth, CA20 1AZ (on the Wasdale Road)
019467 25322
www.gosforthhallhotel.co.uk

Legend claims that the timbers of this 17th-century hall came from a shipwreck. Exposed beams, uneven floors and low doorways add to Gosforth Hall's rich atmosphere and room 11 features an entrance to an old priest's hole – just one fragment of the hotel's fascinating history.

Price: B&B £50–£120 per room or suite per night.

The Pennington 🏊 🐕 🦮 🍴

Ravenglass, CA18 1SD
01229 717222
www.thepennington.co.uk

A stylish beachfront hotel overlooking the south Cumbrian coast and close to Muncaster Castle and the Ravenglass and Eskdale railway. Rooms are modern and plush and include DVD players. The on-site restaurant serves upmarket traditional food and you can choose from 60 different wines and a range of real ales in the lounge bar.

Price: B&B £120 for double occupancy.

INN

Wasdale Head Inn 🏊 🐕 🦮 🍴

Wasdale Head, Gosforth, CA20 1EX
019467 26229
www.wasdale.com

This famous inn is a mile from the tip of Wast Water and surrounded by some of the Lake District's most breathtaking peaks. Lakeland history oozes from every inch of the hotel and after a hard day on the fells you can choose between the award-winning restaurant or a meal in its fabulous bar. Self-catering accommodation is also available.

Price: B&B £54–£59 pppn, large rooms with kitchenettes £108 per room per night, self-catering accommodation £360–£600 per week.

CAMPSITE

Camping Pods 🏊 🐕

Eskdale Camping and Caravan Club Site, Boot, Holmrook, CA19 1TH
01946 723253
www.campingandcaravanningclub.co.uk

Forget shivering under canvas, camping pods are cosy, eco-friendly shelters built with locally sourced wood and insulated with sheep's wool. You'll need all your camping gear except a tent and each pod is heated in winter and sleeps up to four.

Price: £35 per pod per night.

The best... PLACES TO STAY

UNUSUAL

Wasdale Yurt Holiday

Rainors Farm, Wasdale Road,
Gosforth CA20 1ER
019467 25934
www.rainorsfarm.co.uk

Situated on farm land overlooking Wasdale Valley, the yurt at Rainors Farm offers ethnic style luxury under canvas. A wood-burning stove heats this unusual accommodation and toilet and shower facilities are located nearby.

Price: The yurt sleeps up to five people and costs £420–£525 per week or £300–£375 for three nights. Prices include breakfast.

SELF-CATERING

Woodhow Farm

Wasdale, CA20 1ET (on the road to
Wasdale Head from Nether Wasdale)
01946 726246
www.cumbrian-goat-experience.co.uk

A small collection of spacious self-catering cottages gather around this working farm's courtyard. Famous for its goat herds and Herdwick sheep, Woodhow is close to the wilds of Wast Water and a number of small Lakeland communities. It is perfect for those seeking peace and quiet but not complete isolation.

Price: Weekly lets from £350–£700, short breaks from £60 per night. Cottages sleep between two and six.

The best... FOOD AND DRINK

The south-western Lakes is dominated by rural pubs, all of which make full use of local produce and a number serve ale from their own micro breweries. Don't expect to find much in the way of big food stores, instead a couple of excellent village stores in Gosforth and Eskdale cater for the retail needs of self-caterers. This region is especially good for visiting meat lovers, as you'll find two farms selling their own locally bred organic meat and game, much of which is also served in local pubs and restaurants.

▶ Staying in

There are a number of small stores and businesses dotted around this region that anyone who is self-catering and looking for something a bit different from the usual supermarket fare should visit. **Eskdale Stores** (019467 23229 www.eskdalestores.co.uk) at Eskdale Green stocks a range of local Cumbrian foods including locally cured meats and organic products. The store also creates a range of hampers for visitors such as a basket of local produce to start your holiday and a self-catering vegetarian pack.

The Gosforth Bakery (019467 25525) in Gosforth is open Mon–Fri from 8.30am and you can expect to queue alongside locals to sample its freshly baked bread, superb traditional pies, quiches and great cakes. For local meats try **Wasdale Hall Head Farm** (01946 726245 www.wasdalefellmeats.com) at Wasdale Head where you can pick up lamb and beef that's been reared on the fells of Wasdale or arrange to have it delivered.

Country Cuts (01946 726256 www.country-cuts.co.uk) at Bridge End Farm, Santon Bridge sells a range of local poultry and other organic meats in its farm shop which is open daily 10am–5pm and stocks numerous other regional products.

Wasdale cheese is hand-made by the owners of the **Murt Camping Barn** (019467 26044 www.campingbarn.co.uk), which is located on the road between Nether Wasdale and Wasdale Head near the Youth Hostel. Made from unpasteurised local ewe's and cow's milk, the four varieties of cheese can be bought from Murt's and can often be sampled on the cheese boards of local pubs.

Anyone seeking a fish and chip takeaway should head to **Frasers** (01946 823642) on Market Place in Egremont which serves excellent fish and chips, breaded Whitby scampi and veggie breakfasts.

♠ Drinking

Lake District pubs don't come better than **Ritson's Bar at the Wasdale Head Inn**. Named after the former landlord and famous liar, Will Ritson, the bar is a haunt of walkers, climbers, day trippers and locals. It serves ales, such as Liar! brewed by its own Great Gable Brewing Company (www.greatgablebrewing.com) located behind the inn. Other pubs with their own micro breweries include the **Woolpack Inn** (www.woolpack.co.uk) at Boot in Eskdale, which serves ales produced by their Hardknott Brewery and host regular live music nights, and the **Strands Hotel** (www.strandshotel.com) in Nether Wasdale, which brews two ales on site – *Errmmm…. At Wast It's 'Ere* and *T' Errmmm-inator*.

EATING OUT

RESTAURANT

The Brook House Inn and
Restaurant
Boot, Eskdale, CA19 1TG
019467 23288
www.brookhouseinn.co.uk

The restaurant at this charming inn
located in the heart of beautiful
Eskdale is award winning. Its lunch and
evening menu features far more than
the usual pub grub and includes local
meats, trout, seafood and game (mains
start at £9) and the deserts, jams,
chutneys and bread are all home-made.

INN

The Screes Inn
Nether Wasdale, CA20 1ET
019467 26262
www.thescreesinnwasdale.com

Although not completely vegetarian,
the Screes Inn provides an excellent
choice for veggies such as goat's
cheese strudel (£8) alongside more
traditional and meat dishes. The inn
is set amongst magnificent scenery,
which can be enjoyed from outside
tables in the summer.

The Boot Inn
Boot, Eskdale, CA19 1TH
019467 23224
www.bootinn.co.uk

You can choose to eat in the bar,
restaurant or conservatory of this off
the beaten track inn, close to the
Boot station of the Ravenglass and
Eskdale Railway. Local produce

including Eskdale free-range pork and
home-made food fill the menu – all
cooked under the careful eye of the
inn's French chef.

The Lion and Lamb
The Square, Gosforth, CA20 1AL
019467 25242

This down to earth, no frills, locals'
pub has an enormous menu of mainly
traditional pub grub. The inn is
famous for its whale-sized fish and
chips (£10) and lion burgers for
walkers with big appetites.

CAFÉ

The Lakeland Habit
Main Street, Gosforth, CA20 1EJ
019467 25232

The Lakeland Habit, popular with the
locals, is an inexpensive café situated
above a small grocers and newsagents
in the heart of Gosforth. This is one of
the region's few cafés and a good place
to enjoy coffee and cakes, or something
a bit more substantial, before heading
off into Wasdale or Eskdale.

The Woodlands Tea Rooms
Santon Bridge, Gosforth, CA19 1UY
019467 26281
www.santonbridge.co.uk

Located at the Santon Bridge Gift
Shop, this buzzing tea room is the
place to enjoy home-made cakes and
larger snacks. The café is licensed
and open daily for morning coffees,
afternoon tea and lunch – look out for
red squirrels in the surrounding trees.

There's a cluster of pubs – the **Lion and Lamb**, the **Wheatsheaf** and the **Globe** – around the mini-roundabout in Gosforth, all busy with visitors and locals. And the Bridge Inn (www.santonbridgeinn.com) at Santon Bridge and **Bower House Inn** (www.bowerhouseinn.co.uk) in Eskdale are also popular local watering holes.

World's Biggest Liar

It has its roots in the 19th century when Will Ritson, one-time landlord of the Wasdale Head Inn, would spin incredible yarns to visitors who had no idea if he was telling the truth or not. Now every November, the Bridge Inn at Santon Bridge (019467 26221 www.santonbridgeinn.com) invites those skilled at telling barefaced lies to compete for the much coveted title of 'The Biggest Liar in the World'. Liars come from all over the world to compete and past champions include comedienne Sue Perkins – one half of Mel and Sue. Contact the Bridge Inn for details on the exact date each year and get there early to get a seat on the night.

World's Biggest Liar competition

ⓘ Visitor Information

Tourist Information Centres: Lowes Court Gallery, Main Street, Egremont, 01946 820 693; useful websites: www.eskdale.info; www.wasdaleweb.co.uk.

Hospitals: West Cumberland Hospital, Whitehaven, see p.248.

Doctors: Beech House Group Practice, St Bridgets Lane, Egremont, 01946 820203; Seascale Health Centre, 019467 28101; www.seascalehc.co.uk.

Pharmacies: The Pharmacy, Market Place, Egremont, 01946 820 237, 9am–6.30pm Mon–Fri, 9am–5pm Sat; the store in Gosforth sells a limited range of pharmaceutical products; for after hours pharmacies see Whitehaven, p.248.

Police: The nearest police station is in Whitehaven, 01946 692 616.

Supermarkets: A small Co-op in Egremont; large supermarkets in Whitehaven, p.248.

Internet Access: Public library, Wyndham School, Egremont, 01946 820464; public library, Gosforth Road, Seascale, 019467 28487.

Cashpoint: Outside of Egremont, banks are few and far between in this region; HSBC at Gosforth also has ATM.

Bike Rental: Budgie Bikes, Dalegarth Station, Ravenglass and Eskdale railway, 01524 389410, www.budgietransport.co.uk, £1.50 per hour, £9.50 per day.

Taxis: Geoff's Taxis, Egremont, 01946 824554; Gosforth Taxis, 019467 25308.

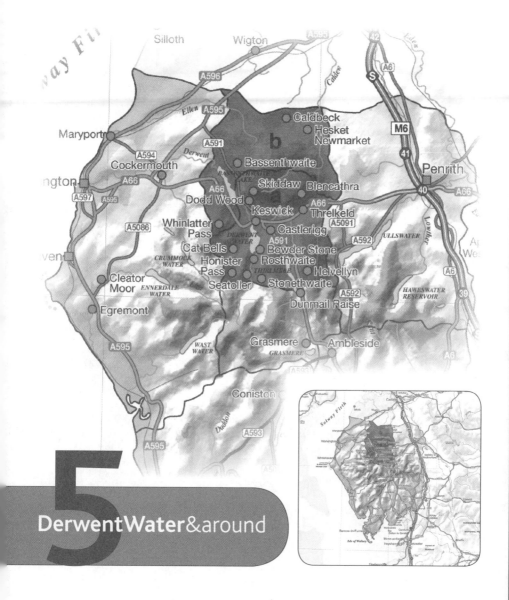

5 DerwentWater&around

a. Keswick and Derwent Water

b. Bassenthwaite and the northern fells

Unmissable highlights

01 Hire a canoe or kayak from Portinscale and paddle out to St Herbert's Island In the middle of Derwent Water for a peaceful picnic, p.232

02 Spend a day at Honister Slate Mine – enjoy an underground tour and, if you're brave enough, climb the Via Ferrata, p.231

03 Take your binoculars to Dodd Wood and try to spot the magnificent ospreys fishing on Bassenthwaite Lake, p.250

04 Visit the spectacularly located Castlerigg Stone Circle and ponder over its many mysteries, p.226

05 Walk up Skiddaw, England's fourth highest mountain, for wonderful views from the summit, p.229

06 Spend some time discovering the lovely, lesser known communities of the northern fells, including pretty Caldbeck, p.251

07 Enjoy the scenery from the water by taking a trip around Derwent Water on the Keswick Launch, p.231

08 Take in a play at the Theatre by the Lake, p.236

09 Spend a day exploring fascinating Borrowdale, visiting Watendlath, Ashness Bridge, the Bowder Stone and the villages, p.227

10 Take the children to Trotters World of Animals to meet gibbons, zebras and birds of prey, p.252

DERWENT WATER AND AROUND

The northern Lake District is a paradise for anyone who loves the outdoors – whether you enjoy getting out there and getting your boots dirty, or simply want to admire the views from a more comfortable vantage point. Steep crags and forested slopes rise from picturesque valleys to the top of some of the highest mountains in England.

From Honister Pass in the west, Dunmail Raise in the south, the edge of the Solway Plain in the north and Blencathra in the east, the area contains three of the major lakes – Bassenthwaite Lake, Thirlmere, which is actually a reservoir that was created by joining up two smaller lakes in 1894, and, of course, Derwent Water itself. Mighty Skiddaw, England's fourth highest mountain, towers over the busy town of Keswick and the iconic peaks of Great Gable and Scafell Pike, England's highest, are accessible from beautiful Borrowdale.

But even if the great outdoors isn't really your thing, you'll find plenty of interesting organised attractions to visit – from museums and a stately home, to mine tours and boat trips.

Finding accommodation in this area isn't difficult – there are quality guesthouses and hotels at every turn. Be warned though, Borrowdale and Keswick get extremely busy during the summer and at bank holidays. September too, once the children have gone back to school, is becoming an extremely popular time for couples and families. Things get a little quieter the further north you go, particularly in the villages that dot the base of the northern fells.

KESWICK AND DERWENT WATER

In terms of mountain locations, there aren't many towns in the UK that can match Keswick. With the dark, massive bulk of Skiddaw looming over it and the pyramid-like Grizedale Pike dominating to the west, this is an excellent location for outdoor enthusiasts or people who simply enjoy magnificent scenery. Walkers, climbers, mountain-bikers, gill scramblers, paragliders... they all flock to this area of the Lakes. If water's more your thing, the much photographed Derwent Water has several marinas where you can hire canoes, kayaks, sailing dinghies, rowing boats, windsurfers and small motorboats.

For something a little more sedate, the classic glaciated landscape of Borrowdale to the south of the town has lots of fascinating sites that can be seen on a driving tour or by using the Borrowdale Rambler and Honister Rambler bus services and the Keswick Launch. Beautiful Castlerigg Stone Circle, just outside the town, is a must and, if the weather closes in – as it often does in this part of the country – there are several unusual museums.

Just as the mountains today drive the local economy by attracting tourists, so, in the past, they generated wealth with their mineral content. From the arrival of German miners in the mid-16th century until well into the 20th century, copper, graphite, slate, lead, coal, cobalt and zinc were all mined here. This heritage is proudly showcased in mining museums in Threlkeld and Keswick, the Pencil Museum and the recently reopened Honister Slate Mine.

The busy, slate-built settlement is the largest town in the northern Lakes and draws in huge numbers of tourists – especially during its many festivals – as well as a fair few shoppers looking for new waterproofs and walking boots in its many outdoor gear shops.

WHAT TO SEE AND DO

 Fair weather

Castlerigg Stone Circle is a photographer's dream. Perched above the town with Blencathra and Skiddaw forming the perfect backdrop, this mysterious site is thought to date from about 3000BC. Neolithic stone axes have been found within the circle, but its use remains a source of speculation. Was it a trading post? An observatory? Or maybe a religious site?

CASTLERIGG STONE CIRCLE, www.english-heritage.org.uk; admission free; open daily; roadside parking nearby.

Castlerigg Stone Circle

The tiny National Trust settlement of **Watendlath** sits high above Borrowdale in one of the area's hanging valleys. 'Hanging' above the level of the glaciated valley floor, it was gouged out by a tributary to the main glacier, and so didn't erode as deeply. Watendlath first got mains electricity in 1978, the last place in the Lake District to be connected. There is a small car park and tea shop in the hamlet. It's worth stopping on the narrow road leading up to the hamlet from the B5289 to enjoy two of the area's best and most famous views of Derwent Water and its surrounding fells – Ashness Bridge and Surprise View.

Further into Borrowdale, a 400-million-year-old lump of rock stops visitors in their tracks. The **Bowder Stone**, dumped here by a passing glacier, is more than 32ft high, about 98ft in circumference and balanced precariously on one edge.

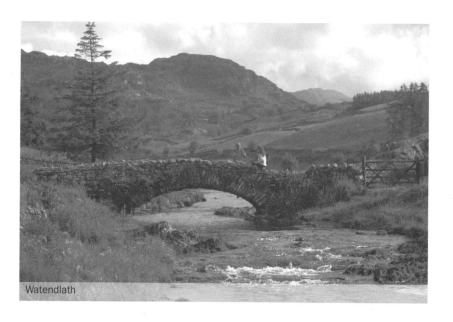
Watendlath

Keswick

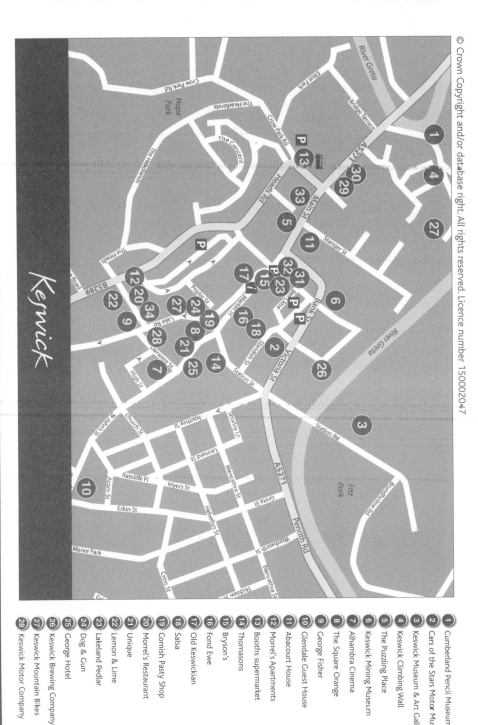

1 Cumberland Pencil Museum
2 Cars of the Stars Motor Museum
3 Keswick Museum & Art Gallery
4 Keswick Climbing Wall
5 The Puzzling Place
6 Keswick Mining Museum
7 Alhambra Cinema
8 The Square Orange
9 George Fisher
10 Glendale Guest House
11 Abacourt House
12 Morrel's Apartments
13 Booths supermarket
14 Thomasons
15 Bryson's
16 Fond Ewe
17 Old Keswickian
18 Salsa
19 Cornish Pasty Shop
20 Unique
21 Morrel's Restaurant
22 Lemon & Lime
23 Lakeland Pedlar
24 Dog & Gun
25 George Hotel
26 Keswick Brewing Company
27 Keswick Mountain Bikes
28 Keswick Motor Company
29 Co-op
30 Launderette
31 Police Station
32 Post Office
33 Star of Siam
34 Bar 26

228

Great Gable

Follow in the footsteps of Victorian tourists by climbing the sturdy wooden ladder to the top. There is no admission charge to the site, which is open at all times, and there is parking nearby.

No visit to the northern Lakes would be complete without donning your boots and taking to some of the area's hundreds of miles of footpaths and bridleways – be it for a short stroll beside the lake or a hike up one of England's highest mountains. **Great Gable** (6.2-mile round walk from Honister Pass) and **Scafell Pike** (8-mile round walk from Seathwaite) are both accessible from Borrowdale; and you can get a head start on the climb up the 3,000ft **Skiddaw** by starting from the Latrigg car park at the end of Gale Road, almost 1,000ft above sea level. From here, it's only three miles to the summit. The smaller, more easily accessible **Latrigg** (5.6-mile round walk from Keswick) and **Walla Crag** (6.4-mile round walk from Keswick) provide great views over Derwent Water and Borrowdale for less effort. The hugely popular **Cat Bells** is best avoided unless you're starting very early in the day and are doing it as part of the **Newlands Round** (about 11 miles). There are literally dozens of walking guidebooks on sale in Keswick to help you choose a route.

One of the newest attractions in the area is the **Honister Via Ferrata**, an adventure climbing system that uses a permanently fixed cable to allow people to climb the old miners' route up the steep and craggy northern face of Fleetwith Pike at the top of Honister Pass. Terrifying or exhilarating, depending on your head for heights, the route includes scrambling on bare rock, a frighteningly narrow metal bridge over a steep drop and a dark, damp tunnel cut into the mountainside by the miners. Harnesses and helmets are provided and climbers are with a guide at all times.

HONISTER VIA FERRATA, Honister Pass (B5289), Borrowdale CA12 5XN; 017687 77714; www.honister-slate-mine.co.uk; adults £19.50, youths (16–17 years) £15, children (under 16) £9.50, family tickets available; minimum height 1.30m; tours depart 11am and 1pm daily.

Honister via Ferrata

The 20th-century caveman

Castle Crag and its woods make for an interesting round walk from Rosthwaite (3.2 miles). Sir William Hamer gave the crag to the National Trust in 1920 in memory of his son and ten other men from Borrowdale who were killed during the First World War. There is a war memorial at the summit.

The crag is crowned by the remains of an Iron Age hill fort. Borrowdale, in fact, is the anglicised version of the Norse 'borgar dalr', which means 'valley of the fort'. The Romans also used it, probably taking advantage of its prominent, strategic position within the valley.

But Castle Crag has been occupied more recently than that. Between the two world wars, two of the crag's caves became the summer home of Millican Dalton.

Dalton was born in Alston, Cumberland in 1867, but his parents moved to Essex when he was young. Sick of being a commuter in southern England and feeling the call of the great outdoors, he left a comfortable career in the City when he was in his 30s to offer adventure holidays to would-be climbers in the Lake District.

Desperate to get back to nature, Dalton lived at first in a tent, then in a split-level quarried cave halfway up Castle Crag. Despite having a waterfall pouring through his roof, he turned one cave into a living area and one into a bedroom, which he called 'The Attic'.

Intelligent and well-educated, Dalton loved to pit himself against the elements. He climbed trees in winter to keep fit for climbing and, on his 50th ascent of Napes Needle, lit a fire on the tiny summit and made a pot of coffee. A dump in the nearby village of Grange helped him make ends meet – by providing basics such as old pans and materials he could make into camping equipment for sale to his climbing customers.

During the London Blitz in 1940/41, he braved snow, ice and sub zero temperatures to remain all winter on Castle Crag.

Sadly, he didn't get to end his days on his beloved fells; he died in hospital in Amersham after contracting pneumonia in 1947 – at the age of 79.

Honister Slate Mine

Honister Slate Mine, located at the top of Honister Pass, is probably one of the best organised attractions in the area. Visitors are kitted out with safety helmets, lamps and battery packs before going deep inside the mountain to see the magnificent caverns and some of the 11 miles of tunnels hollowed out by generations of miners. Workers at England's last working slate mine then show how the stone is made into roof slates.

HONISTER SLATE MINE, Honister Pass (B5289), Borrowdale CA12 5NX; 017687 77230; www.honister-slate-mine.co.uk; adults £9.75, children £4.75; open 9am–5pm Mon–Fri, 10am–5pm Sat, Sun and bank holidays; 3 tours daily; some tours suitable for all ages; minimum height 1m 30cm for 'The Edge' tour.

On the water

Derwent Water is surrounded by some magnificent ridges and one of the best – and easiest – ways to enjoy this scenery is from the **Keswick Launch**. Based close to the Theatre by the Lake, the boats stop at seven jetties around the lake, so you can hop on and off where

KESWICK LAUNCH, 017687 72263; www.keswick-launch.co.uk; around-the-lake tickets £7.90 adults, £3.95 children, £18 families; children under 5 free; single fares also available to any points around the lake.

Keswick launch boat

The islands

Derwent Isle, the most northerly of Derwent Water's islands, was once home to a group of German miners fleeing from the people of Keswick. They were employed by the Company of Mines Royal, which, in 1564, acquired a royal decree to mine and smelt in England. The Germans were forced to leave Keswick after several of them were murdered by local people.

In 1778, the island passed into the hands of Joseph Pocklington. Apart from building a villa, Pocklington also constructed a number of follies including Fort Joseph. This was used during the Derwent Water Regatta, the centrepiece of which was a mock battle where local teams would attempt to land boats on the island and storm the fort's supply of beef and beer while avoiding fire from Pocklington's cannon. The island, a little more sedate these days, is now owned by the National Trust.

The most central of the islands is St Herbert's Island, named after a religious recluse who lived here in the 7th century. He was the long-time friend and disciple of St Cuthbert, Bishop of Lindisfarne. A chapel was consecrated on the island when the cult of St Herbert was revived in 1374.

It is said that the remains of St Herbert's chapel and cell may still be traced at the northern end of the island. A small grotto of unhewn stone stands nearby. This is the New Hermitage, built in the 19th century.

you want – or simply enjoy the entire circuit, which takes about 50 minutes. Additional Santa Specials are laid on in December.

When your boat trip is over, why not take a stroll along the lakeshore to **Friars Crag** for yet another magnificent view of the lake? It's located about a third of a mile south of the landing stages. Simply walk along the lane with the water on your right and, when the path forks, keep straight ahead to the bench on the promontory.

Using your own steam – or at least paddle and wind power – you can hire canoes, kayaks, dinghies, rowing boats, windsurfers and even small powerboats from **Nichol End Marine** and **Derwent Water Marina** in Portinscale, just to the west of Keswick.

NICHOL END MARINE, Portinscale CA12 5YT; 017687 73082; www.nicholendmarine.co.uk; kayaks £5.25 per hour, windsurfers £9.50, motor boats £19 for up to two people; tuition available; open all year; café 10am–4pm, 4.30pm in summer.

DERWENT WATER MARINA, Portinscale CA12 5RF; 017687 72912; www.derwentwatermarina.co.uk), Canadian canoe £10 per hour, windsurfer £15, 4-person rowing boat £10; tuition available; 9am–5.30pm, 10am–4pm Dec and Jan.

Kayakers on River Derwent

Platty+ hires out canoes, kayaks and sailing boats from its base near the Lodore Falls Hotel in Borrowdale. More unusually, an experienced helmsman can take groups out on the lake in dragon boats or in the Gift of the Gael, a replica Viking longboat that can be rowed or sailed, depending on the weather.

PLATTY+, 017687 76572/77282; www.plattyplus.co.uk; 2 hours in Viking longboat £200 for up to 10 people; park in Lodore Falls car park and register with the hotel porter who will issue you with a free parking permit.

Wet weather

Museums

The Cars of the Stars Motor Museum does just what it says on the tin. Located in the middle of Keswick, it is home to the Batmobile, Mr Weasley's Ford Anglia from the *Harry Potter* films and K.I.T.T. from *Knightrider*, which the museum's owner, Peter Nelson, bought from David Hasselhof in 1992. *Only Fools and Horses* fans can see Del Boy's original three-wheeler van and 'the most fantasmagorical car in the history of everything' – from *Chitty Chitty Bang Bang* – is also there.

CARS OF THE STARS MOTOR MUSEUM, Standish Street, Keswick CA12 5LS; 017687 73757; www.carsofthe stars.com; adults £4, children £3; open Easter–New Year/Feb half-term, daily 10am–5pm, weekends only in December.

The **Keswick Museum and Art Gallery** is home to some weird and wonderful exhibits, including a 665-year-old cat, John Ruskin's shoes and Robert Southey's clogs. The musically minded can hammer out a tune on the Musical Stones of Skiddaw.

KESWICK MUSEUM AND ART GALLERY, next to children's play area in Lower Fitz Park, Station Road CA12 4NF; 017687 72297; www.allerdale. gov.uk/keswick-museum; admission free; open Apr–Oct, Tue–Sat and bank holidays, 10am–4pm

CELEBRITY CONNECTIONS

Sir Chris Bonington, probably the UK's most celebrated mountaineer, lives close to Hesket Newmarket in the northern fells. Born in Hampstead, London in 1954, his many achievements include the first ascent of The Ogre and the first British ascent of the Eiger's North Face. He also successfully led the British Everest Expedition of 1975, which put the first Britons on to the mountain's summit, and is an accomplished writer and photographer. He has lived in Cumbria for several decades and has become something of an ambassador for the area, supporting local organisations, encouraging charities and even going so far as to organise a Valentine's card for his beloved Lake District on its 50th anniversary as a National Park in 2001.

The writer and broadcaster **Melvyn Bragg**, born in Wigton to the north of the National Park in 1939, is another famous champion of Cumbrian affairs. Although he no longer lives in the area, he makes frequent appearances in the county, backing local campaigns and charities. Several of his novels are set in Cumbria, including *The Hired Man* and *The Soldier's Return*. He was made a life peer (Lord Bragg of Wigton) in 1998.

Film director **Ken Russell** briefly adopted Cumbria as his home and used Keswick and Borrowdale as the locations for many of his films. *Mahler* was filmed in the area – and included putting a full orchestra on top of Friar's Crag – as were *Tommy* and *The Rainbow*. Living in a cottage next to the Borrowdale Hotel, he became unpopular locally after claiming that scandal in London was nothing compared to that of Cumbria, where wife-swapping, he said, was rife.

CUMBERLAND PENCIL MUSEUM,
Southey Works, Keswick CA12 5NG;
017687 73626; www.pencilmuseum.
co.uk; adults £3, children £1.50; open
9.30am–5pm daily.

The **Cumberland Pencil Museum** bills itself as 'the only attraction in the world devoted exclusively to the rich and fascinating history of the pencil'. Well, it's hard to imagine there being two! It may sound a little dull, but it's a good place to take refuge until the rain passes over.

The history of graphite and pencil-making is brought to life in a fascinating way and youngsters have the chance to put their creativity to the test in the Drawing Zone, where their work can be entered into regular competitions. Borrowdale, incidentally, claims to have made the world's first pencils after the graphite discovered in the valley in 1550 was used to brand sheep.

Take a **drive along the A591** towards Grasmere, recently found to be Britain's 'best drive' in a survey of motorists. Better still, take the 555 bus from Keswick and let someone else do the driving. The journey was recently made even better when United Utilities began felling some of the conifers on its land, making room for native trees and giving road users a better view of the reservoir, Thirlmere. And what a moody, magnificent view it is, even on a rainy day. Interestingly, all the water that flows from here to Manchester, nearly 100 miles away, does so without the aid of pumps – it's all achieved by gravity.

What to do with children...

With no minimum age limit, **Keswick Climbing Wall** is ideal for parents wanting to introduce their children to climbing in a safe, controlled environment. Instruction is available all year round and you can stay all day after your lesson. Located behind the Pencil Museum on the Southey Hill Trading Estate, just a 10-minute walk from the town centre.

Prepare to be well and truly confused when you visit **The Puzzling Place** in Museum Square in the town centre. Interactive exhibits, artwork and sculptures are used to explore optical illusions. One of the most popular features is the Anti Gravity Room, where you'll feel as if you're defying the laws of gravity.

An underground tour of a reconstructed lead and copper mine is one of the highlights of the **Threlkeld Quarry and Mining Museum**, located just outside the village of Threlkeld to the east of Keswick.

KESWICK CLIMBING WALL, Southey Hill, Keswick CA12 5NR; 017687 72000; www.keswickclimbingwall.co.uk; climbing lessons from £9 per person in a group of six (all ages); open daily 10am–10pm, closes 9pm FriMon Apr to Sep.

THE PUZZLING PLACE, Museum Square, Keswick CA12 5DZ; 017687 75102; www.puzzlingplace.co.uk; adults £3.50, children £2.75; open 11am–5.30pm, summer weekdays, 10am–6pm summer weekends; winter 11am–5pm, closed Mon, closed all weekdays Jan.

THRELKELD QUARRY AND MINING MUSEUM, off the B5322, CA12 4TT; 01768 77974; www.threlkeldmining museum.co.uk; underground tour £5 adults, £2.50 children; museum £3 adults, £1.50 (older) children; open daily Mar–Oct 10am–5pm.

... and how to avoid children

LODORE FALLS HOTEL HEALTH AND BEAUTY TREATMENT, off the B5289, 3 miles south of Keswick in Borrowdale, CA12 5UX; 017687 77285; www.lakedistricthotels.net; waterfall treatment (summer only) from £169, including lunch.

The Lodore Falls Hotel in Borrowdale is making good use of the natural facilities on its doorstep by offering unusual spa treatments incorporating a real waterfall. **Waterfall Therapy** incorporates a sauna and an invigorating dip in the crystal clear beck cascading through the grounds followed by more traditional pampering back indoors.

Entertainment

Theatre and cinema

The **Theatre by the Lake** (017687 74411 www.theatrebythelake.com) is home to Cumbria's leading professional theatre company and puts on a popular summer season of six plays. It also hosts visiting groups throughout the year and stages a range of music, dance, talks and comedy events. Some of Keswick's many festivals use the Lakeside location – just a five-minute walk from the town centre – as a key venue.

Theatre by the Lake

Local Knowledge

Chris Higgins is a 42-year-old climbing instructor who lives in Keswick with his wife and two young children. Originally from the West Midlands, he has lived in the area for 13 years. He unashamedly admits that his local recommendations are 'Borrowdale-centric' because, as he says, 'he lives and loves it here'.

Favourite restaurant: The Star of Siam Thai restaurant on Keswick's Main Street. Great Thai food in unpretentious surroundings, and the service is always fantastic.

Favourite pub: Bar 26 on Lake Road, Keswick, isn't just exposed beams, pictures of hounds hunting and the traditional stuff some people still think a pub should be. It has a lovely atmosphere, modern décor and a good selection of beers and wines. All this and free peanuts!

Best view: Looking across Derwent Water on a summer's evening while climbing on Shepherds Crag in Borrowdale. The sky turning a deeper blue as the sun drops behind Cat Bells, the peace of Borrowdale and majestic Skiddaw at the head of the lake.

Best walk: I love Blencathra. There are so many ways to the top it's impossible to get bored. Of all the routes I think Hall's Fell as a way up then a drop down the back along Foule Crag before cutting round on to Sharp Edge to regain the summit and a final walk off Doddick Fell is a wonderful way to see this mountain's many facets.

Best thing about living in the Lake District: If you forget to lock your car at night it will still be there in the morning.

Best thing to do on a rainy day: Put your waterproofs on and do the same thing you would if it wasn't. Surely, that's what living in Cumbria is all about?

Most interesting visitor attraction: Honister Slate Mine's Via Ferrata traverses the front of the mine workings on Fleetwith Pike. It's not extreme in terms of exposure and verticality, but what a wonderful setting, steeped in mining history! It takes me back to a time when things must have been very hard for all those working in the mine, but to have been surrounded by all that must have been quite inspirational.

The independent, 1920s-built **Lonsdale Alhambra Cinema** (017687 72195 www.keswick-alhambra.co.uk) on St John's Street is a breath of fresh air for film-lovers who are tired of the multiplexes. As well as showing the latest releases, it hosts the award-winning Keswick Film Club on Sunday evenings from October to March – a chance to see those 'alternative' British and foreign-language films that the big chains shy away from.

Special events
For ten days in the late winter, authors descend on Keswick to share their love of the written word with Theatre by the Lake audiences. The **Words by the Water Festival** (www.wayswithwords.co.uk) features workshops, book launches and talks by speakers from the worlds of literature, politics and the media. Past speakers have included Jonathan Dimbleby, Melvyn Bragg and the poet laureate Andrew Motion.

The noisy and colourful **Keswick Jazz Festival** (www.keswickjazzfestival.co.uk) takes place in various venues around the town during May. The line-up for 2008 includes Acker Bilk and The Temperance Seven.

It is quickly followed by **The Cumberland Ale Keswick Mountain Festival** (www.keswickmountainfestival.co.uk) where visitors get to try their hand at all sorts of exciting outdoor activities and hear some of the UK's top climbers share their adventures.

The popular **Keswick Beer Festival** (www.keswickbeerfestival.co.uk) is the largest in the north of England, featuring 170 real ales plus bottled beers and ciders. It takes place in June.

Late summer is the time for the local **agricultural shows** including Keswick and Borrowdale. This is a good chance for visitors to get a taste of the real Cumbria and watch traditional sports such as Cumberland and Westmorland wrestling.

And as if all that wasn't enough, there's also the **Keswick Film Festival** (www.keswickfilmfestival.co.uk), the **Victorian Christmas Fayre** and the huge **Keswick Convention**, which attracts 12,000 people to Bible teachings and Christian seminars every summer (www.keswickministries.org).

Nightlife
There's live music every Thursday from 9pm at **The Square Orange** (017687 73888, www.thesquareorange.co.uk) a short stroll from the Moot Hall on St John's Street. This simple café bar, which is listed in CAMRA's *Good Beer Guide*, has a laid-back, continental feel to it. It is also open during the day for tapas, panini and some of the best coffee in town. Open Sat–Thu 10am–11pm, Fri 10am–midnight.

The Visitors' Book

Keswick Recommendations

'Whatever the weather Keswick is a great place to go. We like to go down to the lake first for a bit of fresh air. It's easy to park near the Theatre by the Lake and then there are all sorts of activities to choose from — a rowing boat out on the lake, feeding the ducks (particularly popular with our 2-year-old daughter) or a walk along to Friar's Crag with beautiful views up the lake to Castle Crag. The path is nice and accessible and fairly sheltered so good even in the rain.

'Having done that and feeling suitably virtuous after our exercise, we head into Keswick itself. Parking is easy in the big pay-and-display car park and very convenient for George Fisher's — a must for anyone visiting Keswick. It's a fantastic place if you need any kit — ranging from boots to waterproofs to climbing gear. Their service is excellent and — even better — they have a great play area underneath the stairs to keep little people entertained while the adults browse and buy.

'Once the shopping is done, we go upstairs to the homely little café. Their Cumberland sausage sandwiches are yummy and essential for anyone who wants to taste local produce. The restaurant is also child-friendly and they're happy to provide a high chair. Check the specials board for their puddings as they usually have a good wholesome crumble to fill you up for the day.

'The afternoon can easily be spent wandering the streets of Keswick or else we pack Amelia into her rucksack and get out into the fells for a few hours to coincide with her afternoon sleep time. Ideally, we can make it back in time for fish and chips from the Old Keswickian — preferably eaten by the lake overlooking the sunset, but that doesn't often happen!'

Emma Parkin, Gloucestershire

Shopping

You can't fail to notice the plethora of outdoor gear shops in Keswick, which is a constant source of annoyance for people who live there. 'Plenty of places to get outerwear, but where we can buy our underwear?' But love it or hate it, it can't be denied that Keswick is *the* place to go if you're looking for the latest GPS, a good set of waterproofs or just a new pair of walking boots. The big chains are here – Cotswold Outdoor, Blacks, Millets, etc – as are a host of local retailers such as Rathbones and Needle Sports, which specialises in climbing and mountaineering gear. The huge George Fisher store on the corner of Lake Road and Borrowdale Road is now owned by the Scottish Tiso Group.

 The best... **PLACES TO STAY**

HOTEL

The Leathes Head

Borrowdale, Keswick, CA12 5UY
017687 77247
www.leatheshead.co.uk

This comfortable Edwardian country house is on an elevated site, providing superb views of Borrowdale from just about every room, including its spacious, relaxing lounge areas. It proudly boasts a substantial wine cellar and a well-stocked bar, which has 45 single malts and 11 different gins.

Price: B&B and evening meal £64.95–£82.95 pppn in a standard room. B&B by prior arrangement only.

Hazel Bank Country House

Rosthwaite, Borrowdale, Keswick, CA12 5XB
017687 77248
www.hazelbankhotel.co.uk

Awards line the hallway of this traditional Victorian house located in the heart of some of the Lake District's best walking country. The eight rooms are individually furnished and decorated, some with six-foot beds. There is a small honesty bar and an elegant dining room with set menus changing daily.

Price: B&B and dinner £70–£95 pppn.

The best of... THE LAKES AND SHORES

THE LAKE DISTRICT'S MUCH LOVED LAKES DEFINE THIS REGION AND ITS INSPIRING LANDSCAPE. FROM SCREE LINED REMOTE SHORES TO BUSY BOAT FILLED WATERS, EACH OF THE FOURTEEN MAIN LAKES IS UNIQUE IN CHARACTER AND APPEAL. AND NO VISIT IS COMPLETE WITHOUT ENJOYING ONE OF THE MANY WAYS TO GET OUT ONTO THE WATER ITSELF.

Top: View of Buttermere, Crummock Water and the surrounding Fells from Fleetwith Pike; Middle: Castlerigg Stone Circle; Bottom: Rainbow over Wast Water

Top: A boathouse on Ullswater; Middle: Watendlath; Bottom: Muncaster Castle

Top: The tiny church of St. Martin's; Middle: Ravenglass & Eskdale Railway; Bottom: View from Brantwood, Coiston Water

Top: The watermill at Little Salkeld; Middle: Looking down on Haweswater; Bottom: Windsurfers on Windermere

The best... PLACES TO STAY

Lyzzick Hall

Underskiddaw, Keswick, CA12 4PY
017687 72277
www.lyzzickhall.co.uk

Light and airy rooms with wonderful views of the fells around Keswick await guests at the end of the driveway to Lyzzick Hall. The bedrooms are comfortably furnished and the bathrooms spacious. The popular restaurant is also open to non-residents. Pretty gardens and terrace.

Price: B&B £60–£77 pppn. Reductions given for winter breaks.

INN

King's Head Hotel

Thirlmere, near Keswick, CA12 4TN
017687 72393
www.lakedistrictinns.co.uk

The King's Head is on the A591 close to Thirlmere. Dating back to 1649, the building has plenty of character with a cosy bar and dining areas. Most of the rooms have fell views. The four-poster room is particularly pleasant, with a good-sized bathroom with claw-foot bath.

Price: B&B £45– £70pppn.

Langstrath Country Inn

Stonethwaite, Borrowdale, Keswick, CA12 5XG
017687 77239
www.thelangstrath.com

A family-run inn tucked away in a secluded valley, this is a good place to come to escape the Keswick crowds. The cottage was built in 1590, but the building has been converted to provide eight rooms, all of which have been decorated and furnished in a simple, but modern style.

Price: B&B £37.50–£49.50 pppn.

FARMSTAY

Yew Tree Farm

Rosthwaite, Borrowdale, Keswick, CA12 5XB
017687 77675
www.borrowdaleyewtreefarm.co.uk

Prince Charles sometimes stays in this cosy 18th-century farmhouse when he visits Cumbria. Low beams, uneven floors, no TV and no mobile reception give guests a taste of life on a working sheep farm. Most of the breakfast produce is local and the landlady, Hazel Relph, makes her own marmalades and jams.

Price: B&B £35 pppn.

The best... **PLACES TO STAY**

B & B

Ellas Crag

Stair, Newlands Valley, Keswick, CA12 5TS
017687 78217
www.ellascrag.co.uk

This warm and welcoming guesthouse occupies a superb location in the Newlands Valley with paths up on to the fells from the door and a garden full of birds and the occasional red squirrel. Great value for money, the rooms are immaculate. Guests have access to a large DVD collection.

Price: B&B £30 £32 pppn.

Glendale Guest House

7 Eskin Street, Keswick, CA12 4DH
017687 73562
www.glendalekeswick.co.uk

The five clean, comfortable rooms at Glendale are equipped with light wood furnishings making them bright and cheerful. Four rooms are en-suite with modern, tidy shower cubicles. The fifth is a family room with private bathroom. Centrally located, the guesthouse has storage facilities for bicycles and welcomes walkers.

Price: B&B £30–£35 pppn.

Abacourt House

26 Stanger Street, Keswick, CA12 5JU
017687 72967
www.abacourt.co.uk

This Victorian townhouse retains many of its original features, including the wooden staircase. Each of the rooms is individually furnished and includes plenty of storage space. Although located close to Keswick town centre's many pubs and restaurants, Stanger Street is a cul-de-sac, making it a relatively quiet location.

B&B £30 pppn.

SELF-CATERING

Underscar

Applethwaite, Keswick, CA12 4PH
017687 75544
www.heartofthelakes.co.uk

These are tastefully decorated, luxury apartments in a sublime spot under Skiddaw. Everything you need from a holiday home and more – a drying cabinet for wet boots, heated bathroom mirrors to prevent steaming, music system piped into all rooms, a shower that converts to a steam room and a smart, well-equipped kitchen.

One-bed apartments £625–£925 per week; two-bed apartments £850–£1,490; three-bed apartments £995–£1,590.

The best... PLACES TO STAY

UNUSUAL

Skiddaw House

Bassenthwaite, Keswick, CA12 4QX
07747 174293
www.skiddawhouse.co.uk

If you want to escape totally from the world, Skiddaw House bunkhouse has to be the answer. At 1,550 feet, this former shooting lodge occupies a lonely spot on the open fells, more than 3 miles from the nearest road. Only basic lighting is provided, so you'll need a torch.

Accommodation £11 per person for over-21s (YHA members, £14 for non-members), £9 for 16–21-year-olds and £6 for under-16s. No unaccompanied under-16s, self-serve breakfast trolley £2.25, cash or cheques only, no facilities for credit or debit cards, open 1 March–31 October. Groups only in winter.

SELF-CATERING

Morrel's Apartments

34 Lake Road, Keswick, CA12 5DQ
017687 72666
www.morrels.co.uk

Centrally located in Keswick town centre above the owners' popular restaurant, these two apartments are bright and modern with leather suites and widescreen TVs. The kitchens have been finished to a high specification and have dishwasher, microwave and electric double oven. Towels and linen are provided.

Two-bed apartment £295–£520 per week; three-bed apartment £350–£575.

Skiddaw House and Canuck Fell

The best... FOOD AND DRINK

As far as eating out goes, Keswick doesn't yet have the wide range of quality establishments seen elsewhere in the Lake District, but it is slowly catching up as mediocre Chinese and Indian restaurants are gradually replaced by businesses concentrating on good, fresh food produced locally.

Staying in

Despite food retailers being crowded out by the outdoor gear shops, self-caterers shouldn't have too much of a problem finding good quality produce in Keswick town centre. There are two supermarkets, including the small, Lancashire-based chain **Booths**, which, with its emphasis on local produce, has fewer of the big brand names than you'll see in the likes of Tesco and Sainsbury's.

Thomasons, the butcher-cum-deli on Station Street (01768 780169), sells Cumbrian pork and lamb as well as store-made oven-ready dishes and some great pies. Its superb Aberdeen Angus beef is bought in from Stirlingshire.

The reputable **Bryson's** on Main Street (017687 72257 www.brysonsof keswick.co.uk) has been baking bread and cakes for more than 60 years. Its specialities include Lakeland Plum Bread and delicious Borrowdale Tea Bread, all made to secret recipes.

A recent addition to the town is **Fond Ewe** fine cheeses (01768 773377, www.fondewe-cheeses.co.uk), a tiny shop tucked away on Packhorse Court, just around the corner from the Lakeland Pedlar café. As well as stocking cheeses from the Cumberland Dairy, Thornby Moor and Low Sizergh Barn, it also has an olive bar and sells a wide selection of infused oils in attractive bottles that can be refilled from the shop's large decanters. The rich and luxuriously soft Keldthwaite Gold, an award-winning brie made with the milk of Jersey cows, has to be tried!

Yew Tree Farm in Rosthwaite, Borrowdale – not to be confused with Beatrix Potter's farm near Coniston – is a 2,000-acre hill farm, specialising in pure Herdwick sheep meat, as tender as lamb but with the fuller, gamey flavour of mutton. Born in the valley, grown there, butchered there, vacuum-packed there, the meat is fully traceable. The enterprising Relph family, who run the farm, also have a farmhouse B&B and the Flock-in, a busy little café.

Borrowdale Trout Farm (017867 77293) at Seathwaite in Borrowdale sells both fresh and smoked trout as well as its own honey. It is open seven days a week, 10am–6pm, April to October only.

Takeaways

The best fish and chips in Keswick is to be found at the **Old Keswickian**, opposite the Tourist Information Centre (017687 73861, open daily 11am–11.45pm). Upstairs is a restaurant with seating for 60 people.

Barton's on Windebrowe Avenue (017687 72698, open Tues–Sat, 11.45am–1.30pm and 4.30–7pm), a little way back from the ambulance and fire station, is out of the town centre and so gets missed by a lot of tourists. The fish is always cooked in front of you, so you know it's freshly fried.

Salsa, the Mexican bistro opposite the Cars of the Stars museum, does good takeaway tapas, fajitas and enchiladas (017687 75222 www.salsabistro.co.uk, open daily 5.30–10pm).

For a lunchtime treat, the **Cornish Pasty Shop** on Lake Road (017687 72205, open 8am–6pm in summer, 9.30am–4pm in winter) serves up some tasty pasties including beef and Stilton, and broccoli, sweetcorn and cheese. Be warned though–they sell out fast on busy days!

EATING OUT

FINE DINING

Underscar Manor Country House and Restaurant
Applethwaite, Keswick, CA12 4PH
017687 75000
wwww.underscarmanor.co.uk

The conservatory dining room in this grand Italianate manor at the base of Skiddaw is all lace and chiffon. Traditional dishes such as seared fillet of Lakeland beef are cooked using only high quality ingredients. First courses from £9.50, mains £23. Menu Surprise available at £38 per head.

RESTAURANT

Morrel's
34 Lake Road, Keswick, CA12 5DQ
017687 72666
www.morrels.co.uk

This friendly restaurant has a smart look, with etched glass panels breaking up the dining area to give diners a little extra privacy. The menu combines modern and traditional – with starters priced at about £6 and mains from £9.50 to £18.50. Open Tues–Sat from 5.30pm. Pre-theatre bookings taken.

EATING OUT

Unique Fine Dining Restaurant
26 St Johns St, Keswick, CA12 5AS
017687 73400

A relatively new addition to the Keswick dining scene Unique serves good food at prices that are surprisingly reasonable for a tourist town. Local venison steak carved over a delicious sweet potato mash will set you back £12.50; poached plaice with a dill and prawn sauce just £10.95.

Lemon and Lime
31 Lake Road, Keswick, CA12 5DQ
017687 73088

As well as offering main courses from around the world, this bright and cheerful venue gives diners the choice of something a bit different – tapatinis, a form of tapas with a truly international feel. Thai fish cakes, yakitori chicken, black pudding, falafel... One dish costs £2.95, a selection of four is £9.95.

GASTRO PUB
Horse and Farrier Inn
Threlkeld, Keswick, CA12 4SQ
017687 79823
www.horseandfarrier.com

The award-winning head chef in this warm and inviting country pub injects a little imagination into traditional dishes, serving chicken supreme on a herb risotto (£13.95) and seabass with chorizo, sauce vierge and a balsamic reduction (£14.95). Also open for breakfasts 7.30–10am.

CAFÉ
Lakeland Pedlar Wholefood Café
Bell Close, Keswick, CA12 5JD
017687 74492
www.lakelandpedlar.co.uk

Vegetarian café with a wide range of international influences. The breakfast burrito – scrambled egg, veggie sausage, peppers, mushrooms and tomatoes wrapped in a flour tortilla blanket and served with cheese, sour cream and salsa – will keep you going 'til dinnertime (£7.10). Open 9am–5pm, later in the summer holiday.

The Flock-In
Rosthwaite, Borrowdale, CA12 5XB
017687 77675
www.borrowdaleherdwick.co.uk

This tiny café, popular with walkers, is part of a working sheep farm. Most of the dishes are based on the home-produced Herdwick sheep, including warming stews and the now famous Herdi-burger. Open Feb to Nov 10am–5pm, closed Wed (also closed Thurs in Nov).

🍷 Drinking

If it's real ale you're after, your best bet is the **Dog and Gun** on Lake Road. It's a fairly small, traditional pub, but the local beers make it worth the squeeze on busy summer weekends. Selections include beers from the Keswick Brewing Company just down the road and Yates in Aspatria, which was set up in 1986 by former Jennings head brewer Peter Yates. A few hundred yards away, the **George Hotel** on St Johns Street offers Jennings beers as well as regular guest ales.

Out of town, head for the wonderful **Middle Ruddings** in Braithwaite. More of a country inn than a pub, this hotel is run by Andy and Liz McMaster, a friendly couple who are clearly passionate about their beers. The rotating selection of beers comes from 18 Cumbrian breweries and Andy is happy for guests to order in other beers in advance – as long as he knows it's good stuff.

Established by Phil and Sue Harrison in the spring of 2006, the **Keswick Brewing Company** (017687 80700 www.keswickbrewery.co.uk, The Old Brewery, Brewery Lane, Keswick CA12 5BY) is one of the latest additions to Cumbria's blossoming beer scene. The couple sold their Keswick guesthouse to open the micro brewery, which they are pretty sure is on the site of the old Atkinsons brewery which closed in 1897. Their products include Thirst Pitch, Thirst Ascent and the golden bitter Thirst Winter. Guided tours (£5.50) and tastings by arrangement.

ⓘ Visitor Information

Tourist Information Centres:
Moot Hall, Market Square, Keswick,
017687 72645, open every day,
9.30am–4.30pm (5.30pm mid-March
to 31 Oct).

Hospitals: Minor Injuries Unit,
Keswick Cottage Hospital, Crosthwaite
Road, Keswick, CA12 5PH, 017687
67000); Penrith Community Hospital
(see p.280) can also deal with minor
injuries; for more serious problems,
West Cumberland Hospital,
Homewood, Hensingham, Whitehaven,
CA28 8JG, 01946 693181; or
Cumberland Infirmary, Newtown Road,
Carlisle, CA2 7HX, 01228 523444.

Doctors: Castlehead Medical Centre,
Ambleside Road, Keswick, CA12 4DB,
01768 772025, weekdays
8.30am–6pm; Bank Street Surgery, 9
Bank Street, Keswick, CA12 5JY,
01768 772438, weekdays 9–10am,
5–6pm, Saturdays 9–10am; Cuedoc,
01228 401999, out-of-hours
emergency doctor service.

Pharmacies: Boots, 017687 72383
open every day; Co-op Pharmacy, Main
Street, Keswick, 017687 72108,
closes 12.30pm Saturdays; JN Murray,
Station Street, Keswick, 017687
72049, 9am–5.30pm Mon–Sat; late
pharmacy on a rota basis.

Police: Bank Street, Keswick, 017687
72012.

Supermarkets: In Boothes, Keswick,
next to bus station; Co-op, Main Street,
Keswick, with launderette next door.

Parking: Several large car parks
dotted throughout town centre and at
Lakeside, all pay and display, and
regularly patrolled by wardens; on-
street parking is tight and drivers
must display a disc showing their time
of arrival, discs available from Tourist
Information Centre.

Internet Access: Post Office, corner
of Main Street and Bank Street;
Northern Light Gallery, St John's
Street, Keswick, 017687 75402;
public library, Heads Lane, Keswick,
near the bus station.

Car Hire: Keswick Motor Company,
Lake Road, opposite George Fisher;
017687 72064, closed Sundays.

Left Luggage: The Launderette, Main
Street, next to Co-op, 017687 75448,
8am–7pm, £1 per item.

Bike Rental: Keswick Mountain Bikes,
017687 75202/75752,
www.keswickmountainbikes.co.uk,
outlets behind the Pencil Museum in
town centre at the Lakeland Pedlar
café, daily 9am–5pm; from £17 for a
full day. Experienced mountain bike
guides also available for £150 per
day; Keswick Motor Company, Lake
Road, 017687 72064, closed
Sundays, £10 half day, £15 full day.

Taxis: Davies Taxis, 017687 72676,
www.daviestaxis.co.uk; KLM Taxis,
017687 75337, www.klmtravel.co.uk.

BASSENTHWAITE AND THE NORTHERN FELLS

Bassenthwaite Lake lies to the north of Keswick, flanked by Skiddaw to the east and the Whinlatter forests to the west. There are few villages here – just a scattering of hamlets and centuries-old inns. Driving up the A66 from Keswick towards Cockermouth, you get a clear – and sad – sense of coming to the 'end' of the Lake District as the surrounding countryside begins to flatten out and fells become replaced by fields and farms. But don't despair, there is still lots of spectacular fell scenery in this area, particularly around Coledale. And, it being on the edge of the National Park, this is one of the quieter parts of the Lakes.

Quieter still are the settlements dotted along the base of the Northern Fells – Uldale, Caldbeck, Hesket Newmarket and Mungrisdale. These are some of the National Park's best-kept secrets; pretty villages that seem almost untouched by tourism. Sheep and friendly fell ponies, unique to the area, wander the quiet country lanes. Caldbeck, nestling in a lovely valley with its duck pond, interesting churchyard, old mills and gentle walks, is definitely worth a visit.

Nature lovers come to this area to appreciate the solitude of the rolling, grassy hills of the Northern Fells and to watch the wildlife, including the famous ospreys. One of the top attractions, apart from the wonderful assets that nature has bestowed on the area, is lovely Mirehouse, tucked in at the base of the fells with the brooding mass of Skiddaw looming over it. Children of all ages will love Trotters World of Animals and if you're here at midsummer, you can always go ghost-hunting on lonely Souther Fell!

There are also plenty of interesting places to stay and to eat at, some of the best being hidden away in beautiful lakeside locations or in the forest itself – historic inns, converted stately homes, and pubs and cafés that pride themselves on serving up quality, local produce.

WHAT TO SEE AND DO

 Fair weather

If you visit the Bassenthwaite area, you must at least *try* to see the **ospreys** that nest beside the lake. These magnificent fish-eating birds of prey returned to

LAKE DISTRICT OSPREY PROJECT, for Dodd Wood viewing platform, park at Old Sawmill Tearoom car park, CA12 4QE and follow waymarkers; 017687 78469; www.ospreywatch.co.uk; admission free; Dodd Wood viewing area and Whinlatter exhibition open Apr–Sept.

Cumbria in 2001 after a 150-year absence and now look set to stay. They spend the summer in the county, arriving in April and returning to Africa in September, having reared a small family of two or three chicks. A viewing area has been set up in Dodd Wood and volunteers will help you spot the birds through powerful binoculars. Seeing them fishing is quite a sight! Cameras are also trained on the huge nest and bird-lovers can watch the ospreys on large video screens in the Visitor Centre at Whinlatter Forest.

AIR VENTURES PARAGLIDING SCHOOL, 07830 281986; www.airventures.co.uk; tandem flights £35–£95, taster days £135; based near Bassenthwaite; all flights depart from this area; telephone for directions and further details.

For a completely different perspective on Bassenthwaite Lake and its surrounding fells, Gordon Oliver will take you for a breathtaking tandem **paraglide**. Alternatively, if you've got a whole day to spare, why not try the taster day? After being shown emergency procedures and how the equipment works, you learn how to handle the canopy. Then it's up, up and away for an afternoon of short, independent flights.

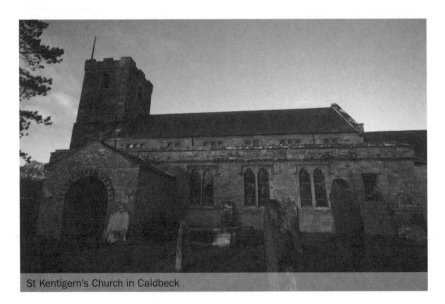

St Kentigern's Church in Caldbeck

The 12th-century **St Kentigern's Church** in Caldbeck is the resting place of the famous 19th-century huntsman, John Peel, as well as Mary Robinson, the Maid of Buttermere (see p.194). On the riverbank behind the church is St Mungo's Well, a spring made holy by Kentigern. The pretty conservation village of **Caldbeck** itself is worth some exploration. Take a walk from the car park, past the duck pond and up to the Howk, the name given locally to the picturesque ruins of an old bobbin mill located in a stunning gorge. Alternatively, head in the opposite direction to Watersmeet, an enchanting 'island' in the woods. Where the River Caldew meets Cald Beck, the channels practically encircle a small, wooded glade, leaving it almost entirely cut off from everything around it. This is a particularly lovely spot in the spring when woodland flowers fill it with colour and fragrance. Ask in the Old Smithy for directions.

The Northern Fells form a mass of rounded hills on the very edge of the National Park. Aside from Skiddaw and Blencathra, the **walking** experience here is very different from elsewhere in the Lake District; instead of bare rock, you'll feel grass under your boots, and you're unlikely to meet the crowds that you'll find on Cat Bells or Helvellyn. For peace and solitude – and the occasional fox or hare – head up High Pike (5-mile round walk from Fellside), Carrock Fell (4-mile round walk from near Calebreck), Knott (8-mile round walk from Green Head) or haunted Souther Fell (4.7-mile round walk from Mungrisdale).

Local Legends: the ghosts of Souther Fell

It was on Souther Fell, on Midsummer's Eve in 1735, that William Lancaster's servant saw a troop of ghostly horsemen crossing the fell.

Exactly a year later, Mr Lancaster and his family saw the same sight. All were ridiculed when they told of the huge numbers involved, ascending a stretch of the fell that no rider would attempt.

So, a few years later, again on Midsummer's Eve, Mr Lancaster took 26 companions with him to witness the spectacle. They all saw the horsemen and even went to investigate the ground they had ridden on, finding no sign of hoofprints or other evidence that horses had passed that way.

Wet weather

Wander around the elegant **Mirehouse** to the sound of live piano music. The house, built in 1666, is home to a collection of letters from Wordsworth, Tennyson, Southey, Thomas Carlyle and John Constable. But the really good thing about this house is that it feels as if it might actually be someone's home, rather than merely a relic of the past. And, if the sun shows itself, head out into the sprawling lakeside grounds to discover the children's playgrounds, a heather maze and a rhododendron tunnel. Unlike other, stuffier houses, there is plenty here to keep children entertained. As well as four adventure playgrounds, regularly updated children's nature notes are provided to keep the youngsters occupied while the adults enjoy a stroll.

MIREHOUSE, 3 miles north of Keswick on A591, CA12 4QE; 017687 72287; www.mirehouse.com; house and grounds £5.60 adults, £2.80 children; grounds only £2.80 adults, £1.40 children; open Mar–Oct; gardens, lakeside walk and tea room, daily 10am–5.30pm, house Sun and Weds only, 2pm–5pm.

 ## What to do with children...

Located at the northern end of the lake is **Trotters World of Animals**, a chance for young and old alike to meet gibbons, zebras, an assortment of reptiles and the only Canadian lynx in the UK. Events throughout the day enable visitors to handle some of the animals, and the birds of prey put on regular flying displays. The site also has play areas, picnic benches, a tea room and an indoor soft play climbing centre – enough to make a day of it.

TROTTERS WORLD OF ANIMALS, follow brown signs on A591 and A66 from end of Bassenthwaite Lake, CA12 4RD; 017687 76239; www.trottersworld.com; £6.50 adults, £4.80 children, open daily 10am–5.30pm/dusk.

Whinlatter Forest Park is home to miles of walking and cycling trails as well as a great little café. The Amazing Badger Sett, a warren of low passageways built into a small earth-mound, gives young wildlife enthusiasts a chance to discover what it's like to live underground. New mountain bike trails and a Go Ape! high-wire forest adventure course are set to open in 2008. The osprey exhibition is open April to September (see above).

WHINLATTER FOREST PARK, Whinlatter Pass (B5292), Braithwaite CA12 5TW; 017687 78469; www.forestry.gov.uk; admission free; open all year.

The foolish Bishop

As you travel up the A66 from Keswick to Cockermouth, you can hardly fail to notice the lump of bright, white rock about halfway up the fellside above Thornthwaite. This is the Bishop of Barf. Barf is the name of the fell, formerly known as Barrugh Fell and probably deriving from the old Norse for mountain (berg). The 'Bishop' part is a longer tale...

In 1783, the rather foolhardy Bishop of Derry was staying at an inn in Thornthwaite when, after a little too much to drink, he had a wager with the locals. He claimed that he could ride over Barf to Whitehaven. The next day, he and his horse headed up the steep, scree-covered fell. His wager – and his life – came to a sudden end when he slipped and plunged down the fellside. The white rock 700ft up the fell marks the place at which he fell and is still regularly whitewashed today.

The Bishop of Barf

Entertainment

Special events
The **Hesket Newmarket Agricultural Show** is held at the end of the summer. This traditional event includes livestock judging, terrier racing, children's competitions and a chance for grown men to wear their underpants as overpants in the Cumberland and Westmorland wrestling. For further information and details on exact dates contact Keswick's Tourist Information Centre.

The best... PLACES TO STAY

HOTEL

Armathwaite Hall Country House

**Bassenthwaite Lake, Keswick,
CA12 4RE
017687 76551
www.armathwaite-hall.com**

Wood panelling, grand staircases, open fires and rich, deep colours – all that you'd expect of a 17th-century hall. What you don't expect though are plasma screens in the bathrooms, iPod docking stations and activity clubs to keep the kids entertained. A wonderful mix of the traditional and the modern.

Price: B&B £105–£175 pppn.

The Cottage in the Wood

**Whinlatter Forest, Keswick,
CA12 5TW
017687 78409
www.thecottageinthewood.co.uk**

Great care and thought has gone into the design of this calm and tranquil hotel in the middle of the forest. The owners, Kath and Liam, are warm, friendly and enthusiastic – they clearly love their work. Liam's cooking, using local produce as much as possible, is becoming famous locally.

Price: B&B £84–£120 per room per night. Special rates apply for five nights or more.

INN

The Pheasant

**Bassenthwaite Lake, Cockermouth,
CA13 9YE
017687 76234
www.the-pheasant.co.uk**

This mellow, centuries-old inn is the sort of place you can't wait to come back to after a cold day on the fells – open fires, exposed beams and home-made scones all in a peaceful setting on the forest edge. The spacious rooms are furnished with king-size beds and soft chairs.

Price: B&B £70–£90 pppn, single rooms £75–£80.

FARMSTAY

Kiln Hill Barn

**Bassenthwaite, Keswick, CA12 4RG
017687 76454
www.kilnhillbarn.co.uk**

This smallholding beside the A591 and close to Bassenthwaite Lake offers simple, but comfortable and good value accommodation in a converted barn. The rooms, all of which are en-suite, have plenty of space and some have lake views.

Price: B&B £32 pppn (or £210 per week); dinner £13 extra.

The best... **PLACES TO STAY**

B&B

Boltongate Old Rectory

Boltongate, Ireby, CA7 1DA
016973 71647
www.boltongateoldrectory.com

A calm atmosphere and elegant surroundings await guests at this small B&B, which won the title of Bed and Breakfast of the Year at the 2007 Northwest Tourism Awards. Towelling dressing gowns provided. En-suites have underfloor heating. Peaceful village location close to the edge of the National Park.

Price: B&B £44–£55 pppn. Dinner by prior arrangement at £30 per person.

SELF-CATERING

Bassenthwaite Lakeside Lodges

Scarness, Bassenthwaite, Keswick, CA12 4QZ
017687 76641 or 0845 4565276
www.bll.ac

A peaceful, relaxing location beside Bassenthwaite Lake. This family-friendly site offers a range of self-catering accommodation, sleeping up to six people. Each lodge has french doors leading to a private patio complete with gas barbecue. The particularly spacious, top-of-the-range lakeside cabins have uninterrupted views of the lake and fells beyond.

Price: £378–£1,049 per week.

The best... **FOOD AND DRINK**

Staying in

Self-caterers can buy Fairtrade produce such as rice and other basic ingredients from the **Old Smithy** in Caldbeck (016974 78246), but for fresh produce you will need to travel into one of the nearest towns – Keswick, Cockermouth or Penrith (see the relevant listings for more details).

Alternatively, for people staying in the Northern Fells villages, nearby Wigton has a small, but good selection of local shops. For fruit and vegetables, greengrocer **Lightfoot's** on High Street (016973 44383) is open 8am–5pm Mon–Fri and 8am–4pm Sat. The butcher **R J Harrison** on King Street (016973 42192) sources most of its meat locally and is open 7am–5pm six days a week.

Carolyn Fairbairn began making cheese using milk from her small herd of goats in 1979. Within a year, she was also using the cows' milk from a neighbouring farm. Since then, **Thornby Moor Dairy** has built up a solid reputation locally, appearing on menus in many of the county's best restaurants. The shop at Crofton Hall, Thursby, near Wigton (01697 345555) is open to the public. Products include the full-flavoured goat's cheese Tovey, a rich ewe's milk cheese called Croglin and the traditional Cumberland Farmhouse.

Takeaways

Luigi's on King Street in Wigton (016973 49208) does decent pizzas and will deliver within a reasonable distance. (Open 4.30pm to midnight most days and until 1am on Fridays. Closed Mondays and Tuesdays.) For fish and chips, **George's Plaice** on High Street, Wigton (016973 44187) is open 4pm–8pm.

EATING OUT

FINE DINING
Overwater Hall
Ireby, CA7 1HH
017687 76566
www.overwaterhall.co.uk

Dinner in this Georgian mansion is like stepping back in time in terms of its grand surroundings and quality service. A typical main course might be Thirlmere venison pan-fried in Cumbrian air-dried ham, served with grilled Lakeland haggis and fondant potato on a port and elderberry sauce. Five courses £42.50.

GASTRO PUB
The Pheasant
Bassenthwaite Lake, Cockermouth,
CA13 9YE
017687 76234
www.the-pheasant.co.uk

The menu changes daily at this charming and serene award-winning inn. Start with pan-fried breast of wood pigeon served with mulled blackberries and carrot purée and then savour the steamed fillet of red bream in a saffron and prawn chowder. Three courses cost £29.95, four courses £33.75.

EATING OUT

The Snooty Fox
Uldale, CA7 1HA
016973 71479
www.snootyfox-uldale.co.uk

This traditional Cumbrian village pub serves up some imaginative dishes using mostly local produce. There's a wide range of vegetarian dishes and a long list of specials. Starters are £5.25 and main courses from £8.75 to about £15. Whatever you choose, have the chips with it – they're to die for!

The Mill Inn
Mungrisdale, Penrith, CA11 0XR
017687 79632
www.the-millinn.co.uk

Located on the eastern edge of the northern fells, the Mill Inn has a reputation for good quality, no-nonsense food. A hearty meal of spicy Cumberland sausage with spring onion mash and vegetables costs £8.95. The pies are so good that the owners had to find alternative premises to meet demand.

CAFÉ
Watermill Café
Priest's Mill, Caldbeck, CA7 8DR
016974 78267
www.watermillcafe.co.uk

The first floor of this mill has been sympathetically restored to house one of the area's most popular cafes. The Watermill proudly serves up a range of light, wholesome lunches made using mostly local produce. Meals around £6.50–£7.25; soup, £3.15. Open 9am–5pm (4.30pm in winter).

Siskins Café
Whinlatter Forest Park, Braithwaite, Keswick, CA12 5TW
017687 78410

You may have to wait a while for your food in this busy café in the Whinlatter Visitor Centre, but the end result is worth it. Panini and sandwiches £5, filled ciabattas £5.10, large and imaginative salads from £6.20. Breakfasts served 10–11.30am. Lots of children's meals and delicious, home-made cakes.

🍷 Drinking

By far the most famous pub in the area is the **Old Crown** in Hesket Newmarket (016974 78288), which became Britain's first co-operative owned pub a few years ago when 125 villagers, including Sir Chris Bonington, clubbed together to stop it falling into the hands of a major brewery. The cosy, traditional bar serves a range of distinctive, full-flavoured beers produced at the Hesket Newmarket Brewery, also owned by a local co-operative. These include the award-winning Doris' Ninetieth Birthday Ale (ABV 4.3%) and the dark, malty Blencathra Bitter (ABV 3.2%). Brewery tours for a minimum of eight people are available by arrangement only.

ⓘ Visitor Information

Tourist Information Centres: See Keswick.

Hospitals: Minor Injuries Unit, Keswick Cottage Hospital; Minor Injuries Unit' Penrith Community Hospital (p.280); for more serious problems, West Cumberland Hospital, Homewood, Hensingham, Whitehaven, CA28 8JG, 01946 693181; or Cumberland Infirmary, Newtown Road, Carlisle, CA2 7HX, 01228 523444.

Doctors: Caldbeck Surgery, Friar Row, Caldbeck, 016974 78254, www.caldbecksurgery.co.uk (dispensing practice), Mon–Fri 8am–6.30pm; Cuedoc, 01228 401999, out-of-hours emergency doctor service.

Pharmacies: Co-op, King Street, Wigton, 016973 42445, Mon–Sat 8.45am –5.30pm (6.30pm alternate weeks); Pharmacy, The Square, Dalston, 01228 712506; also Keswick, Cockermouth (see p.208) or Penrith (see p.280).

Police: Bank Street, Keswick, 017687 72012; Station Road, Wigton, 0845 3300247.

Supermarkets: The nearest are in Keswick, Cockermouth (see p.208) and Penrith (see p.280); for those staying along the northern edge of the National Park, Wigton may be nearer, Somerfield, Station Road, 016973 45232.

Parking: Free car park in Caldbeck. Pay and display at Forestry Commission sites.

Internet Access: See Keswick.

Car Hire: See Keswick.

Left Luggage: See Keswick.

Bike Rental: See Keswick.

Taxis: Station House Taxis and Minibus, Wigton, 016973 43148.

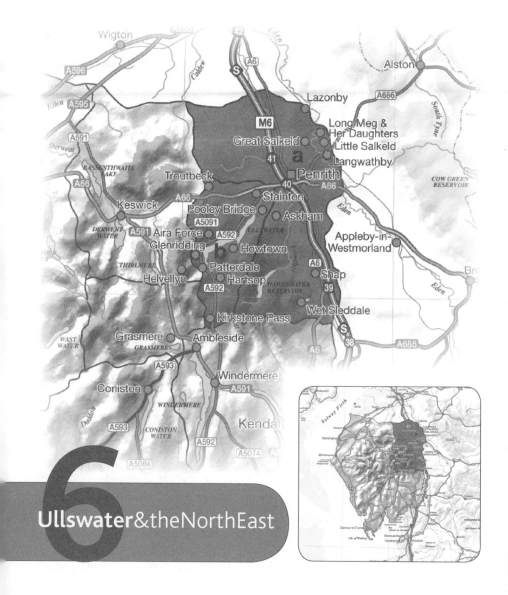

6

Ullswater&theNorthEast

a. Penrith and around

b. Ullswater

Unmissable highlights

01 Stroll through a beautiful arboretum to the base of the magnificent Aira Force waterfall, p.283

02 Enjoy a trip across the lake from Glenridding on the Ullswater 'Steamer' and then walk back from Howtown along the lakeshore, p.285

03 Take your binoculars to the far end of Haweswater and try to spot England's elusive golden eagle, p.266

04 Climb Helvellyn, England's third highest mountain, via the narrow and exposed Striding Edge, p.283

05 Treat yourself to afternoon tea at Cumbria's most famous hotel, the Sharrow Bay, and enjoy the spectacular views down the lake, p.295

06 Saddle up and enjoy a sedate horse ride over the rolling and grassy eastern fells, p.287

07 Watch a 'Giant Movie' on Rheged's enormous cinema screen, as big as six double decker buses, p.290

08 Visit the mystical site of Long Meg and Her Daughters and ponder over the mysteries of the stones, p.262

09 Wander through the High Head Sculpture Valley to see fascinating artwork in a gorgeous woodland setting, p.271

10 Spend a day with the whole family splashing about in the water chutes and slides at Center Parcs' Whinfell Forest site, p.270

ULLSWATER AND THE NORTH-EAST

Breathtaking isn't an adjective to be bandied about on a daily basis, but it is the only word that accurately describes some of the wild, mountain scenery on the north-eastern edge of the Lake District.

Approaching from the south, your first encounter with the area is the view from Kirkstone Pass, one that is sure to stop you in your tracks and make you take a long, deep breath in. Standing at the haunted inn that has occupied this 1,500ft high gap in the mountains' defences for centuries, you look down the winding A592 as it cuts through the steep scree and boulder-strewn slopes – all the way down to Brothers Water and the fells beyond.

The narrow, rugged valley below is home to isolated farmhouses and a few small hamlets and villages – Hartsop, Patterdale and Glenridding being the first you encounter. Beyond that, after you pass below the inhospitable cliffs of the magnificent Helvellyn range, the valley begins to widen out and you reach the scattered settlement of Watermillock and then Pooley Bridge.

This is where the drama of the Lake District proper ends and you enter pretty, rolling countryside alongside the rivers Eamont and Lowther as they meander their way past attractive villages and historic sites to a rendezvous with the River Eden just east of the interesting market town of Penrith.

Further south and on the far eastern edge of the National Park, the lonely fells are home to England's last golden eagle. The drowned village of Mardale is here too – below the waters of Haweswater reservoir. Looking east from here, way beyond the Lake District, you can see across the lovely Eden Valley to the highest hills of the long Pennine chain.

Needless to say, this area, like much of the rest of the Lake District, is beloved of anyone with a passion for the outdoors – divers, kayakers and sailors find Ullswater satisfies their every need, while the fells promise both excitement and serenity for climbers, walkers, horse-riders, even skiers.

But that's not to say you have to be fit and active to enjoy the Lake District's north-eastern corner; there are also stately homes, castles, countless galleries and artists' studios, and even a 'village' built into a man-made hill.

Accommodation here tends to be of a very high quality – with some of the north's most beautifully located hotels situated along Ullswater's long shoreline. Eating out too is always a pleasure with superb cafés and award-winning pubs hidden away in the most unlikely of places. And let's not forget the Sharrow Bay – one of Cumbria's three Michelin-starred restaurants.

PENRITH AND AROUND

The market town of Penrith lies just to the east of the Lake District National Park. Built largely from the red sandstone found throughout the Eden Valley, it is an attractive town with a rich and interesting history. The lore, legends and language of Celts, Romans, Saxons and Vikings have all played a part in enriching the culture of the area. The two oldest streets, Burrowgate and Sandgate, date from the 13th century, and many of the town's old yards and buildings are on sites that follow the plan of the medieval settlement.

The region is home to castles and fortified towers built by barons and feudal chiefs during the violent times when England and Scotland fought for power. Some of these, such as Brougham Castle and Hutton-in-the-Forest are open to the public.

With an ancient history comes much myth and speculation. A legendary giant and King of All Cumbria, is said to be buried in the Giant's Grave in St Andrew's churchyard in the town centre. Beyond Penrith's borders, the ancient henge sites of Mayburgh and King Arthur's Round Table, the stone circle known as Long Meg and Her Daughters and various scattered standing stones all add to the area's atmosphere of mystery.

Maybe it is this sense of the unknown, coupled with a stunning and varied landscape, that attracts artists and writers to the area. There are plenty of opportunities to visit galleries and studios in the villages and hamlets surrounding Penrith.

Although the countryside is not as spectacular as in the National Park itself, it is still absolutely gorgeous. Walking in the wooded gorges of the Eden Valley at sunset or cycling through out-of-the-way villages all along the edge of the eastern fells is truly inspiring.

The agricultural industry, particularly livestock farming, plays a big part in the area's economy and, because of this, there are plenty of shops, restaurants and cafés that source a huge amount of their produce locally. The result is that consumers get particularly high quality food. If you're planning a meal out, plan two or three instead, because you'll be spoiled for choice.

WHAT TO SEE AND DO

Fair weather

Located at the foot of the Pennines and close to the River Eden near Little Salkeld, **Long Meg and Her Daughters** has to be one of the most impressive and enigmatic stone circles in Britain. The most famous of the stones is Long Meg, a 13ft tall piece of red sandstone standing slightly apart from the circle of almost 60

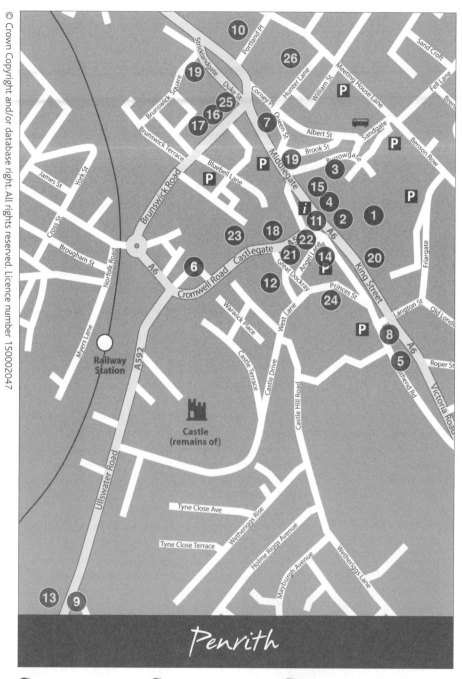

Penrith

① St Andrew's Church	⑩ Brooklands Guest House	⑲ Townhead Fish & Chip Shop
② Tudor House	⑪ J&J Graham	⑳ Cagneys
③ Noah's Ark	⑫ Gordon Clark	㉑ Courtyard Chinese Restaurant
④ George Hotel	⑬ Cranstons	㉒ Gianni's
⑤ Penrith Leisure Centre	⑭ Star Fruits	㉓ Grant's
⑥ Penrith Playhouse	⑮ The Fish Cellar	㉔ Bewicks Coffee House
⑦ Lonsdale Cinema	⑯ Brunswick Deli	㉕ Arragon's Cycle Centre
⑧ No 15	⑰ The Toffee Shop	㉖ Police Station
⑨ North Lakes Hotel	⑱ The Little Chippy	

Long Meg

'daughter' stones made from granite. There are faint outlines of mysterious spiral carvings and a cup and ring mark on Long Meg, possibly dating from the Bronze Age.

Long Meg can be reached by taking the Glassonby road out of Little Salkeld and then turning down a narrow lane on the left, about half a mile from the village. Alternatively, pick up one of the walking booklets published by the East Cumbria Countryside Project and follow a fascinating route from the village and along the River Eden. This also takes in Lacy's Caves, a series of caverns carved into the red sandstone on the riverbank by the local squire Colonel Lacy who entertained his guests here in the 19th century.

Long Meg and Her Daughters (grid reference NY571372) is open at all times and there is no admission fee.

BROUGHAM CASTLE, Brougham, Penrith CA10 2AA; 01768 862488; www.english-heritage.org.uk, adults £3, children £1.50; open daily Apr–Sept, 10am–5pm.

The romantic ruins of medieval **Brougham Castle** are located on the banks of the River Eamont, near the site of a Roman fort guarding the ford. The 13th-century keep survives as do many of the buildings later added by the powerful Clifford family. In the 17th century, the property was one of many castles and churches restored by Lady Anne Clifford. An exhibition at the site includes stones from the Roman fort.

Beautiful **Shap Abbey** is hidden away in a secluded river valley on the edge of the eastern fells. It was built by a small group of Premonstratensian canons in the late

Shap Abbey

SHAP ABBEY, SHAP, CA10 3NB; no admission fee; open daily; site managed by English Heritage.

Local legends: Long Meg

There are a lot of spooky legends associated with Long Meg and Her Daughters. The mysterious circle is said to be the petrified remains of a coven of witches – or a witch and her daughters – who were turned to stone by a Scottish wizard, Michael Scot, for profanities on the Sabbath. The site is supposedly endowed with magic, so that it is impossible to count the same number of stones twice. If you do manage to do so, then the magic is broken (or, alternatively, you are cursed by bad luck).

It is also said that when the local squire, Colonel Lacy, attempted to destroy the stones in the early part of the 19th century, a terrifying storm broke out and the labourers fled in fear of black magic. A prophecy states that if Long Meg were ever to be shattered, she would run with blood.

12th century. Originating from northern France, these 'white monks' sought out particularly isolated and lonely locations for their abbeys. And they weren't wrong with this one – although it is only about a mile from the A6 north of Shap, it feels very much off the beaten track. A substantial amount of the 15th-century west tower remains.

There are a number of standing stones in fields within easy walking distance of the abbey.

Keld Chapel is thought to have been a 'chantry' owned by the Shap canons, dating from about 1350. The custom of saying Mass for those who had died became popular in the Middle Ages, some wealthy people even leaving money so that prayers could be said in perpetuity. Religious houses became overwhelmed by this practice, so they sometimes set up 'chantries' which were dedicated to this purpose.

> KELD CHAPEL, grid ref. NY553145, about two-thirds of a mile SE of Shap Abbey; open daily; key in village – see notice on chapel door; National Trust site.

CELEBRITY CONNECTIONS

Wet Sleddale is a bleak and lonely valley to the south of Shap. It's not the sort of place that tourists generally head for – unless, that is, they are fans of the cult comedy film *Withnail and I*. Made in 1987 starring **Richard E Grant** and **Paul McGann**, the film used several locations in the area. Sleddale Hall, now a ruin about halfway up the fellside, is known in the film as Crow Crag, the home of Withnail's Uncle Monty. The view from the fictional cottage is of Haweswater, which is in fact several miles away. Some scenes are set in Penrith and, when *Withnail and I* celebrated its 10th anniversary, the town was offered a special re-launch preview screening. The powers-that-be said no because they thought it didn't show Penrith in a good light.

Sleddale Hall

Mayburgh Henge is a large and impressive circular bank, up to 21ft high, dating from Neolithic times. It contains a single standing stone, close to its centre. Nearby is **King Arthur's Round Table**, a slightly less well-preserved circular enclosure with a surrounding ditch. Local legend suggests this was King Arthur's jousting arena.

There is free access to the sites, which can be found by following the A6 south from Penrith and then turning right at the mini-roundabout in Eamont Bridge.

Pick up the Access For All Walk leaflet at the Penrith Tourist Information Centre and take yourself on a **self-guided walking tour** of this interesting town. Highlights include the **Musgrave Monument** clock tower, built in 1861, the rather grand-looking **George Hotel** and a picturesque Tudor house. **St Andrew's Church**, which includes a medieval tower from the 13th century, is the resting place of John and Mary Hutchinson, William Wordsworth's in-laws. The churchyard also contains the **Giant's Grave**, which, according to legend, is the burial place of a 10th-century king of Cumbria. The four hog-back stones surrounding the grave are said to represent wild boar he killed in nearby Inglewood Forest. The **Giant's Thumb**, nearby, is a fine example of a Norse wheel cross. The whole tour takes about an hour, but does not include a visit to the scant sandstone remains of **Penrith Castle**, which are in the park opposite the railway station (open daily, no admission fee).

HAWESWATER RESERVE, grid ref. NY469108; 01931 713376; always open; Eagle viewpoint open 11am–4pm Apr–Aug.

Nature reserves and gardens

The **RSPB's Haweswater Reserve** is set in a spectacular location at the foot of High Street's eastern cliffs. But it's not really the location that most people come for; it's the area's famous resident – England's last remaining golden eagle.

Golden eagles have been nesting here since 1969, producing 16 young in that time. Sadly, the female bird went missing in 2004, but the male, who is only 10 years old, is still in the area, keeping his eagle eyes open for a passing mate.

ACORN BANK GARDEN AND WATERMILL, Temple Sowerby CA10 1SP; 017683 618930; www.nationaltrust. org.uk; adults £3.40, children £1.70, family £8.50; open Mar–Oct Wed–Sun 10am–5pm.

The serene walled gardens at **Acorn Bank**, sheltered from the worst of the Pennine weather by tall, ancient oaks, is planted with 250 medicinal and culinary herbs. Its orchards are well known for their old English fruit varieties and the National Trust organises an 'apple day'

Haweswater Reservoir

Driving along the road beside Haweswater Reservoir, it is hard to believe that, less than 80 years ago, this used to be a pretty valley dotted with homes and farms. There were, in fact, two villages here – Mardale Green and Measand. Despite much opposition, the construction of the reservoir began in 1929 after Parliament passed an Act giving the Manchester Corporation permission to build. The valley was flooded in 1935, but before that all the homes and farms were demolished. The village church was dismantled and all the bodies in the churchyard were exhumed and re-buried at Shap. In times of drought, the skeleton of Mardale Green becomes visible as the water recedes to reveal stone walls and the village bridge at what is now the southern end of the reservoir.

Sarah Hall's Commonwealth Writers Prize-winning novel *Haweswater* is set in Mardale at the time of the building of the dam.

Haweswater Reservoir

in October to celebrate this fact. The day includes apple bobbing, storytelling, cookery demonstrations, children's music, craft workshops, a treasure hunt, Punch and Judy and Morris dancers. Outside the walls, follow the path through the woods and alongside Crowdundle Beck to the partially restored watermill, which is also open to visitors.

Winderwath Gardens is not far from Acorn Bank in Temple Sowerby and provides a pleasant contrast to the National Trust site for garden lovers. This 4.5 acre private garden includes rockeries, herbaceous borders and mature trees, and is home to many rare Himalayan species. Picnic tables overlook the pond.

WINDERWATH GARDENS, Temple Sowerby CA10 2AG; 01768 88250; adults £3, children free; open all year Mon–Fri 10am–4pm, Sat 9am–12 noon.

HUTTON-IN-THE-FOREST, Penrith CA11 9TH; 017684 84449; www.hutton-in-the-forest.co.uk; house and gardens £7 adults, £5 students, £3 children, £17 family; gardens only £4 adults, £2.50 students, £1.50 children; house open Wed, Thur, Sun and bank holiday Mondays during Easter holidays/May–Sept 12.30pm–4pm; gardens and grounds open daily except Sat, Apr–Oct 11am–5pm.

THE WATERMILL, Little Salkeld CA10 1NN; 01768 881523; www.organicmill.co.uk; tours adults £3.50, children £1.50, families £8; tours at 2pm and 3.30pm on Mon, Tues, Thu, Fri and Sun Feb–Christmas.

Historic sites

Hutton-in-the-Forest is the beautiful, medieval home of Lord and Lady Inglewood. The house has been in the family since 1605 and displays an interesting range of architectural styles as successive generations have added to it. Outside, the wonderful walled garden contains a large collection of herbaceous plants. The grounds are used to host a variety of events, including horse trials and productions of Shakespeare plays.

The Watermill at Little Salkeld is Cumbria's only fully operational watermill. The gorgeous, 18th-century buildings were lovingly restored (and painted pink!) by Ana and Nick Jones in 1975. The owners and their dedicated, enthusiastic team run tours of this fascinating site where you can see a wide range of organic stoneground flours being produced the traditional way – using clean, self-renewing waterpower. The full range of flours is on sale next door in the delightful café.

 # Wet weather

UPFRONT GALLERY, Hutton-in-the-Forest, Penrith CA11 9TG; 017684 84538; www.up-front.com; admission free; open 10am–5pm, closed Mon except bank holidays.

WETHERIGGS POTTERY, Clifton Dykes, Penrith CA10 2DH; 01768 892733; www.wetheriggs-pottery.co.uk; admission free; open daily 10am–4.30pm except Christmas Day, Boxing Day and New Year's Day.

Galleries and studios

The busy **Upfront Gallery** is housed in a converted 17th-century farmhouse that recently won a rural architecture award. About 18 exhibitions are held each year in four different spaces. The gallery also has a popular vegetarian café and is home to the Upfront Puppet Theatre, which stages charming productions during the main school holidays.

Wetheriggs Pottery is so much more than just a pottery. This former industrial site, built in the middle of the 19th century, is now a busy, thriving complex of artists' galleries, studios and shops. Ironwork, ceramics, paintings, glassware and thought-provoking sculptures are created by a group of eight

The Visitors' Book

Visiting Haweswater

'I have been visiting the Lakes with my family twice yearly for almost 24 years.

'One particular area I like to visit is Haweswater. It tends to be one of the less frequented lakes but is no less spectacular than any of the others. Haweswater and the surrounding fells offer many different views, and the opportunity for some breathtaking photography and panoramas. When the lake is low the remains of the drowned village of Mardale can be seen, and in cold weather there is often snow atop High Street and the other surrounding fells.

'On a typical day, we drive down to Haweswater in the morning (a trip that can be very exciting in treacherous weather conditions), park in the car park at the end of the road and then begin a circular walk over the top of High Street, passing the delightful tarn, aptly named Small Water. Atop High Street wonderful vistas open up in all directions and you can enjoy a picnic admiring the fells ponies. On the way back down we walk along a stony path — the Rigg. Quite steep in places, but again with lovely views of the main expanse of water and Blea Tarn.

'From Haweswater we head to Askham, with its old Lakeland houses either side of the village green. From Askham we continue our journey through the Lowther Estate to the remains of the 'fairytale' Lowther castle, taken directly from some ancient story of wizards, knights and captured princesses. Returning home we know we've spent a lovely day taking in the scenery; recording with photographs the views, flora, fauna, waterfalls, lakes and castle that we have seen. Where else could you see so many things in such a short space of time?'

Rich Rumsey, Wiltshire

talented artists based here. There's also a special studio where visitors can let their imaginations run free – throw your own pot, paint a vase or create a mosaic! The Kiln Café serves freshly cooked food and home-baked cakes.

RED BARN GALLERY, Melkinthorpe, Penrith CA10 2DR; 01931 7127670; admission free; open 10am–5pm, closed Wed and Jan/Feb.

Red Barn is a smart, modern gallery over two floors of a converted 18th-century barn and stables. It features contemporary artists and sculptors working in a wide variety of media. Exhibitions change monthly. Located next door to Larch Cottage Nurseries and restaurant La Casa Verde.

LILLIPUT LANE VISITOR CENTRE, Penrith CA11 0DP, next to junction 40 on the M6; 01768 212692; www.lilliputlane.co.uk; entry to Visitor Centre free; tours free for members and up to 5 guests; non-members £3 adults, £2 children, under-12s free; open Mon–Fri 9am–4.30pm, and some bank holidays; no tours on Fridays.

The **Lilliput Lane Visitor Centre** might not be to everyone's taste, but collectors of these twee miniatures will love it. It's located in a life-size replica of one of the company's thatched cottages and visitors can go on a studio tour to see how the models are made.

 ## What to do with children...

CENTER PARCS, Whinfell Forest, signposted off the A66 about 3 miles E Penrith, CA10 2DW; 01768 893000; www.centerparcs.co.uk; day pass, adults £19, children (4–13) £13, under-4s free, families £56; booking essential.

Children will love the pools and water activities at **Center Parcs Whinfell Forest**, which is open to day visitors. The Subtropical Swimming Paradise has water chutes, slides, play areas and the UK's longest falling rapids ride – plenty to scream and shout about. There's also an outdoors Action Challenge, which includes a 13-metre climbing tower if you're feeling adventurous. For more sedate, but still fun family activities, you can take a boat out on the lake or hire bikes and try to spot the cute, but shy red squirrels in the forest.

ASKHAM POOL, Askham CA10 2PN (01931 712474); Shap Pool, Shap CA10 3LR (01931 716379); Lazonby Pool, Barton Dale, Lazonby CA10 1BU (01768 898346); Greystoke Pool, Church Road, Greystoke CA11 0TW (01768 483637); ring individual pools for opening times and admission prices.

To splash about in a more traditional setting, several of the villages around Penrith are, rather surprisingly, home to **heated outdoor swimming pools** – not something you'd expect to find in a county famous for its above-average rainfall and relatively cool climate. Still, on a warm day, it's great fun for all the family. The pools – a well-kept secret –

are used mostly by locals. They can be found tucked away in Askham, Greystoke, Lazonby and Shap and are generally open from June until mid-September. Shap's claims to be the highest open-air pool in England.

There aren't many farms in Cumbria that house wallabies, ostriches, racoons and the rare 'zebroid' – just the one, in fact. **Eden Ostrich World** is located on a working farm at Langwathby Hall in the Eden Valley. The children can enjoy pony rides, a bouncy castle and, in the spring, get to bottle-feed the lambs. If you're lucky, you may even get to witness ostrich chicks hatching from their enormous eggs (May–Oct). And that 'zebroid'? Well, her mother was a Shetland pony and daddy was a zebra. Now, you don't see many of those, do you? The site also has a tea room, adventure playground and an indoor soft play area.

> **EDEN OSTRICH WORLD**, Langwathby Hall Farm, Langwathby, Penrith CA10 1LW; 01768 881771; www.ostrich-world.com; adults £4.95, children (3–15) £3.95; reduced fees Nov–Mar; open daily Mar–Oct 10am– 5pm; closed Tues Nov–March, last entry 3.30pm.

Abbott Lodge is a great place for ice-cream lovers; it makes more than 30 flavours from the extra creamy milk produced by its herd of Jersey cows. The farm has indoor and outdoor play areas as well as ride-on tractors for the under-8s.

> **ABBOTT LODGE, CLIFTON**, Penrith, CA10 2HD; 01931 712720; www.abbottlodgejerseyicecream.co.uk; admssion free; open daily 11am–5pm, except Nov–Easter when closed Mon & Fri; open all bank holidays except Christmas and New Year.

Noah's Ark is a soft play area for under-8s in Penrith town centre (above the Spar shop). It includes a ball pool and a bouncy castle. Newspapers, magazines and refreshments available for mums and dads while the children play.

> **NOAH'S ARK**, 36–40 Burrowgate, Penrith CA11 7TA; 01768 890640; £2 crawlers, £3 walkers, open daily, except Christmas and New Year; weekdays 10am–3.45pm, Sat 10am–4.45pm, Sun 10.30am–3.45pm; closes 1pm Wed except school holidays.

 ## ... and how to avoid children

For a tranquil, cultural afternoon head to the **High Head Sculpture Valley**. Sculptor Jonathan Stamper has chosen an unusual venue in which to display his work. His life-size creations, carved from wood, stone, iron and bronze are positioned along a pretty valley that is also home to otters, herons and kingfishers. Visitors can follow trails through the High Head Sculpture Valley to see his and other artists' work, and they can also visit more traditional indoor galleries and artists' workshops.

> **HIGH HEAD SCULPTURE VALLEY**, High Head Farm, Ivegill, Carlisle CA4 0PJ; 016974 73552; www.highheadsculpture valley.co.uk; adults £2.50, children/concessions £1.50, under-6s free; open daily except Wed, 10.30am–5pm.

Entertainment

Theatre and cinema

The **Penrith Playhouse** is the intimate, town-centre home of the Penrith Players, an amateur dramatic group that puts on about half a dozen productions each year. Shows for 2008 include the musical *High Society*, with well-known songs by Cole Porter, and Ray Cooney's *Run For Your Wife*. The Playhouse is also the venue for several live music events.

Penrith's cosy **Lonsdale Cinema**, (01768 862400; www.penrith-alhambra.co.uk) formerly the Alhambra, has two screens right in the middle of town. They show most of the big blockbusters and devote Sunday evenings to foreign-language and independent films.

Nightlife

No15 Café Bar is bursting at its seams on the third Thursday of every month. This is when it holds its acoustic night – a chance to hear local bands and singers in comfortable surroundings. It's one of the few nights when the popular lunchtime venue also serves evening meals, but pre-booking of tables is absolutely essential.

Special events

Potfest, the oldest potters' market in the UK, is held at the beginning of August in Penrith (www.potfest.co.uk). Up to 150 unselected potters take part in this huge event, which takes place under cover at Skirsgill Auction Mart, just 100 yards west of junction 40 on the M6. This busy, almost frantic event is always preceded by the more tranquil **Potfest in the Park**, an exhibition of selected potters' work in marquees in the grounds of nearby Hutton-in-the-Forest. Entry to the market is free, but admission to Potfest in the Park is £5 for adults (children go free).

Another big August event is the **Lowther Horse Driving Trials** (01931 712378 www.lowther.co.uk). As well as the famous carriage driving trials, in which the Duke of Edinburgh almost always competes, there is a country fair, which includes dog shows, Cumberland and Westmorland wrestling (see p.39), an RAF Falcons parachute display, a ferret demonstration and archery, mini go-karts and quad bikes for everyone to have go at. All this is held in the grounds of Lowther Castle, which looks very impressive from a distance, but then you get a bit closer and notice it's nothing but a shell.

🛏 *The best...* PLACES TO STAY

Wild Rose Wigwams

UNUSUAL

Wild Rose Wigwams 🏄 🛏 🍴 🏊

Ormside, Appleby, CA16 6EJ
017683 51077
www.wildrose.co.uk

If you want the fun of camping, but can't face the chill at night, the Wild Rose wigwams are a great compromise. These small, wooden cabins are heated and well insulated. They include a sleeping platform with foam mattresses, a fridge, kettle, toaster, microwave, TV and lockable door. Open all year.

Price: Nightly rates £12–£16.50 adult, £8–£10.50 child. Minimum nightly charge of £20.

SELF-CATERING

Whale Farm Cottage 🏄

Whale, Penrith, CA10 2PT
01931 712577
www.lowther.co.uk

Farrow and Ball paints and sumptuous Colefax and Fowler curtains add a touch of luxury to this 5-star cottage, which sleeps four. Facilities include a telephone and fax machine, plasma TV with Sky and a wide selection of CDs and DVDs. Superb kitchen leads on to private terrace with barbecue.

Price: Cottage £560–£1,748 per week.

The best... FOOD AND DRINK

Penrith lies at the heart of a proud and hard-working farming community – and this shines through in the town's shops as well as its restaurants and cafés. If the independent retailers and restaurant owners can get it locally, they will – eggs, poultry, cheese, yoghurt, ice-cream, game, beef, lamb, trout, vegetables... And the producers know that this interest in food provenance and buying local is not just about traceability; it's also about quality – something which most of them provide in abundance.

▶ Staying in

Shopping in Penrith is a joy – there are good quality, independent outlets at every turn. One of the largest and oldest of these is **J and J Graham** on Market Place (01768 862281), which has been in business since 1793. Its wide range of fine food and wine, all sold from its very traditional shop opposite the HSBC, includes sticky toffee pudding from Cartmel, hams and bacon from Waberthwaite, Claire's Hand-made Chutneys and local cheeses. Open 9am–5pm, Mon–Sat.

As you'd expect in a town that is just a few miles from one of Europe's largest livestock markets, there are plenty of butchers here. **Gordon Clark** on Great Dockray (01768 868689) hangs meat to improve the flavour. All the produce is sourced locally, some direct from the farmers. **Cranstons** is a name that everyone in north Cumbria associates with good quality meat. The family-run business has two shops in Penrith, including the huge, award-winning Cumbrian Food Hall on Ullswater Road on the way out to the motorway (01768 868680, open 8am–6pm). As well as meat, this stocks a range of cheeses, home-made bread, patés and jams. Its dry-cured streaky bacon recently won an award at Smithfield and, if you're looking for some of the tastiest meat around, try the saltmarsh-fed lamb reared on the Solway.

The best greengrocer in town is **Starfruits** on Angel Square (01768 890255). This large and busy shop also sells home-made cakes and dairy produce.

For fresh fish and shellfish, head to the Devonshire Arcade where **The Fish Cellar** (01768 899408) gets daily deliveries from Aberdeen. It also stocks wild local salmon and, depending on the season, local game.

Brunswick Deli on Brunswick Road (01768 210500) sells cheese, cooked meats, olives, wines, chutneys, filled baguettes and even some good quality ready-meals. It has won awards for its caramel shortcake and its deliciously dense chocolate brownie. Sticking to the sweet-toothed theme, two doors away from the Brunswick Deli is *the* best fudge you will ever taste. Suppliers to the royal family, **The Toffee Shop** (01768 862008, www.thetoffeeshop.co.uk) has been making fudge and toffee by hand since 1910 and it seems to have learned a thing or two about this secret art in that time. The only word to describe it is 'wow!'

Penrith hosts a decent-sized **farmers' market** in the Market Square on the third Tuesday of every month (9.30am–2.30pm), but for one of the best markets in the region, you should head a little further south – to Orton (www.ortonfarmers.co.uk). More than 40 producers gather together on the second Saturday of the month to sell their wares. More than just a farmers' market, this has become something of an event with cookery demonstrations, children's competitions and live music. Open 9.30am–2.30pm. Orton is one mile from junction 38 of the M6.

Also out of town, **Ivinson's Farm Shop** (01768 866979, www.ivinsonsfarm shop.co.uk) sells everyday provisions such as vegetables, home-baked bread and dairy goods. All of its meat is sourced locally, and most of the lamb and beef comes from the family's own 140-acre farm. Located close to Wetheriggs Pottery at Clifton Dykes. Closed Mon, except bank holidays.

The **Old Smokehouse** at Brougham Hall just to the south of the town (01768 867772, www.the-old-smokehouse.co.uk) uses it own herb and spice recipes to brine local produce. Salmon, poultry, meat, cheese and vegetables are individually smoked by either cold-smoking or by smoke-roasting over oak in the traditional way. Its spicy Smoked Penrith Pepperpot Sausage has won several awards.

Takeaways

If after all that talk of good, fresh food you're still tempted by a takeaway, there's a wide selection in Penrith. For fish and chips, try **The Little Chippy** on Cornmarket (01768 864508) open daily 11am–11.30pm except Sundays when it opens at 4.30pm – or **Townhead Fish and Chip Shop** on Stricklandgate (01768 864988) 11.30am–1.30pm and 4.30pm–10pm (Sundays 4.30pm–9pm).

You can get a good curry at **Cagneys** on King Street (01768 867503) open daily 5pm–11.30pm, or for a tasty chop suey, head to the Courtyard Chinese Restaurant on Cornmarket (01768 840222) open 5pm–11pm, closed Mondays.

The busiest pizzeria in town is **Gianni's** on Market Square (01768 891791). You can get takeaways from 5.30pm to about 9pm and the restaurant is also open for lunch.

EATING OUT

RESTAURANT
Grants of Castlegate
54 Castlegate, Penrith CA11 7HY
01768 895444

A relatively new wine bar and bistro serving tasty meals in smart, modern surroundings. Attractively-served starters include creative vegetarian dishes such as filo pastry parcels filled with feta, halloumi, sun-blushed tomatoes, red onion and fresh mint (£4.75). Main courses from £9.95 to £17.75. Closed Mondays and Tuesdays.

GASTRO PUB
Yanwath Gate Inn
Yanwath, Penrith CA10 2LF
01768 862386
www.yanwathgate.com

This cosy, friendly inn was named Cumbria Dining Pub of 2007 in *The Good Pub Guide*. Although it serves several local ales, the emphasis is firmly on food. Tease your tastebuds with oysters shucked to order. Main's from £13.95 to £17.95, include Galloway veal chop and belly of wild boar.

Queen's Head Inn
Tirril, Penrith CA10 2JF
01768 863219

A roaring fire, low beams and sandstone flags welcome you to the Queen's Head in the village of Tirril. With restaurant and bar menus as well as a specials board, there's plenty of delicious, good-value food to choose from, including vegetable tagine, and venison, port and plum pie.

CAFÉ
The Greenhouse
Larch Cottage Nursery,
Melkinthorpe, Penrith CA10 2DR
01931 712404
www.larchcottage.co.uk

The Greenhouse is a cut above your average garden centre café. Its small menu consists of tasty, interesting pizzas (smoked salmon, coriander and chilli oil £8.25) and hearty, wholesome lunches with a Mediterranean emphasis – in a friendly, lively atmosphere. Its open-air balcony becomes packed in the summer. Great Italian coffee.

No15 Café Bar and Gallery
15 Victoria Road, Penrith CA11 8HN
01768 867453

This lively, smart café-bar is very popular with locals, including families. Lunches include lamb tagine (£8), Caesar salad (£6.50) and good sandwiches (£4.80–£5.30) with a mouth-watering selection of home-made cakes. Although rushed off their feet, the staff are always friendly. Also open for dinner on Saturdays and 'acoustic nights'.

EATING OUT

Bewicks Coffee House
**1 Princes Court, Rowcliffe Lane,
Penrith, CA11 7BJ
01768 864764**

This small, traditional café is another busy town centre venue at lunchtimes. Welsh rarebit (from £3.95) and jacket potatoes (from £4.95) brush shoulders with home-made houmous (£4.95) and aubergine and feta fritters (from £4.75). Good value for money. Open 9.30am–4pm Mon–Sat, closes 2.30pm Wed.

The Watermill Tearoom
**Little Salkeld, CA10 1NN
01768 881523
www.organicmill.co.uk**

The organic, vegetarian lunches at the Watermill are all made on the premises – right down to the wide selection of breads and the salad cream. Substantial main meals – such as quiche or rarebit cost £6.50, but make sure you leave room for the delicious scones, cakes and desserts.

Drinking

Penrith is full of pubs, but if you're looking for real ale in pleasant surroundings, you'll be disappointed; you'll need to head out to the villages for a really good pint. A little way off the beaten track, tucked away in the Eden Valley, the busy **Highland Drove** in Great Salkeld (01768 898349) has cask-conditioned real ales and a good selection of wines. John Smith's and Theakston's Black Bull are among the regulars, and the guest ale is changed with every barrel. A long, long way off the beaten track is the **Black Swan Hotel** at Ravenstonedale (015396 23204), which recently won a CAMRA award. And, in the back of beyond is the **Mardale Inn**, Bampton, near Haweswater. Recently refurbished, this warm and cosy 18th-century inn is a delightful place to settle down and enjoy an evening with well-kept local beers and a huge range of whiskies.

The **Tirril Brewery** was first established at the Queen's Head Inn in the village in 1999, but it wasn't long before it outgrew its premises. It is now located at Brougham Hall, near Penrith, and is available in bottles as well as on draught at a number of local pubs. Regular brews include John Bewsher's Best (ABV 3.8%), a lightly hopped, golden brown beer; Charles Gough's Old Faithful (ABV 4%), a pale gold, aromatic and well-hopped ale; and Academy Ale (ABV 4.2%), which is darker and more full-bodied.

ℹ Visitor Information

Tourist Information Centres: Tourist Information Centre, Middlegate, Penrith, 01768 867466, 9.30am–5pm Mon–Sat, 1pm–4.45pm Sun, mid-March–31 Oct, stays open one hour later during the summer holidays, Mon–Fri 10am–4pm (10.30am Sat) during the winter.

Hospitals: Minor Injuries Unit, Penrith Community Hospital, Bridge Lane, CA11 8HX, 01768 245300, on the southern side of the town. For more serious problems, Cumberland Infirmary, Newtown Road, Carlisle, CA2 7HX, 01228 523444.

Doctors: Birbeck Medical Group weekdays 8.30am–6pm, 01768 214620; Bishopyards Medical Group weekdays 8am–6.30pm, 01768 245219; Corney Place Medical Group (weekdays 8.15am–6.30pm, 01768 245226 (all at Penrith Health Centre, opposite the hospital on Bridge Lane); West Lane Surgery, Shap, Tuesday mornings and Thursday afternoons only, 01931 716230; Cuedoc, 01228 40199, out-of-hours emergency doctor service.

Pharmacies: Morrisons, 01768 867631, 8am–8pm Mon–Sat, 10am–4pm Sun; Co-op, 8 Middlegate, 01768 862695, 8.45am–5.30pm Mon–Sat; Boots, 3 Grahams Lane, 01768 862735, 8.45am–5.30pm

Mon–Sat; Joooph Cowper, 50 King Street, 01768 862063, 8.45am–5.30pm Mon–Sat); Penrith Health Centre, Bridge Lane, 01768 864761, weekdays 9am–6pm, closed for lunch 12.45pm–1.45pm.

Police: Hunter Lane, Penrith, CA11 7UT, 0845 3300247, manned 8am–midnight.

Supermarkets: Morrisons, Brunswick Road, Penrith, CA11 7JN, 01768 867631; Somerfield, 22–27 King Street, Penrith, CA11 7AG, 01768 891455, Co-op, 19 Durrowgate, Penrith, CA11 7TD, 01768 862366.

Parking: Pay and display car parks at several sites in Penrith, the largest at Southend Road, Sandgate (the bus station) and Bluebell Lane; on-street parking in the town centre is limited and drivers must display a disc showing their time of arrival; discs available from local shops and the Tourist Information Centre.

Internet Access: Penrith Library, St Andrew's Churchyard, CA11 7YA, 01768 242100, 50p for 15 minutes; Giga Bite Café, Eden Rural Foyer, Old London Road, Penrith CA11 8ET, 01768 861650, 25p per half-hour; wi-fi at the Narrowbar Café, 13 Devonshire Street, 01768 891417, £1.50 for two hours.

Car Hire: Westmorland Vehicle Hire, Ullswater Road Garage, Ullswater Road, Penrith, CA11 7EH, 01768 864546.

Bike Rental: Arragon's Cycle Centre, 2 Brunswick Road, Penrith, CA11 7LU, 01768 890344, www.arragons.com, a range of bikes for £15 per day; Slug and Hare Bicycle Company, Bampton, CA10 2RQ, 01931 713386, www.slugandhare.co.uk, £15 per day, tandems £35 per day; Eden Cycle Centre, Brougham Hall, CA10 2DE, 01768 840400, www.cycleactive.co.uk, from £17 per day, trailers and tag-alongs £10.

Taxis: Acclaim, 01768 866842; Ace Taxis, 01768 890731; Clover Leaf Taxis, 01768 210130; Eden Taxis, 01768 865432; Penrith Taxis, 01768 899298.

Spiral carvings on Long Meg

ULLSWATER

Although not the longest or the deepest or even the busiest of Cumbria's lakes, Ullswater is possibly the most beautiful. It snakes its way for almost 8 miles from the small village of Pooley Bridge, nestled at the base of the gently rolling eastern fells, to Patterdale, towered over by giants such as Helvellyn and St Sunday Crag. If you're driving the A592 alongside the lake, prepare to be wowed as you head west and south – and be ready to pull over from time to time; those views are a little too mesmerising to be seen from the wheel of a car. Better still, jump aboard the Ullswater 'steamer' and see it all from the lake.

Although always heaving in the summer months, the village of Pooley Bridge has little to offer the discerning visitor other than the lake itself – there are several places nearby where you can hire boats or bikes to do some exploring. Heading along the southern shores of Ullswater, though, you pass Sharrow Bay before coming to the wild and remote Martindale – walking country for connoisseurs (and anyone hoping to see red deer).

Ascent of Helvellyn

The northern and western shores are where you will find most of the settlements – largely scattered until you reach Glenridding and Patterdale. It is here also that you can visit one of the area's most famous and most photographed natural features – Aira Force – and follow in the footsteps of Wordsworth and his 'lonely' cloud to discover the lakeshore woods that inspired *that* poem.

Glenridding and Patterdale themselves, although only tiny villages, offer a great selection of hotels and B&Bs. You're in mountain country now – at the very foot of Helvellyn and its neighbours. Every year, thousands of people climb Striding Edge to get to the summit and, with steep-sided crags and rocky gullies lining its eastern slopes, this range also contains some of England's best and hardest winter climbing routes. There's even a ski tow up there. If you love the mountains, you'll love Glenridding and Patterdale.

WHAT TO SEE AND DO

 ## Fair weather

Aira Force is one of the most spectacular waterfalls in a national park that's full of them. Visitors can walk right up to the base of the noisy, 21-metre drop and feel the spray on their faces – or their camera lens if they're not careful. Steep steps lead up the side of the falls and on to a stone humpback bridge at the top of the drop. Look over the edge if you dare! The short walk up to Aira Force from the National Trust car park is a delight in itself, passing through an arboretum planted by the Howard family of Greystoke. They were lords of the manor here from the late Middle Ages until they sold the land to the National Trust in 1906. The beautiful woods contain a number of wonderful specimens, including Douglas firs, some fine yews and a Chilean pine or 'monkey-puzzle' tree. There is also a pleasant teashop next to the car park.

> **AIRA FORCE**, near Watermillock, grid ref. NY400202; 017684 82067; www.nationaltrust.org.uk; admission free but charge for parking; open all year.

Walking

Spend any time in Glenridding and you can't fail to notice that walking is the most popular activity here. In fact, you'll feel positively out of place without a pair of stout boots or, in the winter, the obligatory ice-axe dangling from your pack. The Helvellyn range, with its formidable-looking cliffs and narrow arêtes, forms the focus of attention in this area. Probably the most popular walk is to ascend via **Striding Edge** and then to return via Swirral Edge. These narrow routes require a head for heights and, on busy days in the summer, you may find yourself in a long

Lonely as a cloud or a heartbroken knight

William Wordsworth was a frequent visitor to the Ullswater area and wrote three poems about Aira Force, the most well known being *The Somnambulist*. This tells the local legend of two lovers who were parted by war.

As the knight went off to fight, his sweetheart was left at home, worrying about him. Her deep anxiety led her to start sleepwalking along the edge of the steep Aira ravine. When the knight returned, he discovered her asleep and in this precarious position. He touched her and she awoke, losing her balance and falling into the ravine. Needless to say, as in all good legends, the damsel died and the knight built himself a cell on the river bank to mourn his loss.

The woodland nearby, at the southern base of Gowbarrow, is said to have inspired Wordsworth to write his most famous poem, *Daffodils*. Having walked through the woods with him on 15 April 1802, his sister, Dorothy, noted in her diary: 'I never saw daffodils so beautiful. They grew among the mossy stones about and about them, some rested their heads upon these stones as on a pillow for weariness and the rest tossed and reeled and danced and seemed as if they verily laughed with the wind that blew upon them over the lake; they looked so gay ever dancing ever changing.' Two years later, he used Dorothy's observations as the basis of the poem.

Striding Edge

queue of walkers slowly edging their way along. But don't be put off, there are other, easier (but generally longer), routes on to England's third highest mountain.

Other great fell walks from nearby take in St Sunday Crag, Fairfield and Hart Crag (Deepdale Round, 10 miles). Some of the best of the lower fells include Gowbarrow (4-mile round walk from Aira Force car park), Place Fell (7-mile round walk from Patterdale) and Keldas for superb views of Ullswater (a pleasant half-mile stroll from Glenridding). If you want to escape the busier spots, drive out to Martindale, just beyond Howtown, and head up on to Hallin Fell (4.7 miles), Pikeawassa (5 miles) or Beda Fell (6 miles, including Place Fell). The Deer Forest here is home to the oldest native herd of **red deer** in England. You can spot them at any time of the year, but listen out for the eerie noise of the males rutting in the autumn.

The Pennine-like moorland above Pooley Bridge and Askham contains a number of ancient and often mysterious sites, including **The Cockpit** (grid reference NY483222). This is a Bronze Age stone circle, about 90ft in diameter, raised on the inside of a low bank. There are about 73 stones in the circle and a standing stone about 300 yards to the south-west. It acquired its name in more recent history, when it was used for cock-fighting. The stone circle can be found by following the lane up to Roehead from Pooley Bridge and then walking along the clear track for two-thirds of a mile until you come to a large cairn. Turn right here and The Cockpit is to the left, just before the path bears right to ford Elder Beck.

These moors are also home to several Bronze Age stone burial mounds and standing stones. The **Cop Stone** (grid reference NY495216) is 4ft tall and about 3ft thick. It forms part of a man-made bank of around 20 yards in diameter. This bank is believed to be a ring cairn that was recorded in the late 19th century as having more than 10 stones around its perimeter.

All these sites are located on open access land.

On the water

On a calm, sunny day, there's probably no better way to experience Ullswater than from one of the **Ullswater 'Steamers'**. Even in the winter, you can sit on deck and enjoy the invigorating ride or come indoors to the warm saloon where refreshments are available. The boats, which have been operating on these

ULLSWATER STEAMERS, Glenridding CA11 0US; 017684 82229; www.ullswater-steamers.co.uk; single fares £4.80–£6.90 adults, £2.40–£3.45 children, returns £7.60–£11.30 adults, £3.80–£5.65 children, family tickets available; open all year weather permitting.

waters since 1859, stop at Glenridding, Howtown and Pooley Bridge. A popular excursion is to get the boat from Glenridding to Howtown and then walk back along the lakeshore (7 miles). Alternatively, for a quieter day out, walk from Pooley Bridge to Howtown via the Cockpit Stone Circle (5 miles) and then get the boat back. Two-hour buffet cruises run on selected evenings during the summer.

GLENRIDDING SAILING CENTRE, The Spit, Glenridding, CA11 0PB; 017684 82541; www.lakesail.co.uk; kayaks from £8 per hour, canoes £15, dinghies £25 (all subject to additional nominal fee to join Glenridding Sailing Club); open Mar–Oct, 10am–5pm

If you want to get out on the water and you're feeling a little more energetic, you can hire kayaks, canoes and sailing dinghies from **Glenridding Sailing Centre**. Because there is a 10mph speed limit on the lake, you're guaranteed a speedboat-free environment. A safety boat service is available, and shore staff keep a close watch on clients on the water.

Waterside House Campsite (017684 86332; www.watersidefarm-campsite.co.uk; Mar-Oct only) near Pooley Bridge also hires out rowing boats, Canadian canoes and sea cycles, the modern, cooler version of the old pedallo.

Small motor boats and rowing boats are available to hire from a number of other locations on the lake, including **St Patrick's Boat and Bike Hire** (Glenridding, CA11 0QQ, 01768 482393), **Ullswater Marine** (Watermillock, CA11 0LP 017684 86415, www.ullswatermarine.co.uk; motor boats £20 per hour plus £2 per adult) and **Lakeland Boat Hire** (Pooley Bridge, CA10 2NR, 017684 86800 www.lakelandboathire.co.uk).

ULLSWATER CANOE TRAIL LEAFLET, £2, available from Tourist Information Offices, canoe hire shops and Eden Rivers Trust on 01768 866788.

If you have your own canoe or kayak, you may want to pick up a copy of the **Ullswater Canoe Trail** leaflet. Produced by the Eden Rivers Trust, it identifies a number of short canoeing trips, as well as one-day and two-day trips and provides information on where to hire or launch boats. Printed on waterproof paper, it is in an easy-to-use, concertina-style format, with a detailed map on one side and the corresponding text on the other.

Wet weather

DALEMAIN, Penrith CA11 0HB; 017684 86450; www.dalemain.com; house and gardens, adults £7.50, accompanied children free; gardens, adults £5 (£3 in winter); summer opening Mar–Oct, gardens and tea room 10.30am–5pm; winter opening, gardens and tea room only, Sun–Thu 11am–4pm; closed Christmas and Jan.

Dalemain has been home to the same family since 1679. Architecturally, the impressive house includes features from the medieval, Tudor and early Georgian periods. Its fine interior includes some fascinating rooms with Tudor oak panelling, original hand-painted wallpaper and 16th-century plaster ceilings. If the weather's good, the gardens are worth a visit. The Himalayan blue poppies, which flower in the early summer, are particularly pretty. Located on the A592 between Rheged and Pooley Bridge.

 ## What to do with children...

Create! is the new pottery painting studio at **Rheged**, the 'village in the hill' on the A66 a few miles west of Penrith. Open to all ages, you simply purchase a mug, bowl or children's character and then let your imagination and the paints do the rest. Baking takes about 30 minutes and then you can take the finished item home with you. Rheged also has a soft play area for under-5s and an outdoor adventure playground complete with a Roman fort, Celtic roundhouse, giant slide and ramparts.

RHEGED CENTRE, Redhills CA11 0DQ; 01768 868000; www.rheged.com; Create! open 10am–4pm, items £3.50–£6.95; soft play area free up to 6 months old, £1 an hour up to one year, £2.50 over one year; open 10am–5.30pm school holidays.

For grown-ups, Rheged also houses exhibitions, gallery space, restaurants and shops. Built into a man-made hill, it is almost literally a vast warren.

If you want to get out in the fresh air, but you've already been on the lake and you want to give your legs a break from walking, **Rookin House Farm Equestrian and Activity Centre** has plenty of other, interesting options for the whole family. More than 35 well-mannered horses are available for all riders, even complete beginners. You can spend a day or just an hour exploring the local countryside – across farmland, through forests and on quiet country lanes. Qualified escorts and riding hats are provided. Alternatively, why not go on a guided quad bike trek? The centre has quads of three different sizes, the smallest of which are suitable for children aged from six years. Rookin House is also home to the Lake District's only indoor go-kart circuit and has cub karts for young children. Other activities include operating a JCB, clay pigeon shooting, archery and an assault course.

ROOKIN HOUSE FARM, Troutbeck, Penrith CA11 0SS; 017684 83561; www.rookinhouse.co.uk; horse treks £25 per person per hour; full day, experienced riders only, £80 per person; quad bikes £16.50 for 20 minutes; go-karts (min. age 14 years) £15.50 for 25 laps.

The Park Foot camping and caravan site also runs a **Pony Trekking Centre** that offers relaxing, escorted rides over the low-lying fells overlooking the northern end of Ullswater. Beginners are welcome. Children must be aged over five and lead reins are available. Hard hats and waterproofs provided.

PARK FOOT PONY TREKKING CENTRE, Pooley Bridge CA10 2NA; 017684 86696; www.parkfootponytrekking.co.uk; 1 hour £20, 2 hours £35, half-day rides on request; treks start 10am daily; booking advisable.

The Alpaca Centre in Stainton

THE ALPACA CENTRE, Snuff Mill Lane, Stainton CA11 0HA; 01768 891440; www.thealpacacentre.co.uk; admission free; open daily 10am–5pm.

Sheep, yes. Cattle, yes. Even the occasional goat. But an alpaca farm in Cumbria? It's not quite what you'd expect, but there are a growing number of breeders of these llama-like creatures in the National Park. Some hill farmers even use them to guard their sheep. The **Alpaca Centre** at Stainton is one of the largest alpaca farms and welcomes visitors all year round. You can see the animals in their paddocks from the farm's elevated buildings or from the grounds. There are information panels detailing their history and explaining why their wool is so sought-after. The shop sells alpaca coats, jumpers, gloves, hats, rugs and wall-hangings.

… and how to avoid children

A trip to the tiny, isolated church of **St Martin's** is as much to soak up the peaceful atmosphere of remote Martindale as it is to see the building itself. The plain, stone building was constructed in 1634. An enormous yew in the churchyard is thought to be about 1,300 years old. The church, which is lit by candle because it doesn't have any electricity, can be found by following the road from Pooley Bridge to Howtown and then continuing up the steep zig-zags, past the 'new' church of St Peter's (built in 1882) and then taking the next turning on the left. The road ends a little over a mile beyond the church.

Local Knowledge

Andrew Laverick has lived in Cumbria since he was 12. His family moved to Pooley Bridge from Darlington, and he now lives in Sockbridge, near Tirril. A keen mountain-biker, the 37-year-old runs the Catstycam outdoor gear shops in Glenridding and Pooley Bridge and also helps organise the annual Ullswater Walking Festival.

Favourite restaurant: This is a difficult one; I would have to go for the one I end up in the most and that's Indiagate in Penrith. Good food, really friendly service and big, comfy chairs.

Favourite café: Greystones Coffee Shop in Glenridding – it's a lovely place and it's a gallery as well. The food is excellent and I could sit and eat all the cakes all day.

Favourite pub: Queen's Head Inn in Tirril – a proper country pub with friendly staff, a big fire burning away and a pool table and juke box in the back bar.

Favourite activity: I love mountain-biking. From where I live I can be on top of the fells above Ullswater in 20 minutes, and there are some incredible down-hill runs to get your heart going.

Best view: From Heughscar Hill on my regular mountain biking route, looking along the lake towards Howtown. I always stop to admire it, even though I've seen it hundreds of times. I have hundreds of pictures of this same view, in all weather conditions, and it's always good.

Best walk: It's got to be Helvellyn – from Glenridding over by Lanty's Tarn and into Grizedale, then up to the Hole In The Wall, along Striding Edge and back down to the mines. It has a bit of everything and the views from the summit are incredible.

Best thing about living in Cumbria: Where to start? Clean air, very low crime, having so much amazing countryside to play in, but I think the very best thing must be the people. Cumbrians are crazy in the best possible ways.

Favourite treat: The fudge from Penrith Toffee Shop – if it's good enough for the Queen...!

Rheged's giant screen

Entertainment

RHEGED CENTRE, Redhills CA11 0DQ; 01768 868000; www.rheged.com; adults £4.95 for one film, children (5–14) £3, extra movie £3 (£2 children); showings 11am–5pm.

You feel like you're part of the action when you're watching a film on **Rheged's** giant cinema screen. It's as big as six double decker buses and the sound system's pretty amazing too. There are seven showings of special, large-format films each day, lasting up to 45 minutes each. The films do change from time to time, but *Shackleton's Antarctic Adventure* and *Everest*, both with magnificent photography that really draws the viewer in, have been showing for quite a while now.

Special events
Ullswater is the venue every May for a growing **walking festival** (017684 82414 www.ullswater.com). As you'd expect, the week-long event includes lots of guided walks through the area's wild and craggy fells, but there is also live music, entertainment and family steamer rides.

The best... PLACES TO STAY

HOTEL

Sharrow Bay

Ullswater, Penrith, CA10 2LZ
017684 86301
www.sharrowbay.co.uk

For a special treat, nothing beats the Sharrow Bay, the quintessential English country house hotel in a magnificent location beside Ullswater. The service is superb, but not pretentious, and the rooms are both luxurious and homely at the same time. Sit back in the lakeside lounge's huge picture window and relax!

Price: B&B £135–£350 pppn. Single room £120.

Rampsbeck Country House Hotel

Watermillock on Ullswater, Penrith, CA11 0LP
017684 86442
www.rampsbeck.co.uk

Also occupying a wonderful lakeside location is Rampsbeck. All of the rooms in this elegant house have been individually furnished to a high standard. Three have private balconies. The reception rooms are delightfully ornate and there is a terrace for afternoon teas. The 18 acres of grounds are immaculately kept.

Price: B&B £65–£140 pppn. Double for single occupancy available midweek only, £95–£150 pppn.

Glenridding Hotel

Ullswater, Penrith, CA11 0PB
01768 482289
www.bw-glenriddinghotel.co.uk

There are 36 comfortable en suite bedrooms in this Best Western hotel, including several family rooms that can sleep up to five people. Downstairs, the public areas are very traditional and include a restaurant, a bar with flagstone floors and a library with billiards table.

Price: B&B £55–£70 pppn. Single occupancy supplement £25 per night.

INN

Inn on the Lake

Glenridding, CA11 0PE
017684 82444
www.lakedistricthotels.net/innonthelake

The standard rooms are far from standard in this lakeside hotel – all are well furnished with large beds, comfy chairs and plenty of wardrobe space. The spacious four-poster rooms are particularly lovely. The staff are smart and efficient, and there is a children's play area as well as a leisure suite.

Price: B&B £81–£110 pppn, excluding bank holidays when there is a minimum stay of two nights and guests must book on a B&B basis.

The best... **PLACES TO STAY**

Brackenrigg Inn

Watermillock on Ullswater, Penrith, CA11 0LP
017684 86206
www.brackenrigginn.co.uk

Occupying an elevated position beside the road, this 18th-century coaching inn offers superb views of Ullswater. Decorated in warm chocolate browns, the rooms in the main building have a pleasantly modern feel about them. All are en-suite. The stable cottages provide spacious suites and family rooms.

B&B £69–£110 pppn doubles/suites; £38–£48 single rooms. Weekend supplements apply.

FARMSTAY

Deepdale Hall

Patterdale, Penrith, CA11 0NR
017684 82369
www.deepdalehall.co.uk

Built in 1670, Deepdale Hall lies at the end of a farm track near Patterdale. As well as being hill farmers, the Browns provide simple but traditional accommodation in a warm, cosy environment. Food is sourced locally and even the carpets are made from the wool of Cumbria's Herdwick breed.

B&B £35 pppn.

Gill Head Farm

Troutbeck, Penrith, CA11 0ST
017687 79652
www.gillheadfarm.co.uk

This charming 17th-century farmhouse occupies a peaceful location at the foot of spectacular Blencathra. The cosy, oak-beamed sitting room has an open log fire and is the perfect place to relax after a day in the great outdoors. The hearty farmhouse breakfasts are made with local produce where possible.

B&B £28–£33 pppn. Minimum of two nights at weekends.

B & B

Grisedale Lodge

Grisedale Bridge, Glenridding, Patterdale, CA11 0PJ
017684 82155
www.grisedalelodge.co.uk

Slippers are provided for guests at this small, friendly and comfortable B&B between the villages of Glenridding and Patterdale. The bright and airy residents' lounge has a balcony with lovely views across to Place Fell. Popular with walkers, the house has drying facilities – and packed lunches can be provided.

B&B £32 pppn.

 The best... PLACES TO STAY

Styan Bew

Hartsop, Patterdale, CA11 0NZ
017684 82139
www.styanbew-b-and-b.co.uk

A tiny, but delightful B&B in the pretty, stone-built hamlet of Hartsop. Guests have exclusive use of a small area built on to the back of the main cottage. The accommodation manages to be both rustic and modern at the same time. Run by a young, friendly, but unobtrusive family.

B&B £30 pppn.

CAMPSITE

Side Farm Campsite

Patterdale, CA11 0NP
017684 82337

Not only is this a clean, friendly and well-run site, but it also occupies a superb location just above the southern tip of Ullswater. At the end of a bumpy farm track, it's almost a mile from the road and there's some great walking directly from the site.

Adults £5, children £3, vehicles £2. Open Easter to end of October.

SELF-CATERING

Stone Cottage

Grove Barn, Hartsop, Patterdale, CA11 0NZ
017684 82647
www.lakelandstonecottage.co.uk

Stone Cottage, tucked away at the base of the fells, has been tastefully refurbished to create a smart holiday home for six. The well-equipped kitchen includes oak-work surfaces and hand-made units. There are two bathrooms, one of which features green slate floors and walls. Enclosed garden with patio area.

£660–£1,200 per week. Also available for short breaks.

The Byre at Deepdale Hall

Patterdale, Penrith, CA11 0NR
017684 82369

It's hard to believe that cows used to be kept in The Byre at Deepdale Hall; today, it provides superb, modern self-catering accommodation in two downstairs bedrooms. Up the oak stairs is an open-plan area with a well-appointed kitchen and comfortable lounge. Good insulation means it is warm all year round.

£470–£550 per week.

The best... FOOD AND DRINK

Ullswater may not have the choice of restaurants, pubs and cafés that the Penrith area has, but the quality continues to be superb. Hotel restaurants, in particular, tend to be of a very high standard.

If you're self-catering, it might be best to head to Penrith for your main groceries, although there are one or two small, convenience-type stores dotted about as well as at least one good farm shop. There are no dedicated takeaways in the area.

▶ Staying in

The Ullswater valley doesn't have any supermarkets – you'll have to go to Penrith for those. For basic groceries in Glenridding, try the **Glenridding Mini Market** or **Sharmans**, which also has a cash machine and sells camping equipment. Down the road in Patterdale is another, tiny convenience store that doubles up as the valley's Post Office.

Pooley Bridge has a small **farmers' market** that is held on the last Sunday of every summer month 10.30am–2.30pm. The market moves indoors to Rheged from October to March.

Greystone House Farm Shop (01768 866952 www.greystonehousefarm.co.uk) in Stainton, up near the A66, is well worth a visit. The Dawson family has been farming here since 1752 and, after losing their stock in the foot-and-mouth outbreak of 2001, they decided to go organic. Their busy farm shop includes a traditional butcher's counter selling home-produced beef, lamb and pork. There are daily deliveries of fruit, vegetables and dairy produce. Even if you don't come away with any shopping, you'll not want to miss the popular, on-site café. Shop open 10am–5.30pm every day except Christmas Day.

EATING OUT

FINE DINING
Sharrow Bay
Ullswater, Penrith, CA10 2LZ
017684 86301
www.sharrowbay.co.uk

The famous hotel is home to one of
Cumbria's four Michelin-starred
restaurants. Dinner here is an event,
albeit a fairly relaxed one, that has
been honed to perfection over the
past 60 years. Six courses will set
you back £55. Alternatively, take
afternoon tea on a table overlooking
Ullswater (£19.48).

RESTAURANT
Fellbites Café Restaurant
Croft House, Greenside Road,
Glenridding, CA11 0PD
017684 82781
www.fellbites.co.uk

Come 6.30pm, this comfortable, airy
café – located in the main car park –
is transformed into a welcoming
evening venue with a slightly rustic
feel. Dishes such as perfectly pink
duck breast or tasty butternut squash
strudel are excellent value for money.
Two courses £17.50, three courses
£23.50.

GASTRO PUB
Brackenrigg Inn
Watermillock on Ullswater, Penrith,
CA11 0LP
017684 86206
www.brackenrigginn.co.uk

This comfortable, modern restaurant
has an interesting à la carte menu
that is popular with locals. A starter of
roasted figs with blue cheese and
honey costs £5.45, and you'll pay
£14.95 for creamy garlic fish stew
topped with noodles. Bar menu also
available in the cosy darkwood bar.

CAFÉ
Greystone House Farm Shop and
Tearoom
Stainton, Penrith, CA11 0EF
01768 866952
www.greystonehousefarm.co.uk

Above the farm shop is what looks
like a run-of-the-mill tea shop, but the
food here is anything but run-of-the-
mill. The menu is simple and
reasonably priced – quiches,
sandwiches, ploughmans – but the
end result is always above the
average for this type of teashop. And
the home-made cakes are delicious.

🍷 Drinking

In Glenridding, the **Traveller's Rest** pub (017684 82298) and the **Ramblers' Bar** at the Inn on the Lake both serve real ale. The former, also known locally as the Jerry, is a friendly, thriving village pub and you're unlikely to be able to get a seat in one of its two lounge bars on a summer weekend. Among its cask and keg beers are Jennings bitter and Speckled Hen. Walkers and climbers often pop in for some liquid refreshment after an exhausting day on Helvellyn. Perversely, there's not a boot or an ice-axe to be seen in the Ramblers' Bar. Nevertheless, it's another popular spot where you can get a good pint of Theakstons.

Drama in the Dale

If the Ramblers' Bar at the Inn on the Lake seems strangely familiar, that's because it played a prominent role in the BBC drama *The Lakes*. The rather dark series, written by Jimmy McGovern – he of *Brookside* and *Cracker* fame – was filmed around Patterdale and Glenridding in 1998.

The first series saw Danny Kavanagh (John Simm), an unemployed man from Liverpool, move to Cumbria to work in a fictional hotel (a role that is played by the Inn on the Lake). He becomes tangled in the rivalries of the community and, when four girls die in a boating accident, the blame is laid on him. It was an often controversial drama, the second series including a lot of violence and a storyline involving a Roman Catholic priest's relationship with a parishioner.

Patterdale is home to what claims to be the narrowest building in England – the **White Lion Inn** (017684 82214). Enjoy a pint of the local Tirril Brewery ales and feel the building shake in the wind! It's the sort of warm, traditional bar where you can still have a game of darts or dominoes.

The haunted **Kirkstone Pass Inn** (015394 33888) isn't quite the highest pub in England, but, at almost 1,500ft above sea level, it's worth a trip up there for a drink amidst the magnificent natural surroundings. It stands at a remote junction between north and south with fantastic views to a distant Windermere from a lone picnic table outside. Inside are exposed beams and flagstone floors. Beers from local micro breweries at Hesket Newmarket (see p.258), Tirril and Hawkshead (see p.279 and 116) are among the rotating selection of real ales. But remember – alcohol goes to your head quicker at altitude; three pints of Kirkstone Porter and you'll be seeing ghosts!

Further afield, **The Royal** at Dockray (017684 82356) buys in from a number of local breweries, including Jennings, Hawkshead, the Derwent Brewery at Silloth, Hesket Newmarket and Cumbrian Legendary Ales. It also has one of the nicest and largest beer gardens in the area.

Kirkstone Pass

Local legends: Kirkstone Pass

There are many ghost stories associated with Kirkstone Pass and its 17th-century travellers' inn. There are tales of the ghost of Ruth Ray who died while trying to cross the pass in a snowstorm and of a lost hiker who worked at the hotel and now plays poltergeist tricks there.

A coachman dressed in 17th-century clothing mysteriously appeared in a photograph taken in front of the inn in 1993. The ghost turned out to be a descendant of the family photographed. He followed them back to southern England, but has since returned to Kirkstone Pass.

It is also said that there was a hangman's tree in the grounds of the inn, and one of the most famous stories of recent times involves a woman who was hanged here for murdering her child. In 2004, a local newspaper reported that a teenager living at the inn had captured the 'otherworldly outlines' of a young girl on his mobile phone while he was locked in a disused room there. Ghosthunters believe this could have been the ghost of the murdered child.

ⓘ Visitor Information

Tourist Information Centres: National Park Information Centre, Beckside Car Park, Glenridding, CA11 0PD, 017684 82414, daily 9.30am–5.30pm, mid-March to end of October, weekends only in winter 9.30am–3.30pm.

Hospitals: Minor Injuries Unit, Penrith Community Hospital, Bridge Lane, CA11 8HX, 01768 245300, on the southern side of the town; for more serious problems, Cumberland Infirmary, Newtown Road, Carlisle, CA2 7HX, 01228 523444.

Doctors: Glenridding Health Centre, Glenridding, CA11 0PD, 017684 82297, weekdays 10–11am, 4pm–6pm (closed Wednesday afternoons); Cuedoc, 01228 401999, out-of-hours emergency doctor service.

Pharmacies: See Penrith.

Police: Hunter Lane, Penrith, CA11 7UT, 0845 3300247, manned 8am to midnight.

Supermarkets: See Penrith.

Parking: Pay and display car parks in Patterdale, Glenridding, Pooley Bridge, Aira Force and Glencoyne; on-street parking in Glenridding is limited and drivers must display a disc showing their time of arrival, discs are available from local businesses.

Internet Access: Glenridding Cyber Café, Kilner's, next to Glenridding Hotel, £1 per half-hour.

Car Hire: See Penrith.

Bike Rental: St Patrick's Boat and Bike Hire, on the road out of Glenridding towards Patterdale, 01768 482393, summer only; Park Foot Caravan and Camping site, near Pooley Bridge, 017684 86309, £9 half day, £15 full day; Waterside House Camp Site, near Pooley Bridge, 017684 86332, £8 half day, £12.

Taxis: A and S Bailey, Glenridding, 017684 82213 or 07714 575024; Clover Leaf Taxis, based in Stainton, 01768 210130.

FURTHER AFIELD

Carlisle

Although not strictly within the boundaries of this book, Carlisle is too good to miss. Well-kept hanging baskets adorn the beautiful sandstone buildings of this small, quiet city and riverside parks play host to flower shows and summer events.

As soon as you step out of the railway station, Carlisle's rich, but turbulent history makes its presence felt – opposite are the imposing oval towers of the Citadel, once home to the assize courts and a prison. They form a grand southern entrance.

Heading down English Street, through the pedestrianised shopping area, you begin to enter the historic heart of the city – the old Town Hall, built in 1770 and now home to the Tourist Information Centre (01228 625600), and the Guildhall, one of Carlisle's four oldest buildings. Each floor of the half-timbered Guildhall projects out over the one beneath, a way of using less ground to create a larger home.

If it's history you want – and let's face it, Carlisle has plenty of it – the city's three big draws are its cathedral, its castle and the excellent Tullie House Museum.

Founded in 1122, **Carlisle Cathedral** (01228 548151) may be small, but it's perfectly formed. Built from red sandstone, the interior is less austere than many of England's larger cathedrals and includes some stunning stained glass in the 14th-century east window as well as beautiful medieval craftsmanship in the form of 15th-century choir-stalls. As you wander round, don't forget to look up at the

Carlisle Castle

CARLISE CASTLE, 01228 591922; www.english-heritage.org.uk; admission £4.20 for adults, children £2.10; open daily 9.30am–5pm Apr–Sep; 10am–4pm Oct–Mar.

painted ceiling – blue and starry, it's quite a sight! Admission is free, but donations are welcomed.

A short walk from the cathedral is the formidable fortress of **Carlisle Castle** with its 12th-century stone keep. Right in the frontline of centuries of bloody Anglo-Scottish warfare, this is a site that's seen a lot of action over the years. In 1746, it became the last English fortress ever to suffer a siege, when Bonnie Prince Charlie's Jacobites vainly attempted to hold off the Duke of Cumberland. The fortress became their prison and visitors can still see the legendary 'licking stones', which the parched prisoners desperately licked for moisture to stay alive.

TULLIE HOUSE, 01228 618718; www.tulliehouse.co.uk; admission £5.20 adults, under-18s free; open daily 10am–4pm (12pm opening on Sundays) Nov–Mar, 10am–5pm (12pm on Sundays) Apr–Oct.

The underground Millennium Gallery – home to the Cursing Stone, a sculpture that has been blamed for the city's 2005 floods and the foot-and-mouth outbreak in 2001 – links the castle with **Tullie House**. This award-winning museum houses a huge range of interesting archaeological artefacts, as befits a city that has played a major role in the region since at least Roman times, and it is also home to some superb galleries and temporary exhibitions.

Although the Hadrian's Wall long-distance path passes through Carlisle, little remains of the great Roman construction within the city. The best place nearby to see the wall and other border defences is at **Birdoswald Fort** (01697 747602 www.english-heritage.org.uk), about 15 miles north-east of the city.

If you're spending a day in Carlisle – and it is worth at least that – there are literally dozens of places serving lunch. Two of the best are Le Gall (01228 818388), a relaxed and very popular café-bar on Devonshire Street, and Watt's Victorian Coffee Shop on Bank Street (01228 521545), which sells more than 20 different coffees, all roasted on the premises. The cathedral and Tullie House also have good restaurants.

Carlisle to Settle Railway Line

If beautiful scenery and trains are your thing, you'll love the Carlisle to Settle railway line – a 72-mile trip through the Eden Valley and the Pennines. Leaving the suburbs of Carlisle behind, the train quickly enters the lush, rolling countryside that flanks the River Eden. Sitting on the left of the train, travellers peer through the window and down steep-sided, wooded slopes into the impressive sandstone gorge cut by the river.

The Carlisle to Settle railway

Armathwaite, Lazonby, Kirkoswald, Langwathby are the pretty villages here – they sound almost as if they were named with the rhythm of the trains in mind.

Langwathby, towered over by the highest of the Pennine hills, makes for a pleasant stop. It's home to Eden Ostrich World (see p.271), Little Salkeld, with its working watermill (see p.268) and Long Meg and Her Daughters stone circle (see p.262), is only a couple of miles away. The well-kept Victorian station building also houses the Brief Encounter Café, a great little place to stop for lunch, especially in the summer when you can sit outside and enjoy the views across to the Lake District.

The next stop is **Appleby**, a small but pleasant town that was once the county town of Westmorland. The picturesque street of Boroughgate, with some interesting old buildings, links the 12th-century castle (currently closed to the public) with the fine medieval church of St Lawrence. The Tourist Information Centre (017683 51177) can be found in the Tudor Moot Hall on Boroughgate.

Every June, the tranquillity of Appleby is shattered as hundreds of Romany families, some in colourful, horse-drawn caravans, arrive for the centuries-old horse fair, the largest of its kind in the world.

Beyond Appleby, the Carlisle to Settle line edges in closer to the Pennines until it reaches **Kirkby Stephen**. Another interesting market town, its parish church, known locally as the Cathedral of the Dales, contains the 8th-century Loki Stone, one of only two such stones in Europe representing the Norse god.

The River Eden rises close by and visitors can enjoy the riverside Poetry Path with 12 poems carved in stone – and celebrating a year in the life of a hill farmer – along the way. For an illustrated guide, visit the Tourist Information Centre in the Market Square (017683 71199).

What could, until now, be described as a pretty journey, suddenly becomes a lot more dramatic as the train heads up into the real hill country. Although still in Cumbria for a while, this is now the Yorkshire Dales National Park.

CARLISLE TO SETTLE RAILWAY,
www.settle-carlisle.co.uk; standard adult day-return fare from Carlisle to Settle costs £18.90 and the entire journey lasts about an hour and 45 minutes. Kingfisher Railtours (0870 747 2983, www.kingfisherrailtours.co.uk) operates special steam services between Hellifield and Carlisle during the summer; standard class return £49 for adults, £30 for children; for a touch of liveried luxury, step back in time for a silver service luncheon served on board for £145.

The train stops at Dent Station, which at 1,150ft above sea level is the highest mainline station in England and Wales, and passes through the 1.5 mile-long Blea Moor tunnel. Then, emerging from the darkness, it begins to slow down in anticipation of the line's most impressive feat of engineering, the amazing Ribblehead Viaduct. With 24 arches, it towers more than 90 feet above the surrounding moorland.

Nowhere along the line does the history of the construction of this railway make itself more keenly felt than here. The moorland below was once the site of the filthy shanty settlements that housed the thousands of navvies who built the line, including 14 tunnels and 17 major viaducts, between 1869 and 1876.

Now in North Yorkshire proper, the line passes through classic Dales scenery with the Three Peaks – Whernside, Ingleborough and Pen-y-Ghent – dominating the skyline.

The journey continues down the River Ribble, through Horton-in-Ribblesdale, to its final stop, Settle, an attractive market town located beside Britain's largest limestone outcrop.

Index

N

O

P